Lynda Weinman's | Hands-On Training

Includes CD-ROM with Exercise Files and Demo Movies

Photoshop® Elements 2

H·O·T™

Hands-On Training

lynda.com/books

By **Shane Rebenschied**
developed with **Lynda Weinman**

Design: Ali Karp

Photoshop Elements 2 | H·O·T
Hands-On Training

By Shane Rebenschied (developed with Lynda Weinman)

lynda.com/books | Peachpit Press
800 East 96th Street • Indianapolis, IN • 46240
800.571.5840 • 317.428.3000 •
317.428.3280(fax)
http://www.lynda.com/books
http://www.peachpit.com

lynda.com/books is published
in association with Peachpit Press,
a division of Pearson Education
Copyright ©2004 by lynda.com

ISBN: 0-321-20300-3

0 9 8 7 6 5 4 3 2 1

Printed and bound in the
United States of America

H•O•T | Credits

Original Design: Ali Karp, Alink Newmedia (alink@earthlink.net)

Editor: Jennifer Eberhardt

Copyeditor: Darren Meiss

Compositors: Rick Gordon, Deborah Roberti

Beta testers: Grace Hodgson, Laurie Burruss-Myers

Proofreader: Karen Gill

Cover Illustration: Bruce Heavin (bruce@stink.com)

Indexer: Cheryl Lenser

H•O•T | Colophon

The original design for *Learning Adobe Photoshop Elements 2 H•O•T* was sketched on paper. The layout was heavily influenced by online communication—merging a traditional book format with a modern Web aesthetic.

The text in *Adobe Photoshop Elements 2 H•O•T* was set in Akzidenz Grotesk from Adobe and Triplex from Emigre. The cover illustration was painted in Adobe Photoshop 7.0.

This book was created using QuarkXPress 4.1, Adobe Photoshop 7.0, Microsoft Office X, Microsoft Office XP, and Adobe Photoshop Elements 2 on a PC using Windows XP and on an Apple Macintosh using Mac OS X 10.2.6. It was printed on 60 lb. Influence Matte at CJ Krehbiel in Cincinnati, Ohio.

Dedications

For my wife:
Thank you for continually
reminding me that
there's life beyond
the computer screen.

For my kids,
Eva and Ethan (the E's):
Without knowing it,
you make me strive to
be better than I am.

For my family.

Photoshop Elements 2 | H•O•T _____ **Table of Contents**

Introduction

H·O·T
_____
Photoshop Elements 2

A Note from Lynda Weinman

In my opinion, most people buy computer books in order to learn, yet it is amazing how few of these books are actually written by teachers. In this book, you will find carefully developed lessons and exercises to help you learn Adobe Elements 2.0. This book was written by one of lynda.com's most popular instructors, Shane Rebenschied, who not only works professionally as a digital illustrator/artist, but has years of teaching experience at our now-closed training center and works as a current CD-ROM instructor for our products and online training movie subscription library. Shane is a respected teacher for a reason: He knows his stuff, he has patience and respect for his students, he makes you laugh, and he teaches you really cool stuff.

This book is written for beginning Adobe Elements learners who are looking for a great tool to edit photographs and create images for print or screen. The premise of the hands-on exercise approach is to get you up to speed quickly in Adobe Elements while actively working through the book's lessons. It's one thing to read about a product, and another experience entirely to try the product and get measurable results. Our motto is, "Read the book, follow the exercises, and you will know the product." We have received countless testimonials to this fact, and it is our goal to make sure it remains true for all of our hands-on training books.

Many exercise-based books take a paint-by-numbers approach to teaching. Although this approach works, it's often difficult to figure out how to apply those lessons to a real-world situation, or to understand why or when you would use the technique again. What sets this book apart is that the lessons contain lots of background information, advice, and insights into each given subject, designed to help you understand the process as well as the exercise.

At times, pictures are worth a lot more than words, and moving pictures are even better! When necessary, we have also included short QuickTime movies to show any process that's difficult to explain with words. These files are located on the **H•O•T CD-ROM** inside a folder called **movies**. It's our style to approach teaching from many different angles, since we know that some people are visual learners, others like to read, and still others like to get out there and try things. This book combines a lot of teaching approaches so you can learn Adobe Elements as thoroughly as you want to.

In this book, we didn't set out to cover every single aspect of Adobe Elements. The manual and many other reference books are great for that! What we saw missing from the bookshelves was a process-oriented tutorial that taught readers core principles, techniques, and tips in a hands-on training format.

We welcome your comments at **elm2faq@lynda.com**. Please visit our Web site at **http://www.lynda.com**. The support URL for this book is **http://www.lynda.com/products/books/elm2hot/**.

–Lynda Weinman

NOTE | About lynda.com/books and lynda.com

lynda.com/books is dedicated to helping designers and developers understand tools and design principles. **lynda.com** offers hands-on books, CD-ROMs, online subscription-based movie training, conferences, and "expert tips" for design and development. To learn more about our training programs, books, and products, be sure to give our site a visit at **http://www.lynda.com.**

About Shane Rebenschied

Shane Rebenschied graduated from the Art Center College of Design in 1998 with an emphasis on traditional and digital media. Since then, his work has appeared in the Society of Illustrators Los Angeles and New York annuals as well as on numerous book covers and magazines. He is a fan of old paper and stains, and can often be found staring at pieces of corroded, rusted metal. Shane is a professional freelance Illustrator and Macromedia Flash designer/developer/consultant living somewhere in the Arizona desert. He maintains an illustration portfolio site at **www.blot.com**.

Past clients include Scholastic, D'Arcy Masius Benton & Bowles, Tor, Harper Collins, Harlequin, Hodder Headline Plc, Summertime Publishing, Harcourt Brace, Ziff Davis, Hanley-Wood LLC, Spirit IC, *Backpacker* Magazine, *X-Files* Magazine, McGraw-Hill, Vanderbilt University, Flashforward, *Phoenix New Times*, *Miami New Times*, *San Francisco Weekly*, and *Cleveland Scene*.

Our Team

Shane frowning at the camera. (I like to take pictures, not have them taken of me!)

Acknowledgments from Shane

My deepest thanks and appreciation to:

Does anyone ever read this? Oh, they do? Hmmm… ;-)

Lynda Weinman, thank you for being my friend and supporter in my personal and professional life.

Garo Green, for heckling me at 2 a.m. and periodically messaging me "*burp*" over AIM. Your caffeinated ramblings have kept me in good spirits. Thank you for inviting me to your home so your dog could scare my daughter and your bird could bite my son…twice. You're a true friend and mentor.

Darren Meiss, the copy editor at New Riders, for turning my confusing, muddled thoughts into crystal clear, razor sharp statements of genius.

Grace Hodgson and Laurie Burruss-Myers, my beta testers for this book, for making sure that left is left, and what's up is down…err…rather…oh, never mind. Your comments and criticisms have made this a better book than I could have written alone.

New Riders, for being so cool to work with, catering to my every whim, and FedEx-ing me bon-bon's to keep me going at 3 a.m. What? That wasn't you? Hmm…

Apple Computer, for making the coolest computers and software in the world.

Adobe, for allowing me to make images I only dreamed of as a kid.

The Universe, for existing. Is this place cool or what?

You, the reader, for buying this book. Congratulations on wanting to further your knowledge and yourself. Keep learning!

How to Use This Book

Please read this section—it contains important information that's going to help you as you use this book. The following chart outlines the information I cover:

Learning Adobe Photoshop Elements 2 H•O•T
Information in this section:
The Formatting in This Book
Macintosh and Windows Interface Screen Captures
Mac and Windows System Differences
• "Choose" for Mac and "OK" for Windows
A Note to Windows Users
• Making Exercise Files Editable on Windows Systems
• Making File Extensions Visible on Windows Systems
Elements System Requirements
What's on the CD-ROM?

NOTE | The Formatting in This Book

This book has several components, including step-by-step exercises, commentary, notes, tips, warnings, and movies. Step-by-step exercises are numbered, and filenames and command keys are shown in bold so they pop out more easily. Captions and commentary are in italicized text: *This is a caption.* Filenames/folders, command keys, and menu commands are bolded: **images** folder, **Ctrl+S**, and **File > Open**. And URLs are in bold: **http://www.lynda.com**.

Macintosh and Windows Interface Screen Captures

Most of the screen captures in this book were taken on a PC using Windows XP. The only time I used Macintosh shots was when the interface differed from the PC under Windows XP. I made this decision because most of the audience for this book and Adobe Photoshop Elements is running Windows, and I wanted to show the images in this book in a format that the majority of the readers would be familiar with. I also own and use numerous Macintosh systems, so I noted important differences when they occurred and took screen captures accordingly.

Mac and Windows System Differences

Adobe has done a great job of ensuring that Photoshop Elements 2 looks and works the same between the Macintosh and Windows operating systems. However, there are still some differences that should be noted. If you are using this book with one of the Windows operating systems, please be sure to read the following section, titled "*A Note to Windows Users*," carefully.

WARNING | "Choose" for Mac and "OK" for Windows

Throughout this book, you will be instructed to click the **OK** button. This is the correct way to do it on the PC using Windows XP. On a Macintosh running OS X, you will instead see a **Choose** button. The two buttons are interchangeable and do the same thing.

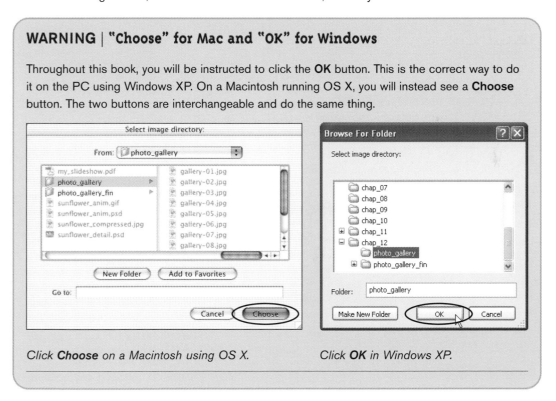

*Click **Choose** on a Macintosh using OS X.*   *Click **OK** in Windows XP.*

A Note to Windows Users

This section contains essential information about making your exercise folders editable, and making file extensions visible.

Making Exercise Files Editable on Windows Systems

By default, when you copy files from a CD-ROM to your Windows 98/2000 hard drive, they are set to read-only (write protected). This will cause a problem with the exercise files, because you will need to write over some of them.

Note: You do not need to follow these steps if you are using Windows NT, Windows XP Home Edition, or Windows XP Professional Edition.

1. Copy the chapter folder from the **H·O·T CD-ROM** to your hard drive.

2. Open the chapter folder and press **Ctrl+A** to select the folder's entire contents.

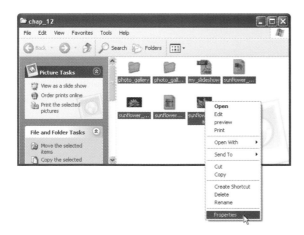

3. Right-click on one of the selected items and choose **Properties**.

4. In the Properties window, uncheck **Read-only**. This will change the setting for all of the selected files.

5. Click **OK**.

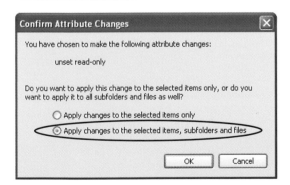

6. If there are other folders inside the chapter folder, Windows 2000 has the option of selecting **Apply changes to the selected items, subfolders and files** to make the contents of all folders editable. Users of earlier Windows systems will have to open each subfolder and repeat Steps 2 through 5.

Making File Extensions Visible on Windows Systems

In this section, you'll see how to turn on file extensions for Windows systems. By default, Windows 98/2000 users cannot see file extensions, such as .gif, .jpg, or .html. Fortunately, you can change this setting!

Windows Users:

1. Double-click on the **My Computer** icon on your desktop. **Note:** If you (or someone else) have changed the name, it will not say **My Computer**.

2. Select **View > Folder Options** (or **Tools > Folder Options** in Windows 2000/XP). This opens the **Folder Options** dialog box.

3. Click on the **View** tab at the top. This opens the **View** options screen so you can change the view settings for Windows.

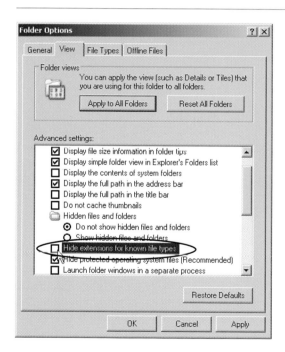

4. Uncheck the **Hide extensions for known file types** check box. This makes all of the file extensions visible.

Photoshop Elements 2 System Requirements

This book requires that you use either a Macintosh operating system (Power Macintosh running System 9.1 or later) or Windows 98, Windows 2000, or Windows NT 4.0, Windows ME, or Windows XP. You also will need a color monitor capable of 800 x 600 resolution and a CD-ROM drive. I suggest that you have at least 256 MB of RAM in your system, because that way you can open Elements and one or two other necessary programs at the same time. More RAM than that is even better, especially on Macintosh computers, which do not dynamically allocate RAM, as Windows does. Although Mac OS X does dynamically allocate RAM, more is always better, *especially* when dealing with high-resolution digital images. Here's a little chart that cites Adobe's RAM requirements, along with our recommendations:

Elements 2 System Requirements		
	Elements Requires	**I Recommend**
Mac	128 MB	256 MB
Windows	128 MB	256 MB

What's on the CD-ROM?

Exercise Files and the H•O•T CD-ROM

Your course files are located inside a folder called **exercise_files** on the **H•O•T CD-ROM**. These files are divided into chapter folders, and you will be instructed to copy the chapter folders to your hard drive during many of the exercises. Unfortunately, when files originate from a CD-ROM, under some Windows operating systems, it defaults to making them write-protected, meaning that you cannot alter them. You will need to alter them to follow the exercises, so please read the "Note to Windows Users" on pages xvi and xvii for instructions on how to convert them to read-and-write formatting.

Demo Files on the CD-ROM

In addition to the exercise files, the **H•O•T CD-ROM** also contains free 30-day trial versions of several software applications for the Mac or Windows. All software is located inside the **software** folder on the **H•O•T CD-ROM**. I have included trial versions of

• Adobe Photoshop Elements 2 (trial version)

• Adobe Reader

• QuickTime 6.3

I.

Background

| What Is Adobe Photoshop Elements |
| Elements versus Photoshop | Image Size/Resolution |
| What's New in Version 2 | Updates |

chap_01

Photoshop Elements 2
H•O•T CD-ROM

This chapter offers a quick overview of some important topics that you'll be dealing with as you read this book and learn Adobe Photoshop Elements 2.0. You need to understand the basic concepts behind digital imaging and Photoshop Elements before you jump in and start working on the exercises. I know you're probably itching to get started, but taking a few minutes to read this chapter will give you a better understanding of many of the topics that I will be addressing later in this book.

What Is Adobe Photoshop Elements?

Simply put, Photoshop Elements is an application that takes many of the features of Adobe's flagship, professional image editing program, Photoshop, and stuffs them into a consumer-level, easy-to-use program. Although Photoshop Elements is geared primarily towards novice computer users, I think you'll find a whole slew of fantastic features that will make your life on the computer easier. Not to mention that Photoshop Elements is "easy on the wallet" as well, oftentimes coming bundled with other items such as scanners and digital cameras. Oh sure, you can use Photoshop Elements to scan in a picture of your sister and give her a few extra eyes and some hairy warts, but its usefulness and capabilities go way beyond that.

Photoshop Elements gives you the ability to easily and quickly do everything from correcting "red-eye" in that otherwise great family photo, to making those old and torn family photos look new again, to easily emailing your favorite photos to friends and family, to automatically creating a Web site with your favorite photos for the whole world to see.

Adobe has certainly outdone itself with this latest version of Elements by adding even more features and capabilities. Whether you are new to the whole computer scene or an advanced Photoshop user, after reading through this book you'll see how Photoshop Elements is a great tool to add to your graphics arsenal.

Elements versus Photoshop

Because Photoshop Elements and Photoshop are similar in name and purpose, understanding which program does what and when you should use one over the other can be confusing. To help clear up some of this confusion, here is a list of some of the things you could do with Photoshop Elements and some things that are better suited for Photoshop. The following chart identifies some common tasks and which program is best suited to complete those projects.

Elements versus Photoshop		
Task	**Elements 2.0**	**Photoshop 7.0**
Getting help; integrated Help such as a Glossary, Hints and How To Windows, Dialog Tips, Smart Messages, and a Help search field in the toolbar	X	
Correcting images; easy-to-use "Quick Fix" window	X	
Extracting images from a video source; "Frame from video" feature	X	
Working with "print quality" image modes; support for CMYK, Lab, and Multichannel images		X
		continues on next page

Elements versus Photoshop *continued*		
Task	**Elements 2.0**	**Photoshop 7.0**
Selecting images with a Selection brush	X	
PDF slideshow export	X	
Attach to E-mail button	X	
Remove red-eye	X	X
Correcting images (change the color, brightness, and so on)	X	X
"Recipes" to guide you through simple image editing tasks	X	
Batch processing images	X	X
Utilizing a File Browser	X	X
Photomerge feature to create panoramic photos	X	
Utilizing Layers	X	X
Ability to save files for the Web	X	X
Utilizing Channels		X
Auto straighten and crop image features	X	

If you are new to image editing or graphics creation, Elements offers a great way to get up and running quickly. The learning curve isn't as steep with Elements as it is with Photoshop, and many features in Elements can be done easily with one click. Let's also not forget cost. After you buy that expensive digital camera, you will be looking to save all the spare change you can. For the price of one Photoshop, you could buy almost seven copies of Elements! (Not to mention the copies of Elements that are bundled with various hardware items such as scanners and digital cameras.) That cost difference isn't just for hoots, however.

But what can Photoshop do that Elements can't? Why would someone want to spend the extra cash to buy Photoshop? *The* main reason (in my opinion) is that Photoshop is geared more towards professionals who require the capability of creating images for high-quality printing (for those of you "in-the-know," that means that Photoshop can create CMYK, Lab, and Multichannel images—a feature Photoshop Elements lacks). Photoshop also gives you more options when preparing to put your images on a Web site and other nifty ways of selecting and modifying an image. Other than that, and the increased power and flexibility of a few different features and tools, Elements is—for the most part—Photoshop with an easy-to-use, helpful, and intuitive interface (and lower price tag!).

Image Size and Resolution

As you work with images from your digital camera, from your scanner, from a frame of video, or from the Web, you are going to be dealing with images that are all different sizes and resolutions (the amount of detail—or pixels—in an image). All of the images you will be working with in Elements are comprised of pixels—tiny squares of color and value (that's brightness/darkness, not tiny squares of high morals).

Throughout this book I refer to the *size* of an image and the *resolution* of an image. You need to under-stand what these two disparate terms mean because they play an essential role in how detailed the image is and how big it is when you print it.

The quantity of those pixels in an image determines how detailed the image actually is. Pixels are measured by a specific unit; in the United States, it is usually inches. So an image that you bring in from your scanner may be 200ppi (pixels per inch), whereas an image that you get off a Web page is most likely 72ppi. Separate from the *resolution* of an image is the *size* of the image—the actual dimen-sions of the image in inches, centimeters, millimeters, and so on. The size of the image is obviously important because it determines how big your image will be when it is printed, posted onto a Web site, or emailed to your friends and family. The size and resolution of an image are related because changing one affects the other. You'll learn more about that in Chapter 3, "*Opening and Importing Images*."

What's New in Version 2.0

Version 2.0 of Photoshop Elements added a few new and greatly helpful features:

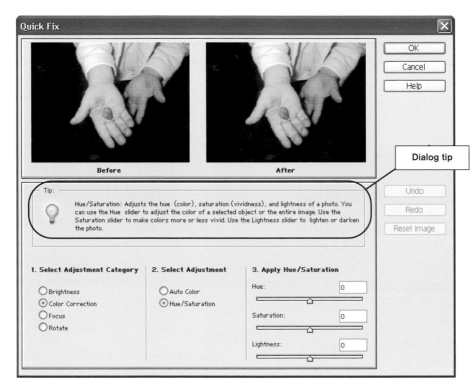

• **Dialog tips:** In Elements, certain complex windows (dialog boxes), or those that offer many options, have dialog tips. Dialog tips are little bits of handy information, relevant to whatever you are trying to accomplish and built right into the dialog window. How useful is that?!

• **Smart Messages:** This is one of those features that makes you say "Now why don't all programs have this?". When you are working in Elements and you trigger an error message for one reason or another, that error message will oftentimes have a link in it. Clicking on the link will give you more detailed information about what that error message means in plain, easy-to-understand terms. Thank goodness!

• **Help search field:** Built in to one of the toolbars is a help search field. Entering in a word or words that you are confused with will provide you with a detailed explanation. I wish life had a built-in search field. *Sigh*

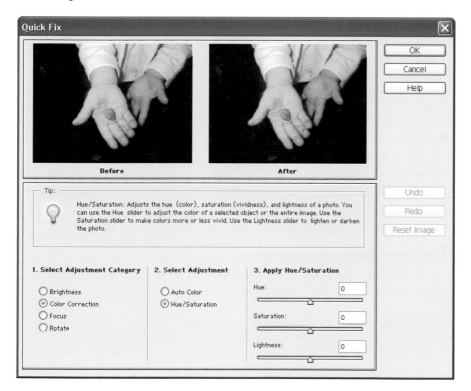

• **Quick Fix:** Quick Fix borrows the same name as my morning ritual of pounding down four cups of black tea in under an hour, and it is a great timesaving feature to boot! Nicely consolidated within one window, you can perform a multitude of color correction and manipulation tasks such as modifying the brightness, color, focus, and rotation of an image, which is a great feature when you're "on the run."

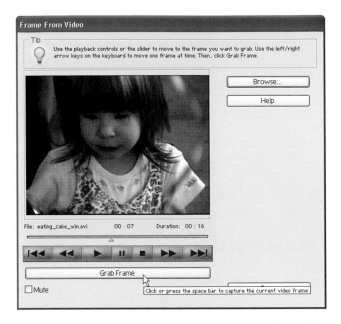

• **Frame From Video:** This feature allows you to select a video file and quickly and easily extract one or more still pictures from that video source. Turn that video camera into a still-shot digital camera with the click of a button! Frame From Video is great for extracting those perfect frames from your home movies.

• **Selection Brush:** Quickly and easily select a portion of your image just by painting! The new Selection Brush tool allows you to select just a portion of your image by painting with your paintbrush, which is a great way to very easily and quickly create a selection. I use this feature many more times throughout this book.

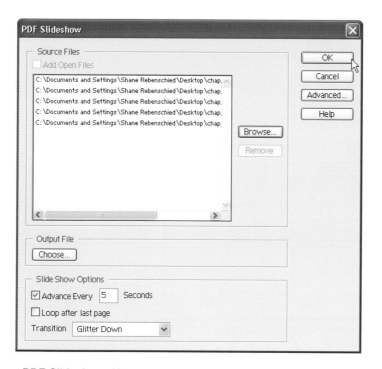

• **PDF Slideshow:** Now you can take a collection of your photos and automatically create an interactive PDF (**P**ortable **D**ocument **F**ormat) slideshow! PDFs are read by the Adobe Reader, which comes bundled for free with many different software packages. As a matter of fact, a free installer for the Adobe Acrobat Reader is on your Photoshop Elements installer CD-ROM. This feature is a great way to spice up that photo trip to the Utah Salt Flats, ensuring complete attention from whoever is viewing it. Because it's a PDF, you're also nearly guaranteed that the recipient probably already has the necessary software (Adobe Acrobat Reader) installed to view it.

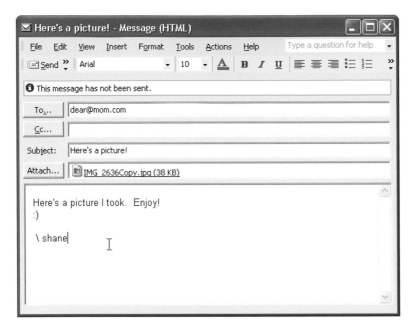

• **Attach to E-mail:** This one-click button allows you to take one of your photos and attach it to an e-mail. Photoshop Elements eliminates all the guesswork by automatically resizing your image to something more suitable for sending via email and compresses it for you as a JPEG. This ensures that the person on the receiving end of the email can download it quickly and will be able to view it with minimal difficulty.

• **Optimization:** Last but certainly not least, Photoshop Elements has been optimized for Mac OS X and Windows XP operating systems. Hurray!

Updates

At the time of writing this book, only three updates to Photoshop Elements 2.0 are available. The first two updates are for Mac users only. The first update addresses an issue with color and certain digital cameras, and the second update addresses an issue with localized language versions of Elements (if you're using Elements in a language other than English) and an automated feature called the WebContactSheet plug-in. The third update is for Windows users and addresses performance issues with certain plug-ins for users with Pentium 4 computers. You can download these updates (as well as any future program updates) from Adobe's Web site at **http://www.adobe.com/support/downloads**.

Now that you have a better understanding of Photoshop Elements, how it compares to Photoshop 7.0, and the differences between image size and resolution, you are going to move on to learning the interface of Adobe Elements in the next chapter.

2.

Interface

Welcome Screen	Interface	Menu Bar
Toolbox	Shortcuts Bar	Palettes
Palette Well	Options Bar

chap_02

Photoshop Elements 2
H•O•T CD-ROM

This chapter offers an introduction to the main items of the Photoshop Elements interface. If you have used other Adobe programs before, such as Photoshop, Illustrator, InDesign, and so on, you should feel right at home in the interface of Photoshop Elements thanks to the commonality of the interface design in the majority of Adobe's applications. You'll be dealing with most of the major interface items as you build projects and work through exercises in later chapters, but this chapter offers a brief tour of a few essential items that comprise the Elements interface.

The Welcome Screen

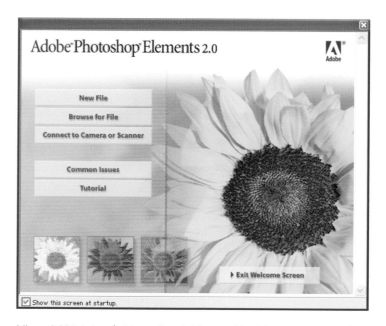

Like a faithful dog (without the slobber and bad breath, of course), Photoshop Elements happily greets you with a welcome screen every time you start the program. From this window you can easily do a variety of common tasks with a single click.

New File

The **New File** button will prompt you with settings to create a new, blank file. (You'll find more about creating new files in Chapter 3, "*Opening and Importing Images*.")

Browse for File

The **Browse for File** button will open up the powerful **File Browser** window, where you can quickly browse through all of the images on your hard drive and get information about each one *before* you open it (a great timesaving feature).

Connect to Camera or Scanner

The **Connect to Camera or Scanner** button brings up the **Select Input Source** window. If you have installed the drivers correctly for your digital camera or scanner, and if those devices are connected and turned on, you should see their names appear from the Import pull-down menu. Simply select a device, and Elements will launch the camera or scanner software, which will take over from there.

Common Issues

The **Common Issues** button will open the **How To** window with links to articles on…well…common issues that you may need resolved when working in Photoshop Elements. Clicking on one of the **Common Issues** links will show you step-by-step instructions (Adobe calls these "Recipes") on how to complete that particular task. It will even offer to complete many of the steps for you if you need extra help!

Tutorial

The **Tutorial** button launches your Web browser to display the help files on tutorials. The tutorials are similar to the How To window (described briefly in the preceding paragraph) but are more in-depth and usually revolve around completing a specific task, such as animating with layers, creating a greeting card, and so on.

▶ Exit Welcome Screen

The **Exit Welcome Screen button** causes a hot tub to appear in your living room and…oh wait. That's in Elements version 3. ;-)

The **Exit Welcome Screen** is pretty self-explanatory. Clicking on it just closes the window and deposits you in the Elements interface.

☑ Show this screen at startup.

Lastly, as you become more familiar with Elements, you may not need the assistance that the welcome screen provides and may grow tired of clicking on the Exit Welcome Screen button each time Elements launches. Adobe realized this and has put a **Show this screen at startup** check box at the bottom of the welcome screen. Uncheck this check box if you don't want the welcome screen to open automatically every time Elements is launched.

Fear not, though. Your old friend hasn't been banished to some great Adobe abyss, never to be seen from again. If you feel that you need access to the welcome screen anew, you can always easily open it back up by choosing **Window > Welcome**.

Photoshop Elements Interface

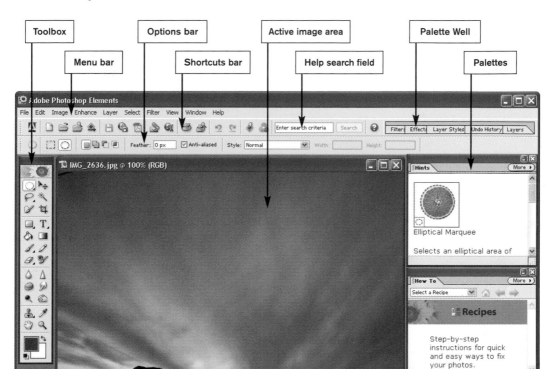

Toolbox

Menu bar

Options bar

Shortcuts bar

Active image area

Help search field

Palette Well

Palettes

Menu Bar

File   Edit   Image   Enhance   Layer   Select   Filter   View   Window   Help

As with pretty much every other program for your computer, Elements has a **menu bar** at the top of the screen. The menu bar is a series of options, all organized by topic. In Elements, the choices are File, Edit, Image, Enhance, Layer, Select, Filter, View, Window, and Help.

Many common and useful tasks in Elements are located inside these menus. For example, if you wanted to adjust the brightness or contrast of an image, you would click on **Enhance > Adjust Brightness/ Contrast > Brightness/Contrast**. You will be using many options from the menu bar over the course of this book, so you'll get plenty of practice learning and understanding where everything is.

Toolbox

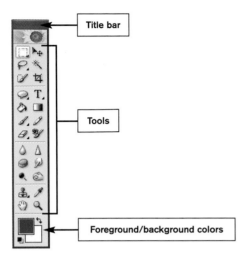

The **Toolbox**, as its name implies, is the box where all your tools are stored. From here you will select all the tools that you'll need to manipulate, select, modify, and work with your images. At the very bottom of the Toolbox is where you can select foreground and background colors for use in your image. You can also reposition the Toolbox (much like many of the other windows in Elements) anywhere you'd like on your screen. Simply drag it from its title bar to wherever you would like to move it.

If you hover your mouse over one of the tools in the Toolbox, the Hints palette (if you have it open) will show you a brief hint, or a little information, about the tool your mouse is hovering over (a *very* useful feature). It's somewhat like those little help balloons that you might have seen before, but on steroids because the hint also gives you helpful links to other related topics!

Warning: Moving your mouse cursor off of a tool in the Toolbox will cause the Hints palette to go back to its default display. If you want to read more in the Hints palette about a tool you're hovering your mouse over in the Toolbox, click on the tool to select it. Then you can scroll through the Hints palette information and click on any available links.

To select a tool to use, simply click on it. The tool that you currently have selected will be highlighted in your Toolbox.

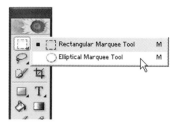

You'll also notice that certain tools in the Toolbox have a small, black triangle just below the lower-right corner of the tool. These tools have additional "hidden" tools. Contrary to the exciting and mysterious name, hidden tools are usually just tools that do similar things, but because of their separate capabilities have been broken off into their own tool. To access one of these hidden tools, simply click and hold on one of the tools that has a black triangle at its lower right, and you'll be presented with a small submenu of the hidden tools.

One other useful item, at the top of the Toolbox, is the Elements logo—a sunflower. Clicking on the sunflower will take you to Adobe Online, a central repository to download updates and add-ons for Elements.

You will learn more about the tools in the Toolbox in greater detail throughout the remainder of the chapters in this book. Rather than describe (in boring detail) what each tool does, I instead prefer to show you how the tools perform in the context of editing or creating a graphic.

Shortcuts Bar

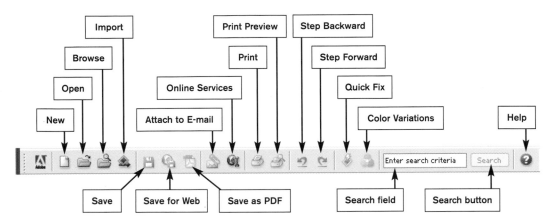

The **shortcuts bar** is essentially a collection of buttons that gives you easy, one-click access to common commands. Everything that you can do in the shortcuts bar you can also accomplish via the menu bar, except it takes fewer clicks with the shortcuts bar, and common tasks are all nicely organized and sorted out in the open for you. One extremely useful feature of the shortcuts bar is the Help search field. Need help with something? Want to know what the Selection Brush is? Type in your question in the Help search field, click the **Search** button, and you're presented with a list of possible answers in a Search Results window. Clicking on one of those results opens your Web browser and displays a detailed answer to your question. How awesome is that?

Here is a breakdown of the buttons on the shortcuts bar and what they do:

Shortcuts Bar Buttons	
Button	**Description**
New	Opens the New Image dialog box, where you can specify settings to create a new image.
Open	Opens the Open dialog box, where you can choose an image to open.
Browse	Opens the File Browser, where you can browse through your computer for an image to open.
Import	Opens the Select Import Source dialog box, where you can choose a device (scanner, digital camera, and so on) to import images from.
Save	Saves changes you've made to your image. If you haven't yet saved your Elements image, clicking the Save button opens the Save As window where you can specify a location/name to save your image.
	continues on next page

Shortcuts Bar Buttons *continued*	
Button	**Description**
Save for Web	Opens the Save for Web window, where you can specify compression settings to save your image in a format suitable for e-mailing or posting to a Web site (GIF, JPEG, and so on).
Save as PDF	Opens the Save window, where you can choose a location/name to save your image as a PDF file.
Attach to E-mail	Can automatically save your image in a format suitable for sending over e-mail (JPEG); automatically launches your default e-mail client, and attaches your image to a new email.
Online Services	Connects to Adobe Online and opens the Online Services Assistant window, where you can download add-ons to Elements as well as connect to online providers such as photo printing companies and online photo sharing companies. Internet access is required for this feature.
Print	Opens the Print window, where you can specify settings to print your image.
Print Preview	Opens the Print Preview window, where you can preview how the image will look and where it will be placed on paper when it is printed.
Step Backward	Undoes the last thing you did to your image. You can keep undoing your changes by repeatedly clicking on the Step Backward button. The number of steps backward allowed is specified in your preferences (the default is 20 steps).
Step Forward	The opposite of the Step Backward button. If you've used the Step Backward button to undo changes, the Step Forward button will redo the changes. Essentially, the Step Backward and Step Forward buttons allow you to go forward and backward through the history of your image.
Quick Fix	Opens the Quick Fix window, where you can easily modify the brightness, color, focus, and rotation of your image.
Color Variations	Opens the Color Variations window, where you can modify—in steps—the color of your image.
Search field	Use this field to enter in a term or terms you want to search the help documentation for. Clicking on the Search button will then perform a search.
Help	Launches Microsoft Internet Explorer and opens the HTML-based help documentation for Elements.

As you can see, the shortcuts bar lives up to its name and has buttons to quickly and easily access many of the frequently used items in Elements. You will practice using many of the shortcut buttons in later chapters.

Palettes

Organized by topic, *palettes* are small, floating windows that give you options and feedback about your images. When you first start using Elements, you may be a little overwhelmed by the quantity of palettes and all of the different options that you're given for each one. After working with a few of the palettes in later exercises, you'll be amazed at how simple Adobe has made it for you. The next section breaks down the different pieces and options of a standard palette.

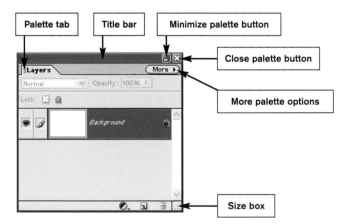

Palettes that you will mostly likely be working with the most are the File Browser, Hints, How To, Layers, Filters, Effects, and Info…heck, almost all of them! You can see a list of the available palettes in the Window menu on the menu bar.

You can reposition a palette on your workspace by dragging its title bar. You can also easily change the size of a palette by dragging at any corner of the palette (Windows only) or by dragging from the size box at the lower-right corner. One other fantastic interface feature is that palettes can be clumped together into a palette group. You can group palettes together by dragging a palette's tab onto another palette.

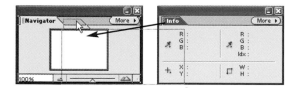

Grouping palettes allows you to customize how the palettes are laid out as well as enabling you to quickly and easily refer back to them. For now, leave your palettes in their default order until you have learned a little more about Elements. If you have already moved them around, you can reset their positions by choosing **Window > Reset Palette Locations**. Once you feel you have a good grasp on the program, *then* go back and reorder the palettes in whichever way you feel is best for your workflow. To ungroup a palette, simply do the reverse of grouping: drag a palette's tab away onto the workspace and it then becomes ungrouped.

"More" button for a palette that is docked in the Palette Well

"More" button for a palette that is not docked in the Palette Well

At the upper-right corner of each palette is a button labeled **More**. Clicking on this button will give you more options for that specific palette. Some (not all) palettes have their own preferences. You can access these palette preferences by clicking on the **More** button at the top of the palette and then choosing **Palette Options**.

Note: When a palette is in the Palette Well, the More button is replaced by a small, white triangle (visible only when you click on a palette tab in the Palette Well).

You will be dealing with various palettes and learning their different options throughout the exercises in later chapters.

The Palette Well

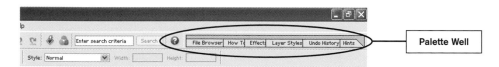

Palette Well

First introduced in Photoshop, the Palette Well was a great solution to the modern day problem of "Where do I put all these stinkin' palettes?!" Located (by default) to the right of the shortcuts bar, the Palette Well is essentially a place to store a few of your palettes that you want easy access to without cluttering up your workspace.

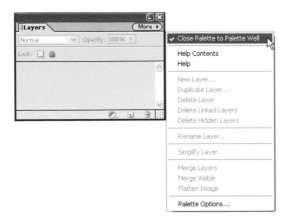

By clicking on the **More** button at the top right of a palette, you can choose the option **Close Palette to Palette Well**, which will make the palette appear in the Palette Well the next time you close that palette. Another way to add a palette to the Palette Well is to simply drag the palette (from its tab) onto the Palette Well.

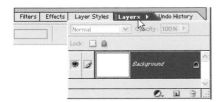

Once a palette has been docked onto the Palette Well, click on its tab and it will open up to display its options. To remove a palette from the Palette Well, simply click on a palette tab to maximize it, then drag the tab off of the Palette Well. At this point in the book, you don't have much experience with the different palettes, so the practicality of the Palette Well may seem somewhat vague to you. But after you have used Elements for awhile, you will find that the Palette Well is a tremendous help in keeping your work environment organized. However, don't put any palettes in the Palette Well that you use often or refer to frequently because the content of docked palettes isn't continually visible (all you see is their tabs poking out of the Palette Well). I like to keep the File Browser, Undo History, Filters, and Effects palettes docked in the Palette Well. Other palettes such as Layers, Hints, and Info I keep out all the time because I use them often. However, in the screenshots in this book, you will see the Layers palette docked in the Palette Well. This was done simply to conserve space in my work environment while taking screenshots. For your own setup, I would still recommend leaving the Layers palette open and not docked to the Palette Well.

Options Bar

By default, the **options bar** is located right beneath the shortcuts bar. It's a unique area of the Elements interface—the options displayed in the options bar will change depending on which tool is currently selected.

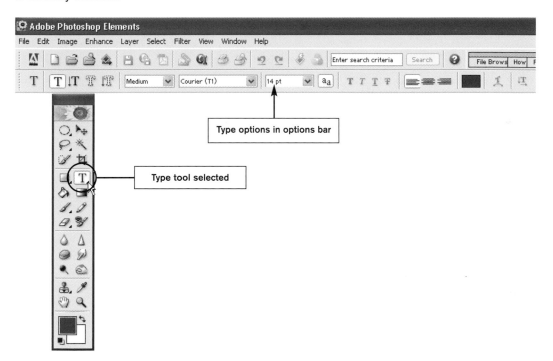

Although some tools have very few options to choose from in the options bar (such as the Arrow tool and the Eyedropper tool), other tools have a large number of options (such as the Type tool and the Marquee tool, to name a few). The options bar is a very important part of the Elements interface. You will use it to modify how a few of your tools perform so that you can create certain effects or accomplish specific tasks. Again, rather than go over each option in the options bar (which would surely put you to sleep), I instead integrate learning about the options bar into the different exercises and examples that you will be building later in this book.

Now that you've had a brief tour of the Elements interface, next you're going to actually start opening and working with images. So batten down the hatches Matey, and shiver me timbers, and all that other good pirate stuff…here is where the fun begins. :-)

3.

Opening and
Importing Images

| Supported Formats | Importing from a Scanner |
| Importing from a Digital Camera |
| Opening Images | File Browser | Place |
| Frame from Video | New Image | Image Modes |

chap_03

Photoshop Elements 2
H•O•T CD-ROM

This chapter walks you through the basic but fundamental steps of opening images, creating new images, and importing images from various sources. You'll learn how to use the File Browser, open scanned and digital camera images, create new images, place vector artwork into another file, grab a frame of video, and change image color modes. If that sounds like a mouthful of new skills, you'll gain confidence by following the exercises and getting a taste of hands-on experience using these features.

Supported Image Formats

As you begin to open and work with images in Elements, recognizing the different kinds of images that Elements can open is important. Images from different sources, such as your scanner, a Web page, or from an e-mail that someone sent you, will come in a variety of different formats. For example, most images on the Internet that look like photographs are probably saved in an image format called JPEG (also known as JPG). This is also a common image format that many digital cameras automatically store the photos you shoot as. However, if you were to scan an image on your desktop scanner, it would most likely be saved as a high-quality format such as TIFF, BMP, or PICT. For reference, here is a list of the different image formats that Elements can open:

Supported Image Formats	
Photoshop	PSD, PDD
BMP	BMP, RLE, DIB
CompuServe GIF	GIF
Photoshop EPS	EPS
EPS TIFF Preview	EPS
Filmstrip	FLM
JPEG	JPG, JPEG, JPE
Generic PDF	PDF, PDP, AI
Generic EPS	AI3, AI4, AI5, AI6, AI7, AI8, PS, EPS, AI
PCX	PCX
Photoshop PDF	PDF, PDP
Acrobat TouchUp Image	PDF, AI, PDP
Photo CD	PCD
PICT file	PCT, PICT
Pixar	PXR
PNG	PNG
Raw	RAW
Scitex CT	SCT
Targa	TGA, VDA, ICB, VST
TIFF	TIF, TIFF
Wireless bitmap	WBMP, WBM

I. ——————————**Importing Images from a Scanner**

Once you have connected your desktop scanner to your computer and correctly installed the software that came with it, scanning images and bringing them into Elements to edit is a breeze. If your scanner software installs either Photoshop Elements–compatible plug-in modules or TWAIN drivers (refer to your scanner's user manual or to the scanner manufacturer's Web site to see if it does, in fact, support these features), follow these steps:

1. From the welcome screen, click on the **Connect to Camera or Scanner** button. This will open the **Select Import Source** dialog box.

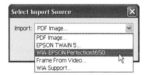

2. If you've installed the software correctly, you should see the name of your scanner from the pull-down menu. In the screenshot above, I've selected my scanner, an **Epson Perfection 1650**.

3. Select your scanner name from the pull-down menu and click **OK**. This will launch your scanner software. From this point you can proceed with scanning your images by following the instructions that come with your scanner software.

Note: These steps don't demonstrate how to scan images from your particular scanner because the process differs widely depending on the brand and model of scanner you are using.

4. After you have scanned your photograph (in this case, a picture of Chopin's grave in Paris), it should appear in a new window within Elements. From here you can edit and modify it (as you'll learn in later chapters) to your heart's content!

The process of scanning a photograph and then opening that photograph in Elements is relatively simple. Most of the work is done by the actual scanner software that came with your scanner. Elements merely acts as a façade for your scanner software.

*Tip: Instead of clicking on the **Connect to Camera or Scanner** button on the welcome screen, you can also access your scanner by choosing **File > Import** and choosing your scanner name there. You should see the same list of input options that you get from the Select Input Source window that you access from the welcome screen.*

Note: If your scanner does not come with Photoshop Elements–compatible plug-ins or TWAIN scanner drivers, you will not see your scanner name listed from the File > Import menu. Instead, you will have to use the scanner software that came with your scanner to scan in your image. From the scanner software, simply save the scanned image as a TIFF, PICT, or BMP, and then open that image in Elements. From Elements, first resave your scanned image as a Photoshop file (PSD), then work with the image as you normally would.

Importing Images from a Digital Camera

The process of importing images from a digital camera is nearly identical to the process of importing images from a scanner. After you have correctly installed the camera software, you can follow these steps:

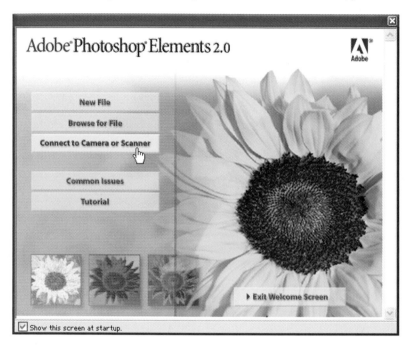

1. From the welcome screen, click on the **Connect to Camera or Scanner** button. If you don't have your welcome screen open, you can open it again by choosing **Window > Welcome**.

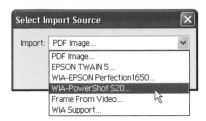

2. Click on the **Select Import Source** pull-down menu and choose your camera name. If you don't see your camera listed here, make sure that you have the camera drivers correctly installed (refer to your camera's user manual for driver installation instructions) and that you're using the latest version of those camera drivers (refer to the camera manufacturer's Web site for the latest drivers). In my case, I've selected my camera, a **Canon PowerShot S20**. Click **OK**.

At this point, Elements will launch the software that came with your digital camera (assuming you installed all the software correctly). Because the bundled software for digital cameras differs widely, these steps don't show this process. Refer to the manual that came with your digital camera for more information on retrieving images from the camera.

After you have selected and imported your image(s) from your digital camera, Elements automatically opens them. From there, you can save the images as Photoshop documents (PSD) and may modify/ edit them.

Note: *Some digital cameras, when connected to your computer, mount themselves on your Desktop the same way a hard drive or CD-ROM does (you'll see a camera icon appear on your Desktop). In this case, you cannot access the camera images from the **Connect to Camera or Scanner** button in the welcome screen, nor from the **File > Import** menu. Instead you can use Elements' **File Browser** feature (which you'll learn about later in this chapter), or you can choose **File > Open** to navigate to and open the digital camera's images. Once you've opened the image(s) in Elements, you can save them as Adobe Photoshop (PSD) documents and can then modify/edit them as you would any Elements image.*

The trickiest part to the process of importing images from a digital camera or scanner is making sure that you install the camera or scanner software correctly. Once you've done that, the rest is a breeze.

3. ————————Opening Images

Showing you how to best use Photoshop Elements without showing you how to open an image would be like showing you how to drive a Ferrari and not giving you the keys. It would be like your parents raising you and teaching you everything there is to know in life, but never letting you leave the house. It would be like…well…you get the point. Opening an image is a very simple but fundamental piece in working with any program.

1. Copy the **chap_03** folder and files from the **H•O•T CD-ROM** to your hard drive.

2. From the menu bar, choose **File > Open**.

*This brings up the **Open** dialog box. This window will look different depending on the operating system you're using (Windows XP, Windows 2000, Mac OS 9, Mac OS X, and so on), but the basic concept remains the same. Within the Open dialog box you can browse, locate, and open any file that is supported by Photoshop Elements (for a list of supported file formats, see the chart at the beginning of this chapter).*

3. From the **Open** dialog box, browse to where you copied the **chap_03** folder. Because I copied mine to the Desktop, I'm going to browse there.

4. Open the **chap_03** folder, and then open the **images** folder. In the images folder, you should see five images. Click once on one of the images to see a small preview of the image. If you're using Windows XP, hovering your mouse over the image will also show you more information about that image, such as the dimensions, when the picture was taken, and so on. This same information is also available on other operating systems; it is just located elsewhere (I show you where in later chapters).

5. Double-click on **IMG_2636**. Elements opens the image.

6. Because you won't be needing this image again in this exercise, close it by choosing **File > Close**.

Double-clicking on an image from your hard drive doesn't always open that image in Elements. That particular file type (JPG, GIF, TIFF, and so on) might not be associated with Elements. Double-clicking on an image file might cause that image to open in a different program. In the Windows version of Elements, Adobe has added an easy way for you to change which image file types should be opened with Elements when they're double-clicked.

By choosing *Edit > File Association* (a Windows-only feature…sorry fellow Macintosh users), you can pick and choose which file types should be opened with Elements when double-clicked.

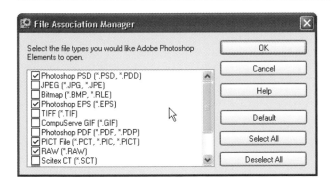

Putting checkmarks next to the different file types will instruct Windows to launch Elements when you double-click an image with one of those file types. Nifty!

Using the File Browser Palette

In the last exercise, you saw how to easily open an image using the File > Open command. In this exercise, you're going to look at a much more "feature-rich" way of opening images that gives you a lot of information about an image before you choose to open it—a very useful feature if you're dealing with large images that take a long time to open. First introduced in Photoshop, the File Browser is my preferred method for browsing and opening images. The File Browser allows you to not only browse and open images, but also move, rename, delete, and rotate images, as well as create new folders. It'll even provide you with a detailed description of the specifics of each image, such as the date the picture was taken, the shutter speed, F-stop settings, and a whole bunch of other information that you never knew existed (if your digital camera stores what's called "EXIF" data; if not, the File Browser will just display basic information about the image, such as file size, dimensions, and so on). Now if I can just get it to file my taxes for me as well…

1. First make sure that you have the File Browser window open by choosing **Window > File Browser**.

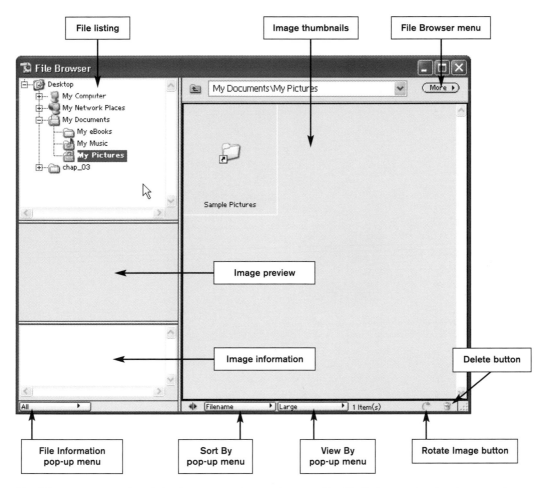

The File Browser window is broken up into four main parts. The file listing section is where you browse through your computer's hard drive. The image thumbnails section is where you see small thumbnails of the images and folders within the directory that is currently selected in the file listing section. The image preview section is where you can see a small preview of an image that you select in the image thumbnails section. Lastly, the image information section gives you various feedback and information about the image that is selected in the image thumbnails section. *whew*

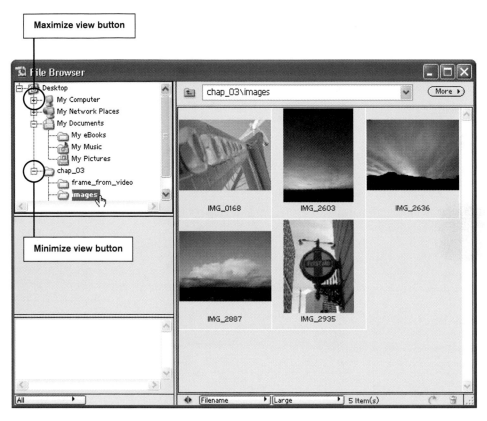

2. In the file listing section, navigate to where you copied the chap_03 files and click on the **maximize view** button to the left of the **chap_03** folder (in the Mac File Browser window, the maximize and minimize icons are gray triangles instead of plus and minus signs). This will expand the folder and display the subfolders. Click on the **images** folder to display the contents of that directory. You should see five image thumbnails appear in the image thumbnails section. Single-click on one of the thumbnails.

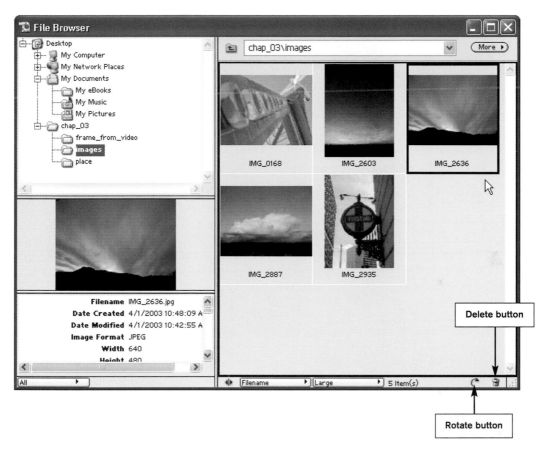

When you select an image from the image thumbnails section, you'll see a larger thumbnail appear in the image preview section and a detailed description appear in the image information section. If your camera stores EXIF data (see the manual that came with your camera), you'll see a very detailed description of the image including the exact time it was taken, the exposure time, the F-stop setting, and a whole bunch of other information that most digital cameras create automatically when you take a photo. How's that for being helpful?

3. Double-click on one of the image thumbnails to open the full-sized image. After you've opened the image, go ahead and close it again (by choosing **File > Close**) because you won't be needing it again in this exercise. I know, I know…opening and closing images is fun and all, but try to stay with me here. Focusss…focussss…

Note: As I mentioned in the introduction to this exercise, the File Browser can do much more than just browse for and open images. Once you have an image thumbnail selected, you can rotate it by clicking on the Rotate button, and you can delete it by clicking on the Delete button. By clicking on the File Browser menu button, you can see that there are many more options available, such as renaming the image (and even options for renaming multiple files at a time [batch renaming], creating new folders, and so on). I'm not going to be the one responsible for causing you to lapse into a coma by going over what each option does here, but you will get a chance to use quite a few of these File Browser features in later exercises.

4. Click on the **File Browser** menu button at the top right of the File Browser palette, and from the pop-up menu choose **Dock to Palette Well**. This docks the File Browser to the Palette Well, where you can easily access it by simply clicking on its tab.

You will be using the File Browser quite a bit throughout the remainder of the exercises in this book, so no need to say goodbye. You'll! be working with it again soon enough. *sniffle*

5. ——————Place

Now that you've seen various ways of opening images, you'll learn one method of combining multiple documents together. In this simple exercise, you're going to use the Place feature of Elements to add a logo to a business card.

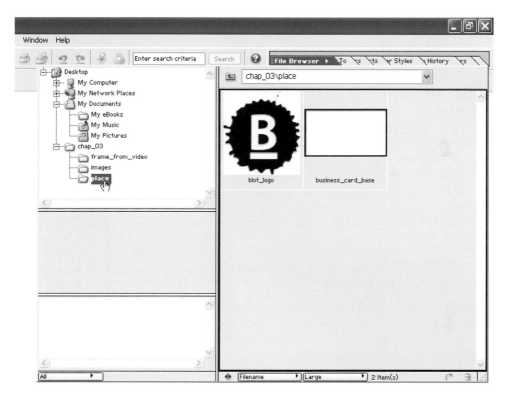

1. Using the File Browser, navigate to where you copied your chap_03 folder on your computer, open the **chap_03** folder, and single-click on the **place** folder within it. You should see two image files: **business_card_base** and **blot_logo**.

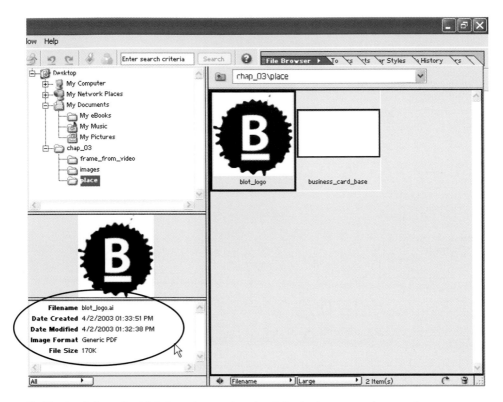

2. Single-click on the **blot_logo** image thumbnail. In the image preview section, you can see that the image is a logo for my illustration business, Blot Illustration. Also note that in the image information section (circled above) you can see that the Image Format is Generic PDF. You're going to use the Elements Place command to add this image file to the other image in the **place** folder, **business_card_base**.

The Place command will only allow you to place PDF, Adobe Illustrator, or EPS (Encapsulated PostScript) files into other images. You'll be learning more about PDF files in Chapter 12, "Elements and the Web." Now that you've seen what format the blot_logo image is in, you're going to open the business card and add the logo to it.

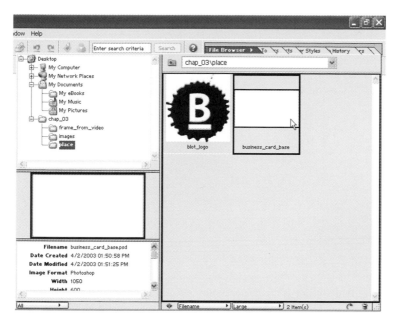

3. In the File Browser, double-click on the **business_card_base** image thumbnail. This will open the image in a new window in Elements.

4. Choose **File > Place**. This will open the **Place** window, which looks and functions much like the Open window you learned about earlier in this chapter. The difference with the Place window, however, is that now you're browsing for a file to place inside the image you currently have open, **business_card_base**.

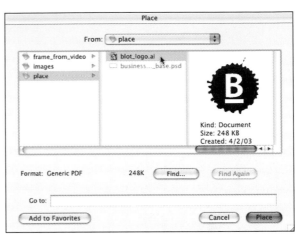

Windows XP   *Macintosh OS X*

5. In the **Place** dialog box, navigate to the **chap_03** folder and into the **place** folder. You should see one file, **blot_logo**. Double-click on it.

Note: The Mac OS X Place window looks a little different than the Windows XP one (pictured above). I've also included a screenshot of the Macintosh Place window (also pictured above) for you Mac users out there…you know who you are. ;-)

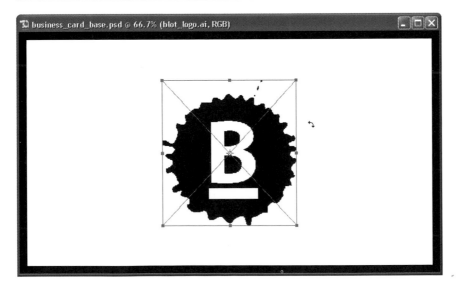

This places the Blot Illustration logo right in the middle of the business card image.

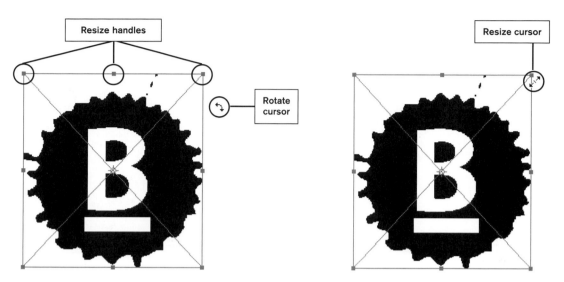

Notice the gray box around the outside of the logo with gray boxes on the corners and the middles of the box. These are called resize handles. Dragging the resize handles around will cause the logo to…well…resize! Also note that moving your mouse cursor over the resize handles causes your cursor icon to change to two opposite-facing arrows.

Tip: Resizing a placed graphic (such as the Blot Illustration logo) might cause the logo to be resized nonproportionally (meaning it might get squished or stretched). To resize a graphic proportionately as you drag its resize handles, hold down the **Shift** key while dragging. Also, if you hold the **Option** key (Mac) or **Alt** key (Windows) as you drag the resize handles, the graphic will resize from the center instead of from the bottom-left.

Moving your mouse cursor off to the sides or to the top or bottom of the graphic, you'll notice that your cursor changes again, this time to a Rotate icon. Dragging your mouse around will cause the placed logo to rotate.

Note: If you're more of a numbers person, you can also resize, rotate, and skew your placed graphic numerically from the options bar.

6. To increase the size of the logo a little, hold down the **Option+Shift** keys (Mac) or **Alt+Shift** keys (Windows) and then drag one of the corner resize handles up.

7. Once you're satisfied with the logo's size, you need to "commit place." I know that this sounds like a very serious thing to do (especially for you bachelors out there who shirk from the word "commit"), but all it means is simply that Elements needs to know when you're finished resizing the placed file. Up until this point the Blot Illustration logo is a vector graphic (see Chapter 7, "*Shapes and Layer Styles,*" for a full description of vector graphics and bitmap graphics). Once you commit place, however, Elements changes it from a vector graphic to a bitmap graphic. From that point on, you shouldn't resize the placed graphic to a larger size, because it will look distorted and unattractive. You can scale a bitmap graphic smaller and it will look fine, but if you scale it larger it will not. To commit place, simply press **Return** (Mac) or **Enter** (Windows). You can also click on the **Commit Place** button in your options bar.

Note: The Place command is essentially designed to place a vector graphic (Adobe Illustrator, PDF, EPS) inside of another image document—in this case, a business card.

*Before you click on the Commit Place button, some of you might be wondering what that **Anti-Alias** check box does. Leaving this check box checked will anti-alias your placed graphic (it will smooth the edges of the graphic) when you commit the place. Unchecking the Anti-Alias check box will alias the graphic (it won't smooth the edges of the graphic; instead it will be jagged) when you commit the place.*

8. Choose **File > Save As**. Name the file **business_card**, make sure that **Format** is set to **Photoshop**, and save it in the **chap_03** folder. You'll be using this business card again in later exercises. After you save the **business_card** file, close it by choosing **File > Close**.

*Note: Performing a Save As on a file will allow you to save your file as a different name and/or in a different location on your computer. That way you won't permanently overwrite the file that you originally opened (**business_card_base**).*

Congratulations! You just merged two separate image files together! That is the fundamental, rudimentary idea behind photo compositing, which you'll be learning about in Chapter 11, "Photo Manipulation."

Video Formats Supported by Elements 2.0

In the next exercise, you'll learn how to import a frame of video into Elements. Don't worry if you don't have any video on your hard drive to import; you'll find a sample movie to work with in the **chap_03** exercise folder. To import your own video files, here is a helpful chart listing the video formats that Photoshop Elements will accept on both Macs and Windows.

Accepted Video Formats		
	Macintosh	Windows
AVI		X
WMV		X
ASF		X
MPG	X	X
MPEG	X	X
M1V		X
MOV (QuickTime)	X	

6.————————**Frame From Video**

Frame From Video is one of the cool, new features of Elements 2.0. Simply, it allows you to grab a frame—or multiple frames—from a video file. Elements won't actually get the video off of your video camera—that you have to do yourself. But once you have your video saved in a format that Elements supports, you can use the Frame From Video feature to grab some still frames from it. Why the heck would you need this? Say you have some video clips—of the kids that you want the grandparents to see, or maybe some vacation footage that you want to show off to your friends—but you don't really want to wait 10 hours while you e-mail them a 50MB video file over your 56k modem. Instead you can just peruse through your movie file, grab some choice frames, and then e-mail them to whomever you'd like. The video camera also doubles nicely as a dual-purpose digital camera, but one that you can sort through and pick out the best pictures from. Granted, the resolution of a still picture taken from a video camera isn't usually digital camera–quality, but if you're just e-mailing a snapshot to some friends or posting pictures to a Web site for family to see, it really makes little difference.

1. Choose **File > Import > Frame From Video**.

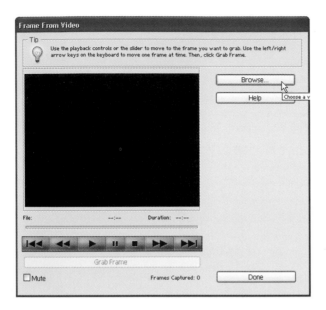

2. This will open the **Frame From Video** window. First you need to select the video that you want to grab a frame from. Click **Browse**.

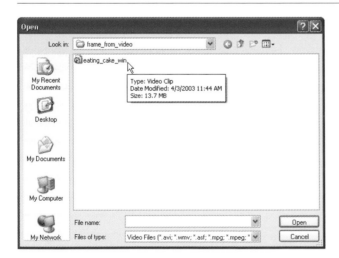

3. The **Open** window will appear. Navigate to the **chap_03** folder and then into the **frame_from_video** folder. If you're running Windows, click on the file **eating_cake_win** and then click **Open**. On a Mac, click on the file **eating_cake_mac** and then click **Open**.

*Note: The file eating_cake_win is encoded as an AVI (**A**udio **V**ideo **I**nterleave) file whereas the eating_cake_mac is encoded as a QuickTime movie file.*

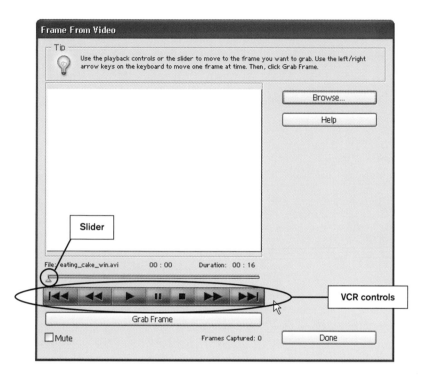

4. Now all that you need to do is pick the frame(s) you want to "grab." There are three methods from which to choose from when reviewing a video clip. You can use the VCR-type controls to play through the video and pause on the frame you want to grab. You can drag the slider back and forth until you've located the frame you want to keep. Or, you can use the left and right arrow keys on your keyboard to navigate through the video clip one frame at a time. Of course, you can also use all three of these methods in combination to find the exact frame that you want.

I use a combination of all three methods. I start with the VCR controls to find the general area of the video I want. Then I switch to the slider to get closer to my preferred frame. Lastly I switch to the ever-so-precise right and left arrows on my keyboard to browse through the video one frame at a time until I've located the exact frame I'm looking for.

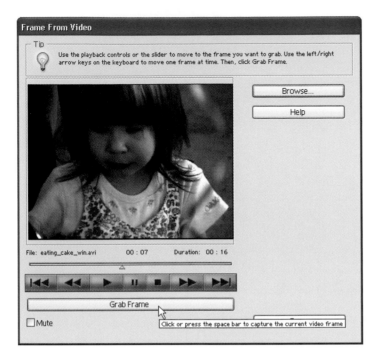

5. Once you've located the frame of the video you want to grab, click **Grab Frame**. You'll notice a slight pause, and then behind the Frame From Video window will appear the frame of video that you grabbed, but now in its own window! Awesome! In later chapters, you'll learn what you can do with those images, including manipulating them, putting them on a Web page, e-mailing them to friends and family, and so on.

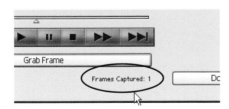

6. You can continue browsing through the video and clicking **Grab Frame** each time you see a video frame that you like. Elements keeps a running tally of how many frames you've captured from this particular clip. When you're done, click **Done**.

7. You won't be needing these images again, so close them by choosing **File > Close**. If you are prompted to save your changes, click **No**.

For those of you that dabble in video, this is a great way to easily pull individual still images out of the video clip to edit, manipulate, or e-mail to friends and relatives.

7. —————————Creating a New Image

In this exercise, you will learn the process of creating a new image in Elements. Just like opening an image, creating a new, blank image is one of the fundamental need-to-knows.

1. Choose **File > New**.

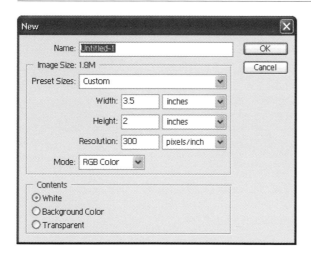

2. Change the settings to match what you see in the image above.

In the screenshot above, I'm creating a new image to design a business card in. It's 3.5 inches wide, 2 inches tall and, because it is going to be printed, is at a high resolution of 300 ppi. The table on the following page summarizes the options you can set when creating a new image.

New Image Options	
Option	**Description**
Name	Give your image a name here (optional). This name is used when saving your file. If you don't enter a name in here, Elements will prompt you for a name when you save the file.
Preset Sizes	Select, from a large list, preset image sizes for common uses such as **Letter**, **Legal**, **5 × 7**, and so on. Alternatively, you can set your own custom image size in the Width and Height fields.
Width and Height	Choose what your measurement unit is (**inches**, **pixels**, **mm**, and so on) and then enter in your dimensions in the Width and Height fields.
Resolution	You can see as you change the number in the Resolution field that it has no effect on the physical size of the image. The resolution determines how many pixels per inch your image contains (although clicking on the Resolution pull-down menu also lets you set the amount of pixels per centimeter). The higher the resolution is, the more detailed the image is when printed. If an image is going to be e-mailed or posted on a Web site, I would suggest setting the resolution to something low, like 72 ppi.
Mode	Allows you to set the mode for this image, such as **RGB Color** (RGB stands for **R**ed, **G**reen, **B**lue, by the way), **Grayscale**, or **Bitmap.** You'll learn about these image modes in more detail in the section that follows this exercise.
Background Layer	Choose what the initial layer contains, such as white, whatever the Background Color is set to in your Toolbox, or to just have it be transparent. (More on layers in Chapter 4, "*Layers.*")

3. Click **OK**. A new, blank Elements window is opened.

You will be creating (and opening) quite a few images during the course of this book, so you'll get plenty of experience with setting and understanding these new image options.

4. You won't be needing this blank image again, so close it by choosing **File > Close**.

What Are Image Modes?

When creating a new image (as you just saw in the last exercise), you have three choices for image modes: **RGB Color**, **Grayscale**, and **Bitmap**. What do these image modes mean and when should you choose one over another?

RGB Color is pretty self-explanatory. If you want to create a color image, you want to set your image mode to RGB Color. Elements—unbeknownst to you for the most part—divides your image up into three "channels:" red, green, and blue. RGB images, on the whole, are mostly used to be displayed onscreen, such as images sent via e-mail or posted onto a Web site. However, most common consumer inkjet printers also print RGB images quite well so don't worry about your images looking like a color disaster when they're printed.

Grayscale is another self-explanatory one. It's used when you want to create a black-and-white image. A grayscale image has no color information, so you'll only be able to work with black, white, and all of the grays in-between. Grayscale images are mostly used when working with black-and-white photography. After you've created a grayscale image, you can easily change it to an RGB color image if you'd like by simply choosing **Image > Mode > RGB Color**.

The last image mode option is Bitmap. An image that has a color mode of Bitmap is comprised of only black or white—no grays and no color. Bitmap color mode images are mostly used for line art (drawings). However, if you are going to edit an image that has an image mode of Bitmap, Elements requires that you change the image mode to something else first, such as grayscale or RGB color.

_____Working with Image Modes

In this exercise, you will learn to change the color mode of an image. You will open a color RGB image and convert it to Grayscale and Bitmap modes, observing how the image changes as you alter the image modes.

1. Open the **File Browser** and navigate to the **chap_03** folder and into the **images** folder. In there, locate the image **IMG_2935** (the first aid sign) and open it by double-clicking on it.

To give you an idea of the different color modes and what they look like, you're going to modify the color mode of this image.

Color mode displayed
in image title bar

You can tell what the color mode is by looking at the image title bar.

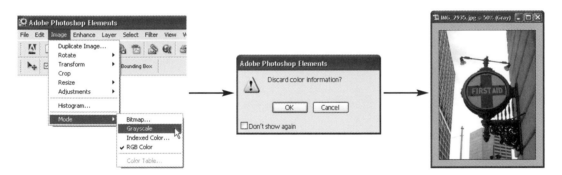

2. Choose **Image > Mode > Grayscale**. You'll then be presented with a dialog box that's there just to make sure that you didn't click on that menu item by mistake. It says **Discard color information?**. And yes, you're purposely converting this image to grayscale, so click **OK**. Once you do that, presto! You now have a black-and-white image.

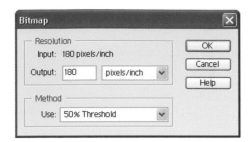

3. Now choose **Image > Mode > Bitmap**. You'll be presented with the **Bitmap** dialog box asking you what you want the resolution of the output image to be as well as what method of bitmap translation you want. Leave the resolution set to **180**, but change the method to **50% Threshold**. Click **OK**.

4. Neat-o! Now you have a stylized version of your image, somewhat akin to a photocopy. As I mentioned earlier, an image with an image mode of Bitmap can only have black or white—no grays and no color. So here is a translation of the original color image, but comprised of only two colors: black and white.

5. You won't be needing this image again, so after you're finished admiring your handiwork, close it by choosing **File > Close**.

You might have noticed under the Image > Mode pull-down menu another image mode called **Indexed Color**. *This mode is primarily used when saving an image as a GIF file, suitable for posting onto a Web page or e-mailing to someone. As such, I don't discuss the Indexed Color image mode until Chapter 12, "Elements and the Web."*

Now that you have some of the basics out of the way, in the next chapter you'll be learning all about layers—the fundamental building block needed to create complex images in Elements. Using multiple layers allows great freedom when creating an image because it enables you to easily combine, overlay, and mix images together to create a unique composition. I bet you're just itching to get started… so what are you waiting for? Read on!

4.

Layers

| What Are Layers? | Layer Basics |
| Non-Destructive Editing | Fill and Adjustment Layers |
| Blending Modes |

chap_04

Photoshop Elements 2
H•O•T CD-ROM

This chapter introduces you to the very important, powerful, and flexible feature known as layers. Layers offer much more control over editing your image. By putting different elements on different layers, you gain the ability to modify one part of your image without modifying any other part. Using layers also opens the door to being able to make changes and alterations to your images without those changes being permanent. By using fill and adjustment layers, you can easily change your entire image with the click of a button. Come one, come all, to the wonderful, feature-filled world of layers!

What Are Layers?

The greatest invention since those little plastic nibs that hold the ends of your shoelaces together is the advent of layers in digital imaging programs such as Photoshop and Elements. The name "layers," by itself, is pretty self-explanatory.

Using layers allows you to put different parts of your image on different, overlapping layers. You can think of layers as transparent sheets stacked one atop another. In the preceding image, Background layer is the bottom-most layer. Clouds layer is above the Background layer, and anything located on the Clouds layer will overlap anything on the Background layer. The Sunflower layer overlaps the Clouds layer, and so on and so forth. Pretty simple concept, eh? The power of layers is evident when you can create one image composition that is actually comprised of many different images, each on its own layer. By putting separate parts of your image on their own layers, you can easily manipulate them separately from the other parts of your image. As you'll see in later exercises, layers give you maximum control over your imagery. I highly encourage you to use them whenever possible.

I. ──────────**Layer Basics—Part One**

1. Copy the **chap_04** folder and files from the **H•O•T CD-ROM** to your hard drive.

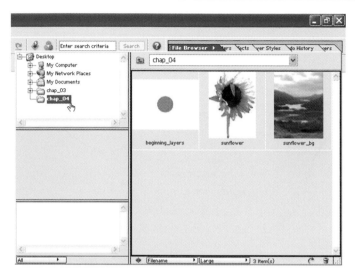

2. Open the **File Browser** window by choosing **Window > File Browser**, and navigate to where you copied your **chap_04** folder. (I copied mine to the Desktop to make it easy to find.) Double-click on the **beginning_layers** file to open it.

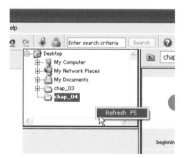

*Note: If you don't see your **chap_04** folder in the File Browser window, right-click (Windows) or Ctrl+click (Mac) anywhere on the file listing portion of the File Browser window. A pop-up menu appears (with one option) that says **Refresh**. Select that option to refresh the file listing, displaying your **chap_04** folder. Elements keeps a cache of the location of your files, and if you've added something (such as copying the **chap_04** folder off of the **H•O•T CD-ROM**) since the last time you used the File Browser, it might not display your new files. Using that Refresh option, however, forces Elements to update its cache.*

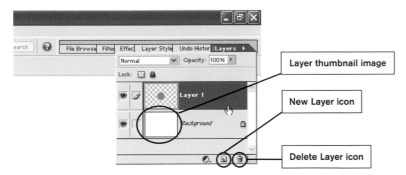

Layer thumbnail image

New Layer icon

Delete Layer icon

3. Once you've opened the **beginning_layers** image, open the **Layers** palette (click on its tab if you've docked it to the Palette Well, or choose **Window > Layers**).

See how this file has two layers, Layer 1 and Background? Whenever you create a new image, by default, Elements creates this background layer for you. (It does this because all images in Elements have to have at least one layer in them. In other words, you cannot have an image in Elements that has no layers in it. Images must have at least one layer.) Also notice the small lock icon to the right-hand side of the Background layer. This means that the layer is partially locked and (in this case) you cannot move it. In later exercises, you'll see how to alter that layer and why you would need or want to.

Note: *Notice that the Layer 1 thumbnail image has a blue circle in it that is surrounded by a gray and white checkered pattern? Whenever you see that pattern, it signifies a **transparent area**. This allows you to instantly see that the entire layer is transparent except for the blue circle. Of course, any part of the image that is transparent will allow you to see through to whatever is in the layer underneath.*

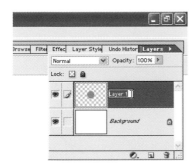

4. Double-click on the layer named **Layer 1**. This will highlight the layer name and allow you to name it something else. Type **blue circle** and press **Enter** (Windows) or **Return** (Mac) to rename the layer. Make sure the blue circle layer is selected by single-clicking on it in the Layers palette.

Note: *In Elements, when you want to modify a layer or edit the contents of a layer, you first need to make sure that layer is selected in the Layers palette (selected layers are highlighted in blue). That's easy enough to do. Just single-click on the layer you want to modify in your Layers palette, and you're good to go.*

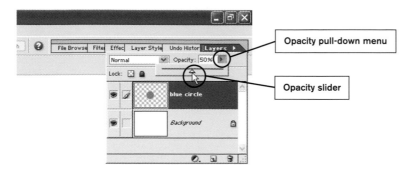

Opacity pull-down menu

Opacity slider

5. Single-click on the **Opacity** pull-down menu, and a slider will pop up underneath it. By dragging the **Opacity** slider back and forth, you can modify the opacity (transparency) of everything that is in the blue circle layer (the layer you currently have selected). Drag the slider to **50%** and then release your mouse button.

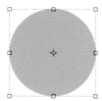

Notice how the blue circle is now lighter than it was. That's because it is now 50 percent opaque, and you're partially seeing through to the white Background layer beneath it.

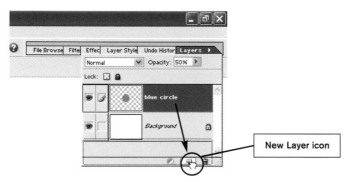

New Layer icon

6. In your Layers palette, drag the **blue circle** layer onto the **New Layer** icon. This will duplicate the blue circle layer, place it above the original in the Layers palette, and automatically rename it **blue circle copy**. Easy!

Note: This is only one way to duplicate a layer. As with most things in Elements, you can do the same thing many ways. This is my preferred method of duplicating a layer—it's quick, easy, and takes fewer mouse clicks than the other methods.

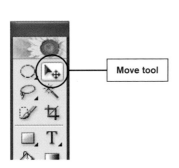

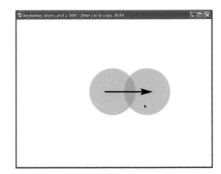

Move tool

7. With the **blue circle copy** layer selected, select the **Move** tool. Drag the blue circle on the document over to the right a little.

Notice how it's darker where the blue circles overlap? That's because you have two overlapping shapes that have their opacities set to 50% (the blue circle copy also has that same 50% opacity because...well...it's a copy). Where the two shapes overlap, they create a darker area. This is just one small example of how using layers can be helpful. By having each blue circle on separate layers, you can move, edit, and manipulate one circle without affecting the other.

What if you wanted to move both those blue circles at the same time? If you were to drag one circle around the image space, you'd quickly notice that even though you were thinking about moving both circles together (sorry...Elements doesn't read minds...yet), only one circle will actually move. There is a way to get the images on both of the layers to move at the same time.

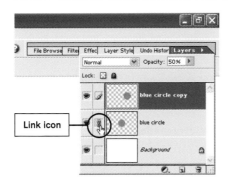

Link icon

8. In the Layers palette, with the **blue circle copy** layer selected, click on the small box between the blue circle thumbnail image and the black eye. (Ohhh...that sounds rather nefarious, doesn't it? I'll talk more about that eye in the next exercise.) You'll see a little chain icon appear in that box. This means that the layer you have selected (**blue circle copy**) and the **blue circle** layer are now linked. Make sure your **Move** tool is still selected and drag one of the blue circles around in the image window. You'll notice that they now move together! When you want to unlink them, simply click on the link icon and they'll be unlinked. You can then move them around independently again.

9. When you are finished moving the circles around the image space, unlink them in the Layers palette by clicking on the chain icon to remove it.

You must be getting sick of those two blue circles by now. In the next step, you're going to change the color of one of them.

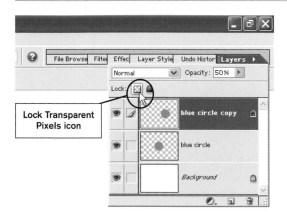

10. Single-click on the **blue circle copy** layer and then click on the **Lock Transparent Pixels** icon.

*When you lock the transparent pixels, you'll notice a small lock icon appear to the right of the **blue circle copy** layer. This lock signifies that you cannot edit the transparent parts of the **blue circle copy** layer. When modifying the color of this circle shape (as you're about to do), you'll want to make sure that you don't edit any other part of the image except the contents of the layer—in this case, a circle. Locking the transparent pixels does just that.*

***Note:** As you can already see, you're working with the Layers palette quite a bit. If it is easier for you, you can undock the Layers palette so that it is always visible as you work with your images (instead of having to click on its tab in the Palette Well every time you want access to it). To undock the Layers palette, click on its tab in the Palette Well to open the Layers palette; then drag the Layers tab off of the Palette Well to a different location on your computer screen. This will make your Layers palette undock and become a free-floating palette that you can place wherever you'd like.*

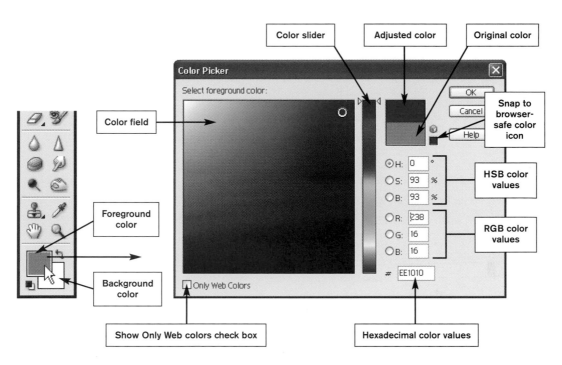

Color slider

Adjusted color

Original color

Color field

Foreground color

Background color

Snap to browser-safe color icon

HSB color values

RGB color values

Show Only Web colors check box

Hexadecimal color values

11. In your Toolbox, single-click on the **foreground color** swatch. The **Color Picker** window will open. From there, you can choose any color under the sun. (To pick a color, drag your mouse up and down the **Color slider** until you have found the color hue that you want. Then drag your mouse around the **Color field** until you've found a value and saturation that you like. For a more detailed explanation of the Color Picker, see Chapter 6, "*Painting and Colors*.") I selected a red color for this example. When you've found the color you want, click **OK**.

12. Choose **Edit > Fill**. This will open the **Fill** dialog box. From the **Use** pull-down menu, make sure **Foreground Color** is selected (you want to fill your object with the foreground color you chose). While you're here, make sure that the **Blending Mode** is set to **Normal** (you'll learn more about blending modes later in this chapter) and the **Opacity** is set to **100%**. Click **OK**.

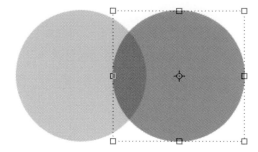

13. Presto! Your **blue circle copy** should now be filled with whatever color you chose. Yippee! This is a great technique for changing the color of artwork in a separate layer. You're done with this image and you won't need it again. Feel free to close the image or save it, print it out, and hang it up on your wall as your first masterpiece!! Bravisimo! ;-)

Note: After completing Step 11, if your whole image (instead of just the one blue circle) fills with the color you picked, go back and make sure you completed Step 10 correctly.

*Note: You'll notice that even though you filled one of the blue circles with a different, 100-percent opaque color, the circle still looks transparent. Why? If you remember back in Step 5, you changed the Opacity of the layer (which you duplicated to create the second circle) to 50%. Even though you're filling one of the circles with a 100-percent opaque color, the layer itself is still set to 50 per-cent opaque. This will cause everything in that layer to also be 50 percent opaque. To see what your circle (that you just changed the color of) looks like without the opacity change, drag the **Opacity** slider (as mentioned in Step 5) up to **100%**.*

There's an enormous amount of things you can do with layers. You'll get plenty of exposure to the layer features you have seen (as well as those you haven't) in later exercises. After working through this exercise, you should have a good understanding of layer basics and how best to select and manipulate them.

Layer Basics—Part Two

Now that you've had a little experience working with layers in the context of simple circles, you're going to reinforce what you've learned. This time, however, you will be working with photographic imagery.

1. Open the **File Browser** window by choosing **Window > File Browser**, and navigate to where you copied your **chap_04** folder. Double-click the **sunflower_bg** file to open the image in Elements.

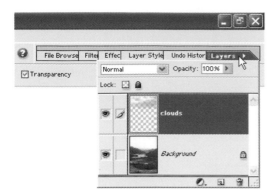

2. Open the **Layers** palette by choosing **Window > Layers**. Single-click on the top-most layer, **clouds**, to select it.

Note how the sunflower_bg image has two layers: Background and clouds. (You might need to expand the size of the Layers palette to see both layers.) Next you're going to add another image (and hence, another layer) to the sunflower_bg image. This technique demonstrates the essence of photo compositing: putting multiple images together to create one composition.

3. Open the **File Browser** again by choosing **Window > File Browser** and make sure you still have the **chap_04** folder selected. This time, double-click on the **sunflower** image to open it.

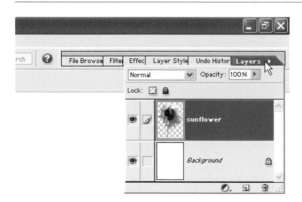

4. Open the **Layers** palette again by choosing **Window > Layers**. This time you'll notice that there are two layers in this image. The layer titled **sunflower** contains…well…a sunflower, and the **Background** layer is just filled with white.

5. Position your two open images, **sunflower_bg** and **sunflower**, so that you can simultaneously see both (as shown above). Make sure that the "active image" (the image you're currently working with) is the **sunflower** image. You can make it your active image by clicking anywhere on it.

6. Open the **Layers** palette and single-click on the **sunflower** layer to make sure it's selected.

Move tool

7. Select the Move tool, and drag the **sunflower** from the **sunflower** image over to the **sunflower_bg** image. When you let go of your mouse button, you'll see that the **sunflower** is now sitting on top of the **sunflower_bg** image!

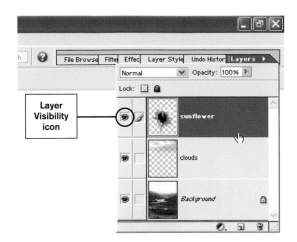

8. Click on the **sunflower_bg** image to make it the active image, and open the **Layers** palette by choosing **Window > Layers**.

*Where before the sunflower_bg image had two layers, it now has three layers. And Elements was smart enough to also name this new layer the same as it was in the sunflower image: **sunflower**. By dragging one image (sunflower) into another (sunflower_bg), Elements automatically creates a new layer to hold that image.*

Note: The reason I wanted you to first select the clouds layer way back in Step 2 was because when you dragged the sunflower over into the sunflower_bg document, Elements automatically created a new layer to hold that sunflower in the layer above the selected layer in your Layers palette. By selecting the clouds layer first, you ensured that the sunflower layer would be created above the clouds layer. Of course, you could have always reordered the layers by just dragging them up or down, but this saves you a little time.

*Tip: You can temporarily turn off the visibility of a layer by clicking on the **Layer Visibility** icon (the small black eye to the left-hand side of the Layers palette) next to the layer that you want to hide or show. This is very useful if, when you're working with multiple layers, one layer is obscuring something that you need to see or edit in a layer underneath.*

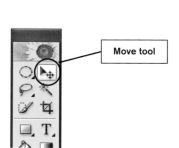

Move tool

9. Select the **Move** tool in the Toolbox, and then drag the sunflower into place.

Notice the dotted line surrounding the sunflower with corner and side boxes along it? Elements auto-matically displays this bounding box around the outside of the image in the selected layer in your Layers palette (you must have the Move tool selected to see this bounding box). Identical to the corner and side resize handles you saw in Chapter 3, "Opening and Importing Images," these resize handles also allow you to easily rotate and scale the image in your current layer. This is one simple demonstration of the power of layers. You can easily scale or rotate the sunflower without altering the sunflower_bg image in the layer beneath it.

10. Choose **File > Save As** and name the file **sunflower_composite**. Make sure the **Format** is set to **Photoshop** and save it in the **chap_04** folder. You'll be utilizing this image again in later exercises.

Non-Destructive Editing

Imagine this. You decide to color your hair fluorescent pink late one evening after a night out with some friends. The next morning, after you've scared yourself silly in the bathroom mirror, you decide that you made a big mistake and you want your old hair back. Easy! Wiggle your nose and your hair returns back to its former (and much less pinkish) color. That would be nice now, wouldn't it? That obscure analogy summarizes the concept of non-destructive image editing in Elements. In many cases (note "many," not "all"), you can easily modify an image so that the changes you make are not permanent. Why make a permanent change if you don't need to? Image editing features such as (I know you don't know what these are yet, please bear with me) fill layers, adjustment layers, and the ability to group layers is your key to non-destructive image editing. When possible, you're going to use one of these methods to make changes to your images that do not permanently alter them. You can, however, easily turn off non-destructive editing with the click of a mouse. In the next two exercises, you're going to learn about ways to use non-destructive image editing to your advantage. Now where's that hair dye…

3. ———————————**Fill and Adjustment Layers**

In this exercise you're going to learn how to modify images non-destructively. To do this, you will be using two types of layers that you haven't seen yet: fill layers and adjustment layers. If you've worked with other image editing programs before and haven't seen this kind of feature, you'll shortly be wondering where it's been all your life.

> **1.** Open the **File Browser** by choosing **Window > File Browser**, navigate to the **chap_04** folder, and double-click on **sunflower_composite** (the file you worked on earlier) to open it.

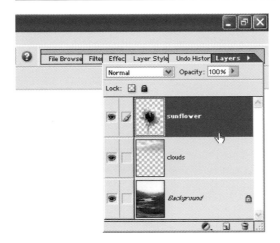

> **2.** Open the **Layers** palette by choosing **Window > Layers**. Single-click on the **sunflower** layer to select it.
>
> *First you're going to add an adjustment layer to adjust the levels of the image. What are levels you say? **Levels** are the highlights, midtones, and shadows that make up your image. This is also called the "tonal range"—throw that term out at a party to get a few ooohs and ahhhs, eh? "Ahh yes. Before I arrived at this party I was at home adjusting the tonal range of my photographic portfolio." Essentially, in layman's terms, it's the brightness/darkness of an image.*

Create New Fill or
Adjustment Layer icon

3. With the **sunflower** layer selected, click and hold on the **Create New Fill or Adjustment Layer** icon. This will pop up a menu. From that menu, choose **Levels**.

You'll learn more about levels in Chapter 9, "Correcting Photos" (and the "proper" way to use levels), but in this example you're focusing more on adjustment and fill layers, not on levels.

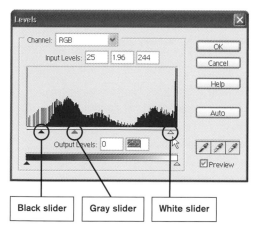

Black slider   Gray slider   White slider

4. The **Levels** dialog box will appear. Drag your **Black**, **Gray**, and **White** sliders so that they match the screen shot above. The black input level (the left-most field) should be at **25**; the gray at **1.96** (or thereabouts); and the white at **244**. If you have your windows positioned so that you can see this dialog box and your sunflower_composite image at the same time, you'll notice the darks and lights in your image changing as you drag the sliders around. Once you've finished setting your black, gray, and white points, click **OK**.

Note: The Levels dialog box allows you to change the white, black, and gray values of an image. By dragging the White slider to the left, you increase the intensity of the image's highlights. Conversely, by dragging the Black slider to the right, you increase the intensity of the image's shadows. As you'll see in Chapter 9, "Correcting Photos," levels are superb at correcting the values of an image.

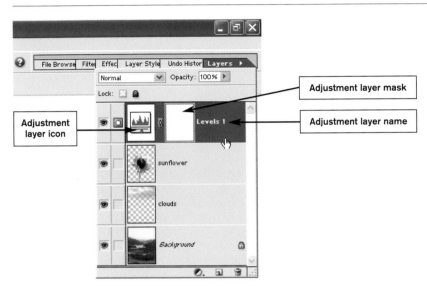

5. Open the **Layers** palette. You'll quickly notice that there is now a new layer above the sunflower layer titled **Levels 1**. This is your new adjustment layer (awww…isn't it cuuute!). To be specific, it's a levels adjustment layer because it's a layer that's adjusting the levels of your image.

Here's the nifty part…

*To see the before/after image, simply toggle the visibility on and off for your adjustment layer. To do that, just click on the **Layer Visibility** icon (the black eye) to the left of the **Levels 1** layer. Congratulations! You're now witness to the flexibility of working with an adjustment layer. In early versions of Photoshop, if you were to change the levels of an image as you just did, it would be a permanent change. Didn't like the levels change you made? Too bad…you were stuck with it. But thanks to adjustment layers, if you don't like the changes, you can simply alter the levels again, hide the layer, or even delete the adjustment layer completely. How awesome is that?*

*Note: To access the Levels dialog box for your adjustment layer, simply double-click on the **adjustment layer** icon and you'll be presented with the Levels dialog box again. If you want to delete the layer, just drag it to the **Trash** icon at the bottom of the Layers palette.*

*Now what if you like the levels changes you just made but you only want to apply those levels to the sunflower—not to everything else in the image? You're about to learn a brilliant way to do just that. It's called **grouping layers**.*

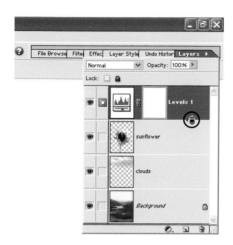

6. Open the **Layers** palette. Hold down your **Alt** key (Windows) or **Option** key (Mac) and move your mouse cursor so that it's between the **Levels 1** layer and the **sunflower** layer. You'll notice that your cursor will change to two overlapping circles. When you see that icon, click.

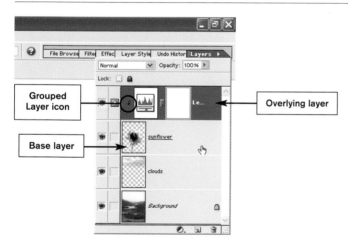

You'll quickly notice a few things have happened in the Layers palette. Most obvious is that the Levels 1 layer is now indented slightly and it has an icon next to it. This is the **Grouped Layer** *icon, and it is telling you that now the Levels 1 layer is being applied only to the layer directly beneath it, the sunflower layer. The sunflower layer and the Levels 1 layer are now a layer group. The sunflower layer is called the* **base layer** *(the sunflower layer name is now underlined to signify that it is the base layer), and the Levels 1 layer is called the* **overlying layer**. *Regardless of the different names of the layer group, you've now told Elements to have that levels adjustment layer be applied only to the sunflower layer (yet another fantastic reason to use layers, and a great example of the power of adjustment layers). Looking beyond the Layers palette, look at your image. Now those levels you set earlier are no longer being applied to the whole image. They're being applied only to the sunflower.*

Note: To ungroup your layer grouping, simply reverse your steps. Hold down your *Alt* key (Windows) or *Option* key (Mac), move your mouse between the Levels 1 and sunflower layers, and click when you see your mouse cursor change to two overlapping circles. The layers will then become ungrouped. It's a snap!

Now that you've seen an example of an adjustment layer, you'll learn about using a fill layer.

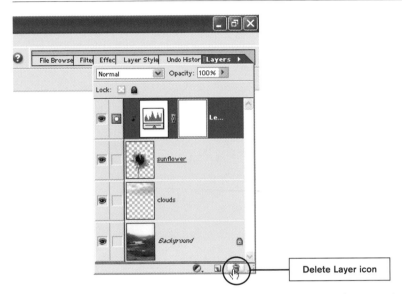

Delete Layer icon

7. Drag the **Levels 1** adjustment layer to the **Delete Layer** icon (the Trash) at the bottom right of the Layers palette. This will, of course, delete your adjustment layer.

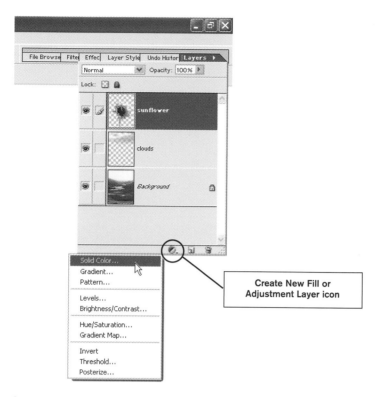

Create New Fill or
Adjustment Layer icon

8. In your Layers palette, once again, single-click on the **sunflower** layer to make sure it's selected. Then single-click on the **Create New Fill or Adjustment Layer** icon. From the pop-up menu that appears, choose **Solid Color**.

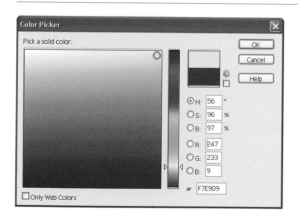

9. The **Color Picker** window will appear. Pick a color…any color. In this example, I chose a **bright yellow** color. When you've found the color you want, click **OK**.

Now don't get scared and run away when you see your image. It is now completely filled with the color you picked! But remember, this is just an adjustment layer. As you saw earlier, you can easily modify, turn on/off, and delete adjustment layers. Your image is still there…it's just underneath a blanket of color.

Next you're going to use a layer grouping to have your fill adjustment layer be applied to only the sunflower layer. Remember how to do that?

10. Open the **Layers** palette. Hold down your **Alt** key (Windows) or the **Option** key (Mac), move your mouse cursor so that it is positioned between the **Color Fill 1** layer and the **sunflower** layer, and click when your mouse cursor turns into two overlapping circles.

As you saw earlier in this exercise, this groups the two layers together. Again, all this essentially means is that now the color fill adjustment layer is being applied to only the sunflower layer instead of to the entire image.

Neat! The resulting image is a sunflower that is now completely covered by the color fill adjustment layer. Leave this image open—you'll be using it again in the next exercise.

Note: To reiterate, the reason why only the flower fills with yellow is because in the sunflower layer, everything else is transparent except for the sunflower. You can easily see this by opening up the Layers palette, looking at the sunflower layer, and noticing how in the layer thumbnail image everything (except for the sunflower) is filled with that gray and white checkerboard pattern (which as I spoke about earlier, represents transparent areas).

Although this exercise was done mostly to give you some hands-on experience with fill layers and grouping layers, the techniques covered are certainly applicable to working with your own digital images. For instance, you could use a fill layer in combination with layer grouping (as you did in this exercise) to silhouette an image in a layer, or you could also adjust the opacity of the color fill layer to give a color tint to the other layer(s) beneath it. There really are myriad effects that you can achieve using these techniques, and I encourage you to explore. You will gain more experience in later chapters, where you will be using more of both adjustment layers and layer grouping.

As I mentioned at the beginning of this exercise, the best thing about adjustment layers is that they're non-permanent. Once you have created an adjustment layer, it's very easy to go back and modify the settings or to just delete it completely—all without permanently altering the image in the slightest. You also learned the powerful feature of being able to group layers together so that one layer affects only the layer directly underneath it and not the entire image. You'll be gaining more experience with these techniques by using them again in later exercises.

What Are Layer Blending Modes?

In the upcoming exercise, you will gain hands-on experience using layer blending modes. Before you get started, the following chart shows the various blending modes, what they do, and what the result looks like using a sample image.

Layer Blending Modes		
Blending Mode	**Description**	**Preview**
Normal	Displays the layer normally without any changes.	
Dissolve	Same as Normal except the edges of the graphic are "randomly replaced," or scattered.	
Darken	Displays only the darker values of an image. The lighter values are replaced (made transparent).	
Multiply	Multiplies (hence the name) the colors of the layer image (called the "base color") with the colors of the layer images beneath (called the "blend color"). This always results in a darker color.	

continues on next page

Blending Mode	Description	Preview
Color Burn	Darkens the color of the layer image to be the same value as the layer images beneath.	
Linear Burn	Similar to Color Burn, but Linear Burn darkens the color of the layer image— by decreasing the brightness—to be the same as the layer images beneath.	
Lighten	Opposite of Darken. Displays only the lighter values of an image. The darker values are replaced (made transparent).	
Screen	Similar to Multiply, except Screen multiplies the *inverse* of the layer image colors with the colors in the layers underneath. This always results in a lighter color.	
Color Dodge	Similar to Color Burn, but instead of darkening the layer image, Color Dodge lightens it to be the same value as the layer images underneath.	

Layer Blending Modes *continued*

continues on next page

Layer Blending Modes *continued*		
Blending Mode	**Description**	**Preview**
Linear Dodge	Similar to Linear Burn, but instead of darkening the layer image, Linear Dodge lightens it—by increasing the brightness—to be the same as the layer images underneath.	
Overlay	Overlay is a complex blending mode. It mixes the colors (using either a Multiply or Screen effect) of the layer image with the colors of the layer images beneath while preserving the highlights and shadows of the image.	
Soft Light	If a color in the layer image is lighter than 50 percent gray, it is lightened; if a color is darker than 50 percent gray, it is darkened.	
Hard Light	Similar to Soft Light, except if a color in the layer image is lighter than 50 percent gray, it is lightened—like if it were screened; if a color is darker than 50 percent gray, it is darkened—like if it were multiplied.	
Vivid Light	If a color in the image is lighter than 50 percent gray, it is lightened by decreasing the contrast; if a color is darker than 50 percent gray, it is darkened by increasing the contrast.	

continues on next page

Layer Blending Modes *continued*		
Blending Mode	**Description**	**Preview**
Linear Light	Similar to Vivid Light. If a color in the layer image is lighter than 50 percent gray, it is lightened by increasing the brightness; if a color is darker than 50 percent gray, it is darkened by decreasing the brightness.	
Pin Light	If a color in the image is lighter than 50 percent gray, the dark parts of the image are replaced (made transparent), and the light parts are unchanged. If the color is darker than 50 percent gray, the light parts of the image are replaced, and the dark parts are unchanged.	
Difference	Compares the color values of the layer image with the color values of the layer images underneath. Depending upon which color values have a greater brightness, Elements will either subtract that color in the layer image from the color in the layer images underneath or vice-versa. Essentially, you end up with a very unique image. ;-)	
Exclusion	Similar to Difference, but the end result is an effect that is lower in contrast.	
Hue	Keeps the luminance (the intensity of the brightness) and the saturation (how colorful or "pure" an image is) the same, but changes the layer image hue (shade of color) to be the same as the layer images underneath. Essentially, it keeps the brightness/darkness and the saturation of the layer image the same, but then changes the actual *colors* of the layer image to match that of the layer images underneath.	

continues on next page

Layer Blending Modes *continued*		
Blending Mode	**Description**	**Preview**
Saturation	Similar to Hue except the luminance and hue of the layer image remain the same while the saturation of the layer image is changed to match the saturation of the layer images beneath.	
Color	Similar to Hue and Saturation except the luminance of the layer image remains the same while the hue and saturation of the layer image is changed to match those of the layer images underneath. The Color blending mode is especially useful for colorizing black-and-white images.	
Luminosity	Similar to Hue, Saturation, and Color modes, except the hue and saturation of the layer image remains the same while the luminosity of the layer image changes to match that of the layer images underneath.	

Blending modes is, in essence, how one layer blends into the other layers underneath it. By default, every layer you create has its blending mode set to Normal. Although there are too many blending modes to cover in this one exercise, I'd still like to show you a few so that you can get an idea of what they're capable of. Blending modes is one of my personal favorite features in Elements that I use, without fail, very frequently in my illustrations. Using blending modes properly can go a long way toward giving your image a beautiful and unique look.

Note: Blending modes can also be assigned to certain tools such as Paintbrush, Pencil, Gradient, and Paint Bucket. That way, as you use the tools, you're working directly with a blending mode. This is very useful if you want to apply a blending mode to a specific brush stroke or area of your image but you don't want to apply that same blending mode to the graphics in an entire layer. You'll learn more about tool-specific blending modes in Chapter 6, "*Painting and Colors.*"

4. ———————Using Blending Modes

In this exercise you will learn how to use blending modes. Utilizing blending modes allows you to modify how the colors and values of an image in one layer are affected by the colors and values of images in other layers underneath it. Sound confusing? Complicated? It's actually quite easy, as you'll see.

1. First, make sure that the image you were working on in the last exercise, **sunflower_composite**, is back to the way it was since the last time you saved it. With the **sunflower_composite** image open, choose **File > Revert**. This will revert your image back to the way it was when you last saved it.

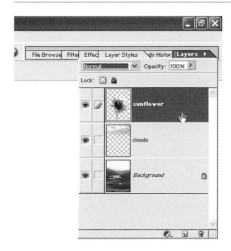

2. Open the **Layers** palette by choosing **Window > Layers**. Single-click on the top-most layer, **sunflower**, to select it.

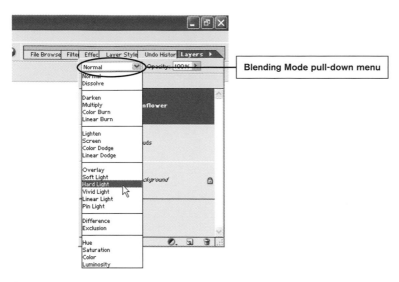

3. Click on the **Blending Mode** pull-down menu and choose **Hard Light**.

before   after

As you can see in the before and after images, the sunflower (after having the Hard Light blending mode applied to it) now has a greater contrast (stronger light values and stronger dark values), and in places, you can even partially see through the sunflower to the layers underneath. Cool! Blending modes are especially useful when doing photo montages and photo compositing. As such, you'll get more experience using blending modes in later chapters.

4. Open the **Layers** palette again, make sure the **sunflower** layer is selected, and from the **Blending Modes** pull-down menu choose **Difference**. Holy psychedelic, Batman! The Difference blending mode is always good for a laugh or two.

5. When you're finished, close this image and don't save changes.

As you can see, you can achieve some very interesting and artistic effects by using blending modes. I encourage you to experiment with different blending modes when working with your images. Sometimes you can be pleasantly surprised with the results. :-)

In the next chapter, you'll be learning all about selecting. Selecting is an important part of image editing because it allows you to select specific portions of an image to work with or modify. In this chapter (Chapter 4), how do you think I got the sunflower to be in its own transparent layer? I selected it using various selection tools and removed it from its background (much like cutting an image out of a magazine). In the next chapter, you'll learn all the tools needed to accomplish such a task. Onward and upward!

5.
Selecting

| About Selections | Pre-Selecting Advice |
| Using Selection Tools |
| Adding and Subtracting from a Selection |
| Moving and Saving Selections | Building an Image |

chap_05

Photoshop Elements 2
H•O•T CD-ROM

Learning how to properly select different parts of your images is one of the need-to-know keystones in Elements. Selecting is the doorway that leads you to more exciting things such as image manipulation, color correction, and photo compositing. As a professional illustrator, I can safely say that when I'm working on an illustration, I spend at least half the amount of time selecting different parts of images before I begin drawing or editing. Whether you want to apply a filter or effect to a portion of your image or cut a part of your image out and paste it someplace else, selecting is the key to performing those tasks. So put on your thinking cap (geez, I hated it when the teacher used to say that) and off we go!

About Selections

Plain and simple, selections are what they sound like. You use various tools and methods to select a portion of your image so that you can apply filters or effects to parts of the image, or to simply extract from the rest of the image—akin to cutting an image out of a magazine. Why would you want to do this? Well, what if I had a picture of a flower, and I wanted to place that flower (*just* the flower) onto a different background (just like you did in the last chapter…not-so-coincidentally)? The only way to do that is by selecting the flower, extracting it from its background, and putting it against a different background. One day I imagine a voice-activated version of Elements that upon hearing me utter "cut out picture of flower" would proceed to extract the image of a flower from its background. In Elements 2, however, you still have to do it the "old-fashioned," manual way. Sure, I will show you other ways to make the process simpler and less time-consuming, but you'll find that selecting portions of your images is still a mostly manual and non-automated task that requires a good deal of time and dexterity. You will certainly be using selections in later chapters (especially Chapter 10, "*Retouching Photos*" and Chapter 11, "*Photo Manipulation*"), so this chapter is meant just as an introduction and overview of the various ways to select portions of an image. Later, you will learn what you can actually do with those selections.

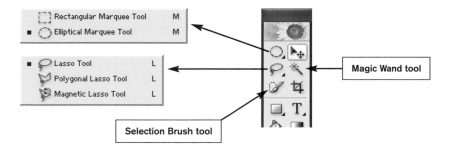

The selection tools that you will be using in this chapter are all located towards the top of the Toolbox. They are the Marquee tools (Rectangular and Elliptical), the Lasso tools (Normal, Polygonal, and Magnetic), the Magic Wand tool, and the Selection Brush tool.

Pre-Selecting Advice

Keep in mind a few of the following details while you are scanning and photographing your images—they'll make a huge difference when you attempt to select portions of those images.

This picture is a scan I made of a live ladybug. I just found her, plopped her on my scanner bed, gently laid a sheet of paper over her, and held the edges down so she wouldn't move while I made the scan.

*Note: No ladybugs were harmed during the production of this book.

Now wouldn't it be nice if you could digitally "cut" the ladybug away from the paper background and "paste" it onto another image? How about…say…that composition you worked on in the last chapter where you placed an image of a sunflower against a landscape? In this chapter, I'll show you how to do exactly that.

When selecting part of an image, whether you want to take a particular part of it and put it into another image, or to just apply a filter or effect to it, you should first evaluate the subject matter. Does the object that you want to select have lots of straight edges? Does it have lots of curved lines? Is it a complex shape? Simple? What kind of background is the object against? A flat color? Textured? Evaluating your subject matter first will enable you to pick the best tool for the job. In this case, your subject matter (a ladybug), has lots of curved lines to its complex shape, but it's against a relatively flat background color.

If you are taking a photograph that you know you will later want to cut objects out of, shooting your subject matter against a flat background color will certainly be *extremely* beneficial. For example, you could use a piece of white or black cloth—you might have also heard the movie term "blue screen" or "green screen." When using special effects, filmmakers often shoot their subject matter against a bright blue or green cloth. This enables the special effects team to easily and digitally cut the subject matter away from the background, allowing them to then place their content seamlessly against any other background of their choosing. This is essentially what you will be doing in this chapter. As you'll see with this ladybug, having a flat color behind your image can save you a lot of time when trying to select it.

I. —————————**Using and Choosing Proper Selection Tools**

In this exercise, you will learn about the various tools that select specific parts of an image. As I mentioned at the beginning of this chapter, learning how to select certain parts of your image is critical to image manipulation, application of filters and effects, and photo compositing. A bit of warning about this exercise—you're going to be learning about a lot of new tools! Normally, once you know what tools work best, you'll go right to the correct selection tool and won't need to use all the techniques you learn in this exercise. For learning purposes, however, you'll get to tinker with a lot of selection techniques to help you get to know the tools a little better. In this particular exercise, the process of getting there is more important than where you're going!

1. Copy the **chap_05** folder and files from the **H•O•T CD-ROM** to your hard drive.

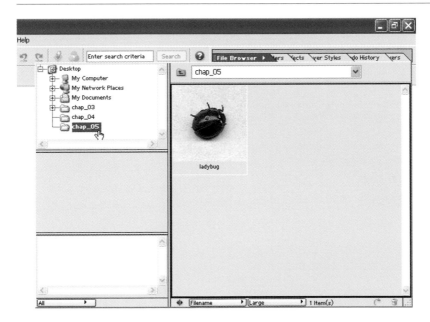

2. Open the **File Browser** by choosing **File > Browse,** and navigate to where you copied the **chap_05** files on your computer. Locate the file titled **ladybug** and double-click on it to open it.

As I mentioned in the last chapter, if you open the File Browser and you don't see the ***chap_05*** *folder, you may need to right-click (Windows) or Ctrl-click (Mac) on the file listing portion of the File Browser window and choose* ***Refresh****.*

Tip: *When the File Browser window is open, you can also refresh the file listing by pressing* ***F5.***

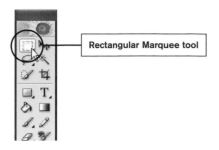

Rectangular Marquee tool

3. It's time to take the Rectangular Marquee tool for a test drive. Click on it in your **Toolbox** to select it. If you have the Elliptical Marquee tool selected, switch back at this time to the Rectangular Marquee tool by clicking–and holding–on the **Elliptical Marquee** tool. When the hidden tools pop-up menu appears, select the **Rectangular Marquee** tool.

4. Position your cursor (which turns into a crosshairs icon) over the ladybug image. Then (not to sound like a bad infomercial) just click and drag to create a selection. When you release the mouse button, the selection is created and you'll see a dashed line that appears to animate. This is your selection, and that animation is called the "marching ants."

Congratulations! You have just created your first selection by using the Rectangular Marquee tool to select part of the ladybug image. At this point, you could add a filter or effect to just the portion of the ladybug image that you selected, or you could cut it out of this image and paste it into another. The Elliptical Marquee tool creates a selection (like you just did with the Rectangular Marquee tool), except, of course, it's elliptical (rounded). If your purpose is to select just the ladybug, the Marquee tools aren't really right for the job. The shape of the ladybug is too complex to correctly select with either of the Marquee tools. Why don't you try the Lasso tools next?

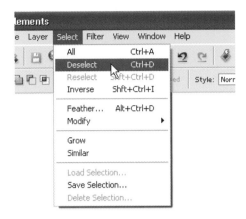

5. Because the selection you just made with the Marquee tool isn't quite the right one, get rid of that selection (called **deselecting**) before experimenting with the other selection tools. To deselect your selection, choose **Select > Deselect**. Because deselecting is such a common practice, you should learn its shortcut key: **Ctrl+D** (Windows) or **Cmd+D** (Mac).

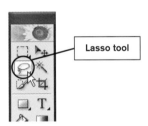

Lasso tool

6. Select the **Lasso** tool by clicking on it in the Toolbox. When you move your mouse cursor over your image, notice how your cursor changes to the shape of…well…a lasso. (The bottom part of the lasso is the actual point from where you draw your selection, by the way.)

7. Drag your lasso icon around the outside of the ladybug to create your selection. Make sure to end up very near where you started dragging. When you've deftly drawn around the entire ladybug, release your mouse button and your selection is created. *Whew.* The Lasso tool requires great dexterity with the mouse, a steady hand, a smooth mousing surface, and very little caffeine. As I'm sure you can see from this example, the Lasso tool is a great way to create more "organic" selections (unlike the simple lines of the Rectangular and Elliptical Marquee tools), but it's not very good at creating precise lines around the edges of a shape. Adobe realizes this, and has given you a few more options with the two hidden Lasso tools: the **Polygonal Lasso** and **Magnetic Lasso** tools.

8. Deselect the selection that you just made with the Lasso tool by using the shortcut key **Ctrl+D** (Windows) or **Cmd+D** (Mac). Select the **Polygonal Lasso** tool by clicking and holding on the **Lasso** tool until the hidden tools pop-up menu appears. Then from the pop-up menu choose the **Polygonal Lasso** tool.

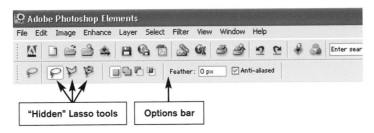

"Hidden" Lasso tools   **Options bar**

Note: *You can also access the hidden Lasso tools from the options bar. Just simply click on the standard Lasso tool in the Toolbox, and you'll see the additional Lasso tools (as well as a few options you'll see later) appear in the options bar.*

The Polygonal Lasso tool functions a bit differently than the standard Lasso tool. To create a selection with the Lasso tool, you dragged your mouse around the object (or the part of the image) that you wanted to select. With the Polygonal Lasso tool, you click from point to point around the image to create your selection. Every time you click your mouse with the Polygonal Lasso tool, it creates an anchor point. If you move your mouse elsewhere on the document you'll notice a line that extends away from the point that you clicked. Clicking again creates another anchor point, and so on and so forth.

9. At this point, go ahead and click with the **Polygonal Lasso** tool around the ladybug to create your selection. Once you've worked all the way around the ladybug, click on the point where you first started clicking (you'll notice that when you get close to the point where you started clicking, the Lasso tool cursor will change to have a small circle at its bottom right; when you see that cursor, clicking will create the selection).

The Polygonal Lasso tool requires less mouse dexterity than the standard Lasso tool, and you can create more precise selections with it to boot. While creating a selection with the Polygonal Lasso tool, you can temporarily have it behave as a standard lasso tool! To do that, simply hold down the Option key (Mac) or the Alt key (Windows). This will turn your polygonal lasso tool into a standard lasso tool (able to create a selection with a curved line) for as long as you hold the Option or Alt key down.

*Tip: When you're using the Polygonal Lasso tool, and you want to remove the last anchor point you created, simply press **Backspace** (Windows) or **Delete** (Mac). *Thanks to Lynda's husband, Bruce Heavin, for showing me that trick a few years ago.*

*Tip: You can also use your standard Lasso tool as a Polygonal Lasso tool. Without any selection currently active, and with the standard Lasso tool selected, hold down the **Alt** key (Windows) or **Option** key (Mac). Then, instead of dragging around your image with the Lasso tool, click around it like you would with the Polygonal Lasso tool. Fantastico—the standard Lasso tool is behaving just like the Polygonal Lasso tool does. When you've completed your selection, release the **Option** or **Alt** key and your selection is created.*

10. Deselect your selection by pressing **Ctrl+D** (Windows) or **Cmd+D** (Mac). In the options bar, click on the **Magnetic Lasso** tool icon to select it. When you do, you'll see some new options appear to the right side of the options bar.

The Magnetic Lasso tool sounds quite mysterious, doesn't it? Just like the other Lasso tools, the Magnetic Lasso tool allows you to make a selection. The difference between the Magnetic Lasso tool and the other Lasso tools, however, is quite dramatic. Whereas the Lasso and Polygonal Lasso tools are very manual, the Magnetic Lasso tool is more automatic. As you move your mouse around the image, the Magnetic Lasso tool constantly tries to find the edge of a shape and snaps your selection to fit it. Ohhhh. The Magnetic Lasso tool works best for selecting images against a high-contrast background. Here's an explanation of those new options that appear on the options bar:

Magnetic Lasso Tool Options	
Option	**Description**
Width	Specifies the area of edge detection the Magnetic Lasso tool uses to find edges of your shape. If an object you want to select has lots of other content around or near it, you probably are going to want to set Width to a low number.
Edge Contrast	Controls how sensitive the Magnetic Lasso tool is to detecting the edges of the part of the image you're trying to select. Enter a higher number to have the Magnetic Lasso tool select the parts of your image that have a high contrast. Conversely, entering a lower number lets the tool select parts of your image with areas of low contrast.
Frequency	Sets the rate at which the Magnetic Lasso tool lays down anchor points around the area that you're trying to select. Entering a higher value allows the Magnetic Lasso tool to add more anchor points around the image, thereby making the selection process go by faster.

For this example, leave the Width, Edge Contrast, and Frequency settings at their default. Width is 10 pixels, Edge Contrast is 10%, and Frequency is 57.

11. With the **Magnetic Lasso** tool, click on the edge of your shape (the ladybug, in this case) to create your initial anchor point. Then, without holding the mouse button down, move your mouse cursor around the edge of the ladybug until you're back to where you started from. You don't need to trace the edge exactly; you just need to trace near it.

That's the beauty (or one of them anyway) of the Magnetic Lasso tool. As you move your mouse around the edges of the ladybug, you'll notice it laying a selection line around the edges of the shape. Exactly where and how close it lays down the selection line is dependent on the settings you specified in the options bar (as discussed in Step 10). When you're near the selection's starting point, the Magnetic Lasso tool cursor will change to include a small circle at its lower right (just like the Polygonal Lasso tool, remember?). Single-clicking when you see that cursor icon will complete the selection (don't double-click—that will deselect your entire selection!).

Tip: *The Magnetic Lasso tool is better when used on image edges with high contrast, so you will get better selection results if you increase the contrast of your source image first and then use your Magnetic Lasso tool to create the selection. You will be learning more about increasing the contrast of images in Chapter 9, "Correcting Photos."*

Although the Lasso tools are a great way of manually creating complex selections, they are still very time consuming and require a steady hand. Next you're going to learn to use the Magic Wand tool to easily create selections with a simple click.

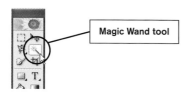

Magic Wand tool

12. Deselect the selection you made with the Magnetic Lasso tool by pressing **Ctrl+D** (Windows) or **Cmd+D** (Mac). Next, click on the **Magic Wand** tool to select it.

Magic Wand tool options

Once you've selected the Magic Wand tool, you'll notice a few new options in the options bar.

Magic Wand Tool Options	
Option	**Description**
Tolerance	This is the most important Magic Wand tool setting. A low Tolerance specifies that fewer colors will be considered similar to the one that you click on, whereas a higher Tolerance specifies that more colors will be considered similar. Essentially, the lower the tolerance, the fewer pixels will be selected around where you clicked; the higher the tolerance, the more pixels will be selected. For now, though, leave the Tolerance option set to the default 32.
Anti-aliased	When this box is checked, the edges of your selection will be smoothed (anti-aliased). In most cases, you will probably want to leave this checked.
Contiguous	When this box is checked, only the pixels that are directly contiguous (adjacent) to each other will be selected. Unchecking this check box will cause pixels with a similar color to the one you clicked on to be selected over the entire image.
Use All Layers	When this box is checked, the Magic Wand tool selects pixels that span all of the layers in your image.

13. Move your mouse cursor over onto the white area of the ladybug image and click.

Presto! Instant selection. Now isn't that a heck of a lot easier than using the manual Lasso tools?
As you can see, however, the selection runs a little wide around the side of the ladybug that is in
*shadow. You can make the selection cinch up closer to the ladybug by setting the **Tolerance** to a*
higher number, which means that the Magic Wand tool will consider more pixels similar to the one
you clicked on.

14. Deselect your selection by choosing **Select > Deselect**. With the Magic Wand tool still selected,
set the **Tolerance** in the options bar to **125**. Lastly, move your mouse cursor over to the image and
click on the white (paper) area of the ladybug image again.

Great! Now you've created a selection again, but this time you'll notice that the selection runs up much closer to the edge of the ladybug. You can see that in some parts of the ladybug, the selection actually runs into the ladybug itself, but that's easily corrected using the other selection tools, as you'll see in the next exercise.

Some of you might be saying, "Wait a second! I didn't select the ladybug, I selected the paper!" This is most certainly true. Because the ladybug is all different colors and values but the paper is generally one solid color (which is much easier to select with the Magic Wand tool), you selected the paper. To select the ladybug, you simply want to tell Elements to take your selection and invert it—so that everything currently selected is not, and everything not selected is. Capisce? This is a very easy thing to do in Elements.

---

15. Choose **Select > Inverse**. Now, instead of the paper being selected, the ladybug is. Magic!

*From this example, I hope you can see how, in some cases, the Magic Wand tool can save you a lot of time when selecting an object. Where the Magic Wand tool fails, however, is when you want to select a portion of an image against a textured, patterned, or complex background. In that case, you need to bring out the big selection gun: the **Selection Brush**.*

The Selection Brush is a new and novel way to create selections in Elements—by just painting with the paintbrush. By specifying a few options and then "painting" with the Selection Brush on your image, you're actually defining a selection! After using the Selection Brush, you'll probably never go back to the Lasso tool again! Aren't you glad you learned it the hard way first?

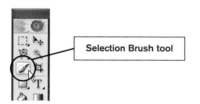

Selection Brush tool

16. Deselect your selection once more by pressing **Ctrl+D** (Windows) or **Cmd+D** (Mac). In your Toolbox, click on the **Selection Brush** tool to select it.

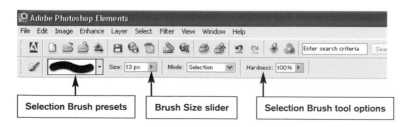

Selection Brush presets · Brush Size slider · Selection Brush tool options

As with the other selection tools, when you select the Selection Brush tool you'll see some new options in the options bar.

Selection Brush Tool Options	
Option	**Description**
Selection Brush presets	From the Selection Brush presets pull-down menu, you can choose the style of brush you want to use when defining your selection. You'll gain more experience with brushes in Chapter 6, "*Painting and Colors*." For now, just leave the brush set at its default which is a hard, round, 13-pixel-wide brush.
Size	Click on the little arrow to the right of the Size field. From the slider that pops up, you can specify a size for your Selection Brush. **Tip:** You can quickly change the size of your brush by pressing the **]** and **[** (bracket) keys to make your brush size larger and smaller, respectively, without the hassle of accessing the Size slider. How about that?! Using the keyboard to dynamically change the size of the Selection Brush is *very* useful—especially when moving from selecting large areas to smaller, more detailed areas. *With thanks again to Lynda's husband, Bruce, for showing me that trick so long ago.
Mode	This selects whether you want to paint with a selection or a mask. With the Mode set to **Selection**, where you paint with the paintbrush is what becomes your selection. With the Mode set to **Mask**, where you paint (by default) is covered in a 50 percent transparent red color. With the Mask feature, you're essentially painting the area of your image you want to mask out, or hide. After painting a mask, if you choose **Selection** from the pull-down menu, you'll see that everything but what you painted is selected. The advantage of using the Mask mode is that if you choose a different brush preset, you can actually see the different brush edges, such as hard, soft, and so on, as you're painting with them. When you're using the Selection mode brush, you can't see the different brush edges.
Hardness	The Hardness slider specifies how "hard" the edge of the brush is. A higher value denotes a hard-edged brush; a low value signifies a soft-edged brush. Again, you won't really see a difference while you're creating a selection with the mode set to Selection. You'll notice this while working with the mode set to Mask.
Overlay Opacity and Overlay Color	If you have your mode set to Mask, you can also set how opaque your mask color will be. By clicking on the Overlay Color box, you can also specify what color to use as well.

17. The default brush size of **13** is a little too small to work with for this image, so set your brush size to **30 px**. You can do this by either dragging the Brush Size slider or by typing **30** into the **Size** field and pressing **Enter** (Windows) or **Return** (Mac). Leave the **Mode** set to **Selection** and the **Hardness** set to **100%**.

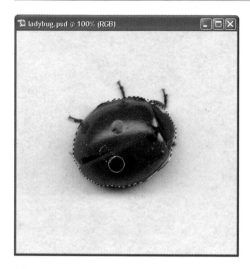

18. Move your mouse cursor onto the image of the ladybug and drag your mouse around to start defining a selection. Simply, you're "painting" a selection onto the ladybug. I used the **30 px** brush to first draw around the outside edge of the ladybug (ignoring any small parts like legs) and then filled in the center area. Then, press **[** (left bracket key) until your brush size is **7 px**, which will give you a nice, small Selection Brush tool so that you can define the legs as well. As you paint with the Selection Brush, you're adding to the selection you already have. Don't worry about being a little messy and selecting small areas that are a little too far outside of your shape; I'm going to show you next how to remove (by painting) parts of the selection.

*Tip: If you really want to make sure your selection is just perfect, you can zoom closer into the lady-bug for more precise selecting. Normally, you can just select the Magnify tool in the Toolbox and then click on the area of the image you want to zoom into. But to prevent confusion that would be caused by flipping back and forth between the Magnify tool and the Selection Brush tool, use the keyboard shortcut instead. To zoom into your image, press **Ctrl + +** (that's the Ctrl key and the plus sign key on Windows), or **Cmd + +** (that's the Command key and the plus sign key on a Mac). You can keep pressing that keyboard shortcut to zoom closer into the image. Now that you're nice and close, you should be able to more easily select small areas of an image, such as the legs of the ladybug. When you're ready to zoom out, press **Ctrl + -** (Windows) or **Cmd + -** (Mac). Like the zoom-in keyboard shortcut, you can press it repeatedly to zoom further and further out of the image.*

19. Hold down the **Alt** key (Windows) or **Option** key (Mac) and drag the **Selection Brush** icon over the areas of the selection that hang too far outside of the ladybug shape. You'll notice that as you drag the Selection Brush over the selection, it'll actually remove that part of the selection.

Neat! By using this method, you can easily add and subtract from a selection until you have selected the exact part of the image you want.

---

20. Leave your ladybug image open with your selection still active—you will be using it again in the next exercise.

How Do I Add or Subtract from a Selection?

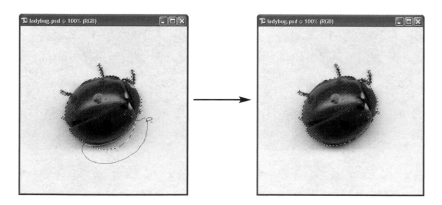

Subtracting from a selection works the same way with the Selection Brush as it does with all of the other selection tools. To subtract from a selection you already have, hold down the **Alt** key (Windows) or the **Option** key (Mac) while you're using your selection tool. Where the two selections overlap, that part of the selection gets deleted.

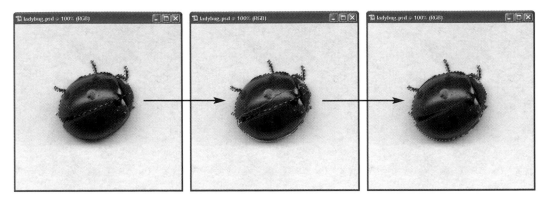

Adding to a selection with the other selection tools isn't as easy as it is with the Selection Brush tool. When using another selection tool *besides* the Selection Brush tool, hold down your **Shift** key while using the tool to add to any selection that you already have.

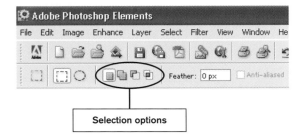

Selection options

When using the Marquee, Magic Wand, and Lasso tools, you can also specify—in the options bar for each tool—how the selection will interact with other selections (if any). The circled options above are **New Selection**, **Add to Selection**, **Subtract from Selection**, and **Intersect with Selection**, respectively.

Now that you've seen how to create selections using a wide variety of selection tools, in the next exercise you will learn how to move those selections around and how to save them for later use.

2. ——————————Moving and Saving Selections

In this exercise, you will learn how to move and save your selections (now that you've slaved long and hard over them to make sure that they're perfect). Saving a selection in particular is very useful because you can then recall that selection at any time you want for any other purpose. Anytime you have a complex selection that you would rather not spend the time to re-create, save it because you never know when you may need it again.

1. With the **ladybug** image from the previous exercise still open, select any of your selection tools *except* the Selection Brush tool. Position your selection tool cursor over the selection and drag it to a new location.

You can move the selection anywhere else in the image that you'd like. This is often very useful if your selection is off by a little bit—you can move it back into the correct location by simply dragging it. You can also use the arrow keys to nudge a selection in small increments.

Note: *Logic would suggest that you should use the Move tool if you want to* move a selection, yes? *What actually happens, though, is that Elements moves the part of the image you have selected, not the selection itself. If you need to move your selection, you must have a selection tool selected first.*

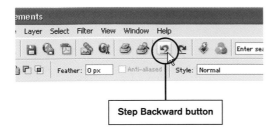

Step Backward button

2. Click on the **Step Backward** button in your shortcuts bar—and keep clicking on it if need be until your selection is back where it was, on top of the ladybug. You need it back in its original location because next you will learn how to save your selection.

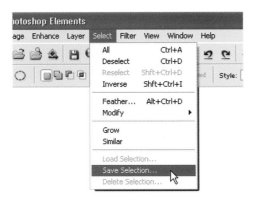

3. Choose **Select > Save Selection**.

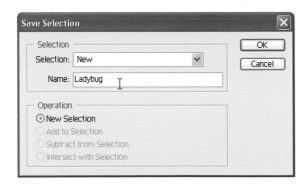

4. From the **Save Selection** dialog box, leave the **Selection** pull-down menu set to **New** (there aren't any other options to choose from at this point anyway), and in the **Name** field, type **Ladybug**. Click **OK**.

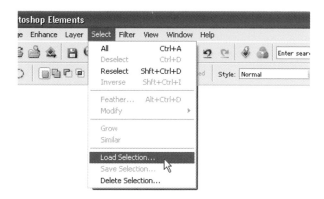

5. Now for the moment of truth…take a deep breath…and deselect your hard-earned ladybug selection by pressing **Ctrl+D** (Windows) or **Cmd+D** (Mac). Now you're going to resurrect it. Choose **Select > Load Selection**.

6. From the **Load Selection** dialog box that appears, leave the **Selection** pull-down menu set to **Ladybug** and click **OK**.

Yayy! Like the phoenix rising from the ashes, your selection is now back on the ladybug image in the exact same place. As I mentioned earlier, saving a selection is very useful when you've spent a lot of time making a selection and you don't want to lose it. It also allows you to save the selection for later use while you continue to work on other parts, or other layers, of your image.

7. Leave the ladybug image open and the selection active—you will be using it again in the next exercise.

In the next exercise, you will take what you've learned so far in this book to combine two images together in a simple photo composite.

Building an Image

In this exercise you're going to combine the ladybug image with another image that you worked on in Chapter 4, "*Layers*," called **sunflower_composite**.

1. Open your File Browser by choosing **File > Browse** and navigate to the **chap_04** folder. In the **chap_04** folder should be **sunflower_composite**, the image you worked on and saved in Chapter 4. Double-click on it to open it.

2. At this point you should now have two images open in Elements. You should have the **ladybug** image open—with its selection still active—and the **sunflower_composite** image open. Position them next to each other so that you can see both at the same time.

3. Select the **Move** tool and drag the selected **ladybug** over onto the **sunflower_composite** image and release your mouse button.

In the sunflower_composite image, the ladybug that you dragged over may or may not be on top of the sunflower. It all depends on which layer you had selected in the sunflower_composite image when you dragged the ladybug onto it. You need to make sure that the ladybug is on top of the sunflower and that it's the proper size and orientation.

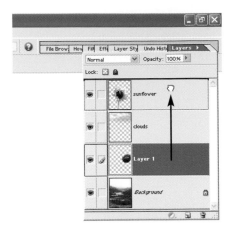

4. Make sure that your **sunflower_composite** image is the active image (click on its title bar) and open the **Layers** palette by choosing **Window > Layers**. If your ladybug layer (which is probably titled **Layer 1**) is below the **sunflower** layer, drag the ladybug layer so that it is above the **sunflower** layer.

The reason why you need to do that—of course—is because you want the ladybug to be positioned like it is sitting on top of the sunflower.

Next you're going to…holey baloobey! That's one giant ladybug that's about to swallow that sunflower whole! Run for the hills Bessie-Sue!

Voila! The ladybug is now in the sunflower image and is positioned on top of the sunflower! This is similar to the exercise in Chapter 4, "Layers," where you dragged the sunflower image onto a different background image, except this time you selected the ladybug yourself using selection tools, and effectively cut it out and moved it into another image! You should give yourself a huge pat on the back (not too hard now—I still need you around to read the rest of this book) because you've now learned the basics of photo compositing…and you've done it from scratch to boot! In the next steps, you're going to make that ladybug look like it's part of the whole sunflower image by decreasing its size, rotating it, and applying a blending mode.

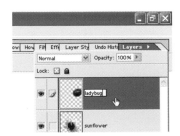

5. While you have the Layers Palette open, rename your ladybug layer (by double-clicking on the layer name) to **ladybug**, of course.

6. Make sure the Move tool is still selected, hold down the **Alt** key (Windows) or the **Option** key (Mac) and the **Shift** key, and drag down one of the top corner resize handles (around the outside corner of the ladybug), thereby making the ladybug smaller. Holding down the **Alt** (Windows) or **Option** key (Mac) while you drag resizes the ladybug from its center (instead of from the bottom left). Holding down the **Shift** key while you drag resizes the ladybug proportionately. Once you have the ladybug at the size you want it, press **Enter** (Windows) or **Return** (Mac) to commit to the size transformation you just made.

7. Is that box around the ladybug image getting in your way? If so, you can temporarily hide it by making sure your Move tool is selected and then unchecking the **Show Bounding Box** check box in your options bar. Want the box back again so that you can easily resize/rotate the image? Just recheck the **Show Bounding Box** check box.

For now, uncheck the Show Bounding Box check box so you can easily see the blending mode you will be applying to the ladybug.

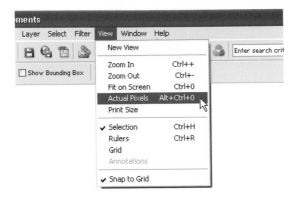

8. To best see the blending mode changes you will be making in the next step, make sure you are viewing your image at 100% by choosing **View > Actual Pixels**. If you're viewing your image at less than 100% (actual size), it will zoom in. If you're viewing your image at greater than 100%, it will zoom out.

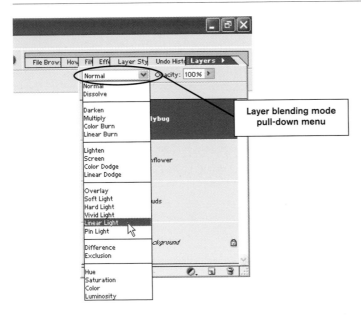

9. Open the Layers Palette by choosing **Windows > Layers** and make sure the **ladybug** layer is selected. From the blending mode pull-down menu, choose **Linear Light** as the blending mode.

Linear Light (as you saw from the blending modes table toward the end of Chapter 4, "Layers") essentially makes the image on that layer more vivid. It brightens the lights and darkens the darks based on the values of the sunflower image that's behind it.

The end result! If you listen verrry quietly, you can almost hear her calling "coomme heere little aphid's aphid's...comme heeerre..." ;-)

Note: *If you see a small, white "halo" around the outside edge of the ladybug, it's there because you selected part of the ladybug's white background. To fix it, go back to the ladybug image and use the selection techniques you've learned thus far to reselect the ladybug and avoid selecting any of the white background. Then in the sunflower_composite image, throw away the old ladybug layer by dragging the layer to the Trash icon at the lower right of the Layers Palette, and then repeat Steps 3 through 9.*

---

10. So that you don't get confused later, place the checkmark back into the **Show Bounding Box** check box (you can do this by making sure the Move tool is selected and placing a check mark in the **Show Bounding Box** check box).

---

11. Save your **sunflower_composite** image by using the keyboard shortcut **Ctrl+S** (Windows) or **Cmd+S** (Mac). I recommend that you memorize this keyboard shortcut because saving is something you will do quite frequently.

---

12. Close the ladybug image, and if prompted to save your changes, click **No** (Windows) or **Don't Save** (Mac).

In this chapter you learned how to use the different selection tools. As you use those tools to select different parts of your own images, you'll gain more experience with understanding which selection tools work best for different types of images. You also learned the beginnings of photo compositing by cutting the ladybug out from its background, adding it to a completely different image, and making a few changes to make that ladybug look like it belongs in that photo. Photo compositing is kind of like applying makeup (well...uhhh...so I'm told)—when it's done correctly, you should never notice it. Good photo compositing shouldn't look like photo compositing at all. It should just look like one, cohesive image.

In the next chapter, you will be learning about painting, drawing, and colors. See you there!

6.

Painting and Colors

| Painting and Drawing | Erasing |
| Modifying Colors |

chap_06

Photoshop Elements 2
H•O•T CD-ROM

"I'm not an artist!" you might be saying to yourself. "I don't need to know about painting and colors." In this chapter, I'm not going to show you how to paint a pretty picture using the various drawing and painting tools in Elements. If you want to learn that, you should enroll at an art school or take evening art classes at your local community college. What I *am* going to demonstrate is how the painting and drawing tools work, and how to pick and swap around colors. In this chapter, you will focus more on the tools than how best to apply them. In later chapters, you will apply what you learned in this chapter towards more advanced exercises such as photo correction, retouching, and compositing. You don't need to be an artist to be able to understand the painting tools and color selection; you just need to follow along—and have fun for goodness sakes!

I. ———————Painting and Drawing

In this exercise, you're going to learn the basics of the paintbrush, drawing, and gradient tools. As you read further in this book, you will build on some of what you learn in this exercise and chapter. Initially, in these first few exercises, you will be working only with the colors black and white (and the grays in-between), which will allow you to concentrate on the new tasks you're learning and will prevent you from getting sidetracked or confused by dealing with multiple colors. Later in this chapter, however, you will be introduced to the Color Picker and how to choose various colors.

1. Create a new image document by choosing **File > New**.

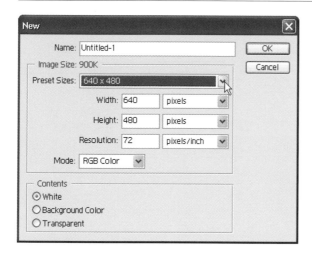

2. In the **New** dialog box, click on the **Preset Sizes** pull-down menu and, from the list of image presets, choose **640 x 480**. Make sure your resolution is **72 pixels/inch** and the **Mode** is **RGB Color**. Under **Contents**, make sure that the **White** radio button is selected. Click **OK**.

This will create an image for you that is 640 pixels wide by 480 pixels high, has a resolution of 72ppi, is color, and has a white background. Although the resolution of this image is low (72ppi), you will just be using it for learning purposes. If you wanted to print this image, you would set the resolution to something higher, like 300ppi.

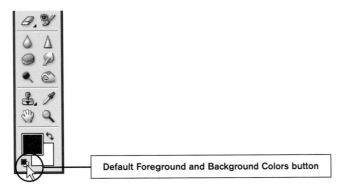

Default Foreground and Background Colors button

3. To make sure that you're using the same colors as I am in this exercise, first set your foreground and background colors to their defaults. You can do this by clicking on the **Default Foreground and Background Colors** button, which is placed just down and to the left of the foreground and background color swatches in the Toolbox. Later in this chapter, I'll go more into detail about those foreground and background color swatches and on color itself.

4. Select the **Pencil** tool by single-clicking on its icon in the Toolbox.

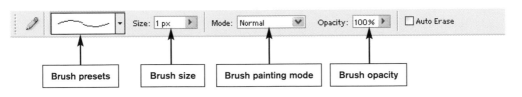

Brush presets   Brush size   Brush painting mode   Brush opacity

5. One of the first things you should do before drawing with the Pencil tool is to set up the pencil options in the options bar.

Pencil Tool Options

Option	Description
Brush presets	A pull-down menu where you can easily select a brush size and shape. **Note:** The Pencil tool draws with an "aliased" line, meaning that the edges of the line will be jagged (also called "stair-stepped") and not smooth. If you want the edges of your line to be smooth, use the Paintbrush tool, which has an "anti-aliased," smoothed edge. You'll learn more about the Paintbrush tool coming up next.
Brush size	A slider that allows you to choose what size your pencil (or paintbrush) draws with.
Brush painting mode	In Chapter 4, "*Layers*," you learned about layer blending modes. Layer blending modes allow you to control how an image in one layer blends into the images on other layers beneath it. Brush painting modes are very similar in that they control how what you draw or paint blends into the images on other layers (or the same layer) underneath them. For more information about blending modes, flip back to Chapter 4 and read the section "What Are Layer Blending Modes?".
Brush opacity	Also in Chapter 4, "*Layers*," you learned about layer opacity. Layer opacity allows you to change the opacity of your imagery on a layer-by-layer basis. Brush opacity is very similar, except instead of controlling the opacity of the layer, it controls *just* the opacity of what you're drawing or painting.
Auto Erase	With Auto Erase unchecked, your Pencil tool behaves just like if you were drawing on paper. If you draw over a line, it just draws on top of it. But with Auto Erase *checked*, if you draw on top of a line you've already drawn, it'll use your background color to draw over that line instead.

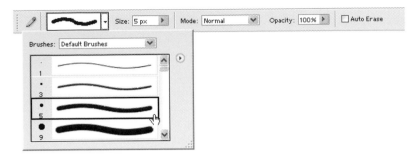

6. Click on the **Brush Presets** pull-down menu and choose the **hard round 5 pixels** brush. Leave the **Mode** set to **Normal**, the **Opacity** set to **100%**, and leave **Auto Erase** unchecked.

Note: The brush preset thumbnails will look a little different on a Mac. They have a tapered, pointed edge. The brushes and their effects are the same on both Mac and Windows—just the thumbnail images differ. By hovering your mouse over one of the brush presets, Elements will pop up a small yellow box that states the name of the brush preset.

Tip: So that you have maximum control over anything you draw, you should always create a new layer to draw on.

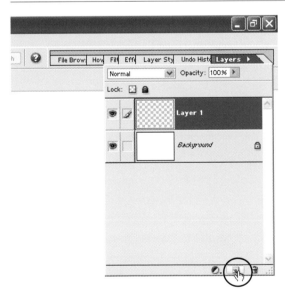

7. Open the **Layers** palette by choosing **Window > Layers** and click on the **Create a New Layer** icon. This will create a new layer (titled **Layer 1**) above the Background layer.

8. Move your mouse cursor onto your image document, and start drawing! Go crazy! And yes, this is a sketch of me *before* I've had my morning tea. Remember, if you make a mistake, you can always click the **Step Backward** button in the shortcuts bar, or press the undo keyboard shortcut, **Ctrl+Z** (Windows) or **Cmd+Z** (Mac).

By default, you can undo the last 20 things you did. You have no idea how many times I've wished that life had an undo button. I'm still waiting for Life version 2 to come out...ho-hum.

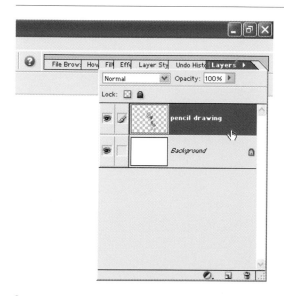

9. If you don't already have it open, open your **Layers** palette (by choosing **Window > Layers**). Rename **Layer 1** (which has your drawing on it) to **pencil drawing**. Remember, to rename a layer, simply double-click on the layer name in the Layers palette.

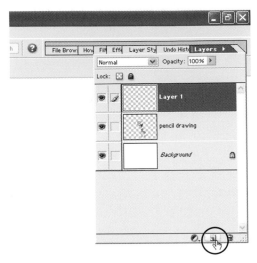

10. Create a new layer by clicking on the **Create a New Layer** icon. Next you're going to be painting with the Paintbrush tool, so this is the layer that the paintbrush drawing will go on.

11. Single-click on the **Paintbrush** tool icon in the Toolbox.

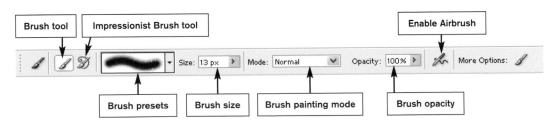

Just like the Pencil tool, before using the Paintbrush tool you should set the options for the Paintbrush tool in the options bar. As you'll notice, many of the options for the Paintbrush tool in the options bar are identical to the Pencil tool options. However, a few options are different:

Paintbrush Tool Options	
Option	Description
Brush tool and Impressionist Brush tool icons	Allow you to switch between the Brush tool and the Impressionist Brush tool. By simply selecting the Impressionist Brush tool and then "painting" with it over an image, it will make the part of the image that you paint on look like an impressionistic painting.
Enable Airbrush	Treats your paintbrush as an airbrush. The longer you hold your mouse button down on a spot, the darker and larger that spot will grow—simulating paint from the airbrush building up.
More Options	Gives you access and control over the brush dynamics such as brush shape, scattering, size, and color. By modifying the brush dynamics, you can get some really great, hand-drawn paintbrush styles.

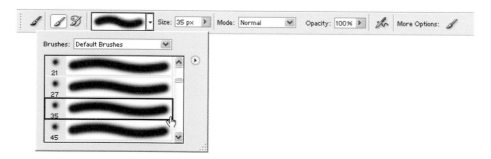

12. From the **Brush Presets** pull-down menu, select the brush **soft round 35 pixels**. Set the **Mode** to **Normal**, the **Opacity** to **100%**, **Enable Airbrush** off (button not depressed), and make sure that the standard **Brush** tool is selected (on the far-left of the options bar) and not the Impressionist Brush.

13. Before you start painting, first make sure that you have the correct layer (**Layer 1**) selected in the Layers palette. Then, just like you did with the Pencil tool, start painting!

In this example, I've drawn a rather ominous but tiny rain cloud above my "self portrait." As you can clearly see in this example, the Pencil and Paintbrush tools draw very different lines—the Pencil tool draws a line with a hard edge, and the Paintbrush tool draws with a very soft edge. When picking a drawing tool for your own future use, you can simply choose which tool you want for the job at hand. Do you want a soft-edged or a hard-edged line?

You'll be using the Paintbrush tool many more times throughout this book, so you'll get plenty of experience using and working with it in later exercises. Next you're going to learn about the basics of the Gradient tool, which, of course, allows you to create gradients.

14. Open the **Layers** palette (if you closed it, you can open it again by choosing **Window > Layers**) and rename the layer (by double-clicking on the layer name) with your paintbrushed image on it to **paintbrush drawing.** Then create a new layer by clicking on the **Create a New Layer** button.

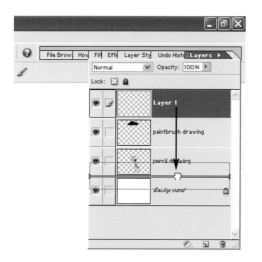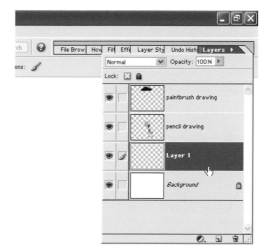

15. In the Layers palette, drag the new layer (titled **Layer 1**) down so that it's underneath the **pencil drawing** layer. The gradient that you are about to create is going to go in this new layer, but in this example the gradient needs to be *behind* the pencil and paintbrush layers.

16. Single-click the **Gradient** tool in the Toolbox to select it.

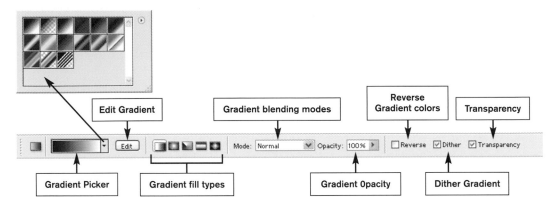

As with the other painting and drawing tools that you've seen thus far in this chapter, the Gradient tool has a variety of options that you can set. Here are descriptions of those features that differ from the Pencil and Paintbrush tools, which were described earlier:

Paintbrush Tool Options	
Option	**Description**
Gradient Picker	Clicking on the small, black triangle to the right of the Gradient Picker will pop open a small window that gives you access to some prebuilt gradients. Single-clicking on a preset gradient will select it for your use.
Gradient fill types	Single-click on one of these five buttons to define the style of gradient you want. For your reference, here's a table outlining the different gradient fill types:

Linear Gradient creates a gradient in a straight line starting with the foreground color and ending with the background color.

Radial Gradient creates a gradient in a circle pattern with the foreground color in the middle and fading to the background color around the outside.

Angle Gradient creates a gradient that sweeps around your starting point in a counterclockwise direction.

Reflected Gradient is similar to the linear gradient except that the Reflected Gradient creates an opposite gradient that moves away from your starting point in the opposite direction. This mirror gradient effect gives the Reflected Gradient its name.

Diamond Gradient creates a gradient in the shape of a diamond. Bling bling.

continues on next page

Paintbrush Tool Options *continued*

Option	Description
Reverse Gradient colors	Fairly self-explanatory—it reverses your gradient colors. If your gradient went from black to white, clicking on the **Reverse** check box would change the gradient so it went from white to black.
Dither Gradient	This adds a little bit of "noise" (dithering) to your gradient. What the heck do you need this for? When working with smooth gradations (such as a gradient), you might notice something called "banding." Banding is where your supposedly smooth gradient appears to have "bands" in it, or areas where the gradient has clumped together. This is especially prevalent if your monitor is set to thousands of colors (instead of millions) or if you're exporting your image as a GIF (more on GIFs in Chapter 12, "*Elements and the Web*"). By checking the **Dither** check box, Elements will add a slight amount of dots (called "noise") to your dither, which will reduce the banding effect.
Transparency	There is a preset gradient in the Gradient Picker pull-down menu that fades from whatever your foreground color is to transparent. You can also design a gradient to have transparent colors in it. Leaving the **Transparency** check box checked will allow your gradient to have transparent colors in it. Unchecking the check box will disallow transparent colors in gradients.

17. With your **Gradient** tool still selected, in the options bar make sure that **Linear Gradient** is the currently selected gradient type, **Mode** is set to **Normal**, **Opacity** is at **50%**, **Reverse** is unchecked, **Dither** is checked, and **Transparency** is checked.

18. Before you create the gradient, first double-check that you have **Layer 1** selected (which you created in Steps 14 and 15). Move your mouse over onto your image document and position your cursor so that it's near the top of the image window. Then, simply drag down until the cursor is a few inches above the bottom of the image window. By dragging the mouse cursor, you're defining where the gradient starts and where it ends.

19. When you let go of your mouse button, you should see your gradient fill the background of your image. Yay! Now, in my example, thanks to the gray background and a dark rain cloud overhead, my self-portrait is ready to go. Happy days! (Note the sarcasm in my voice.)

20. Feel free to save your masterpiece, or just close it without saving the document. Either way, make sure your image is closed before continuing to the next exercise.

In this exercise you were introduced to the Pencil, Paintbrush, and Gradient tools. As you've seen, there are quite a few options that you can configure for each tool. Even though you will be gaining more experience with some of these tools in later chapters, I still highly encourage you to experiment and play around with the different tools and options. I can't begin to tell you how many times I've discovered a neat effect or something I didn't know about before just by experimenting.

2. _____Erasing

Now that you've learned the basics of painting and drawing, you should also learn how to erase those mistakes…er…I mean, those "creative errors." In this exercise you're going to learn about the Eraser tools: Eraser, Background Eraser, and the Magic Eraser.

1. Copy the **chap_06** files and folders from the **H•O•T CD-ROM** to your hard drive.

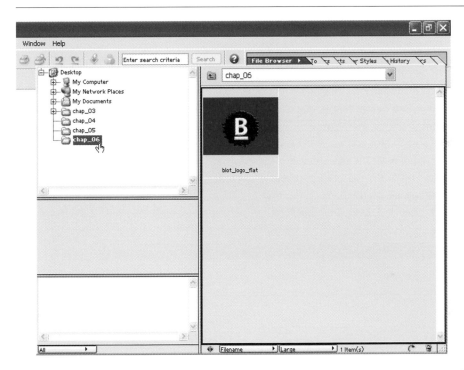

2. Open the **File Browser** by choosing **File > Browse**, and navigate to where you copied the **chap_06** files to on your computer. Locate the file titled **blot_logo_flat** inside the **chap_06** folder, and double-click on it to open it.

As you can see, it's the Blot Illustration logo again. But you'll also notice only one layer, **Background**, when you open the Layers palette (by choosing **Window > Layers**). Now what if (in a real-world example), this is the file that "the client" has given you, along with instructions to take the logo and put it on their stationery and on their Web site. "Aww great," you say to yourself. "This logo is against a red background. Both the stationery and the Web site have white backgrounds! I need to find a way to get the logo off of the red background so I can integrate it into the stationery and the Web site." In this exercise, you are going to look into using the Eraser tool to erase the red background, leaving you with the logo against a transparent background—perfect for transplanting onto a Web site or stationery.

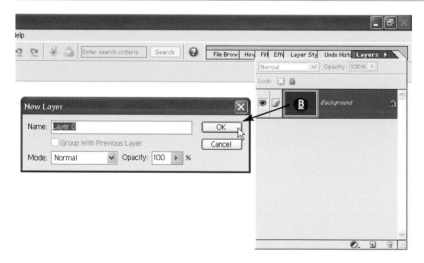

3. The first thing you need to do is change the default **Background** layer into a normal layer. The **Background** layer, as mentioned previously, is a special type of layer in Elements, and you cannot edit it because it is locked. To change it into a normal layer, double-click on the layer. When the **New Layer** dialog box appears, simply click **OK**.

*Now you'll notice in the Layers palette that the layer is no longer titled **Background**; instead it is titled **Layer 0**.*

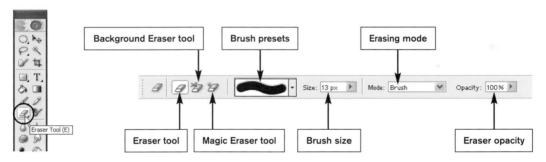

4. Single-click on the **Eraser** tool in the Toolbox to select it. As with other tools, you should learn about a few options (in the options bar) before continuing.

Eraser Tool Options	
Option	**Description**
Brush presets	The same as the Pencil and Paintbrush Brush presets, this pull-down menu allows you to select a brush shape and size to do your erasing with.
Brush size	This slider allows you to select, in pixels, the size of the brush that you will be using to do your erasing.
Erasing mode	From this pull-down menu, choose whether you want your Eraser tool to act like a brush (anti-aliased [smooth] edge), pencil (aliased [jagged] edge), or block (just a plain, non-resizable square).
Opacity	This slider allows you to determine at what opacity you will be erasing with. For example, if the Opacity slider is at 50%, whatever you are erasing will be 50% opaque.

5. In the options bar, make sure that the **Eraser** tool is selected, **Size** is set to **30 px** (pixels), **Mode** is set to **Brush**, and the **Opacity** is **100%**.

6. Move your mouse cursor over onto your image document; then drag your mouse around the logo, attempting to erase all of the red areas.

Although you can see that it is *in fact erasing the red, this would be a painstaking task to erase just the red areas while leaving the logo intact. The Eraser tool does a great job erasing parts of an image, but in this case, for this task, the regular Eraser tool isn't quite the right tool for the job.*

7. Repeatedly click on the **Step Backward** button in the shortcuts bar until you're back to the unaltered image. If you continue to click on the **Step Backward** button, but your image won't go all the way back to the way it was when you first opened it, it's probably because you made more than 20 alterations to the image (20 is, by default, how many steps backward you can go). So to get the image looking the way it did when you first started, choose **File > Revert**. The image will then revert back to the way it was when it was last saved.

*Note: If you press the **Step Backward** button too many times, or if you choose **File > Revert** to revert the image back to the way it was when it was last saved, you will have also undone the changing of the* Background *layer to a normal layer. Before you continue, make sure you open the Layers palette* **(Window > Layers)** *and check that your layer (the only layer) isn't titled **Background**. If it is, you'll simply need to repeat Step 3.*

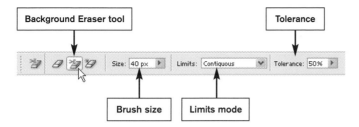

8. In the Toolbox, make sure you have the **Eraser** tool selected. Then in the options bar, single-click on the **Background Eraser** tool to select it.

Once you choose the Background Eraser tool, you need to set a few options (also in the options bar). The following chart explains what the possible options are, and the next step will instruct you how to best set your options for this particular image.

Background Eraser Tool Options	
Option	**Description**
Brush size	Same as the standard Eraser tool, this sets the size of the eraser brush.
Limits mode	**Contiguous** erases areas that are connected *only* to each other. **Discontiguous** erases the color you are sampling/erasing wherever it appears under the brush.
Tolerance	Similar to the Tolerance setting you saw with the Magic Wand tool in Chapter 5. The higher the tolerance percentage, the more colors will be considered similar to the one you're sampling and, therefore, more area will be erased. The lower the tolerance percentage, the fewer colors will be considered similar to the colors you're sampling, and fewer areas will be erased.

9. In the options bar, set **Size** to **40 px** (either by dragging the **Size** slider until it reaches **40**, or by typing **40** in the **Size** field and pressing **Enter** [Windows] or **Return** [Mac]). Set **Limits** to **Contiguous**. (The Limits mode is irrelevant in this case because the background you're erasing is one solid color. If the background was textured, however, you would most likely want to select **Discontiguous**). Set the **Tolerance** to **50%**.

10. Move your mouse over onto the image document, and start dragging your mouse cursor around the outside of the logo. As you drag the Background Eraser, always keep the crosshairs over the color(s) that you want to erase (in this case, the red). Like magic, you'll see the color being wiped away very cleanly all the way up to the edge of the black in the logo. Nifty! And yes, to make it easier to erase the small areas, you can zoom closer into the image if you'd like. Press the keyboard shortcut **Ctrl++** (that's the Ctrl key and the plus sign key on Windows) or **Cmd++** (Mac) to zoom into the image; **Ctrl+−** (Windows) or **Cmd+−** (Mac) will zoom out of the image.

Note: While using the Background Eraser tool, if you still see a small fringe—or halo—around the outside edge of the logo, you can tell Elements to consider more *colors similar to the red background color. In the options bar, simply increase the Tolerance percentage by dragging the* **Tolerance** *slider up. Then next time you use the Background Eraser tool, it should erase more of that halo away because it considers more colors to be similar, and thereby within its range to erase.*

---

11. Repeatedly click on the **Step Backward** button in the shortcuts bar (just like you did in Step 7) until your image is back to where the background is a solid red.

Note: Again, if you press the **Step Backward** *button too many times, or if you choose* **File > Revert** *to revert the image back to the way it was when it was last saved, you will have also undone the changing of the* Background *layer to a normal layer. Before you continue, make sure you open the Layers palette* **(Window > Layers)** *and check that your layer (the only layer) isn't titled* **Background.** *If it is, simply repeat Step 3.*

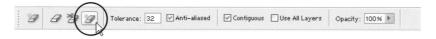

12. In the Toolbox, make sure you have the **Eraser** tool selected. Then in the options bar, single-click on the **Magic Eraser** tool to select it.

After you choose the Magic Eraser tool, you need to set a few options in the options bar. (These options are identical to the Magic Wand tool's options, by the way.) The following chart explains the possible options for this tool. In the following step, you'll be instructed how to set the proper settings for the image at hand.

Magic Eraser Tool Options	
Option	**Description**
Tolerance	The most important option is the Tolerance setting. A low Tolerance specifies that fewer colors will be considered similar to the one that you click on, whereas a higher Tolerance specifies that more colors will be considered similar. Essentially, the lower the tolerance, the fewer pixels will be erased around where you clicked; the higher the tolerance, the more pixels will be erased. For now, though, leave the **Tolerance** option set to the default **32.**
Anti-aliased	The Anti-aliased check box toggles whether or not you want the edges of what is erased to be smoothed (anti-aliased). In most cases, you will probably want to leave this check box checked.
Contiguous	The Contiguous check box sets whether or not you want only the pixels that are directly contiguous (adjacent) to each other to be erased. Unchecking this check box will cause pixels with a similar color to the one you clicked on to be erased over the entire image.
Use All Layers	The Use All Layers check box is fairly self-explanatory. Do you want to use the Magic Eraser tool to erase pixels that span all of the layers in your image or not?
Opacity	This slider allows you to determine at what opacity you will be erasing with. For example, if the Opacity slider is at 50%, whatever you are erasing will be 50% opaque.

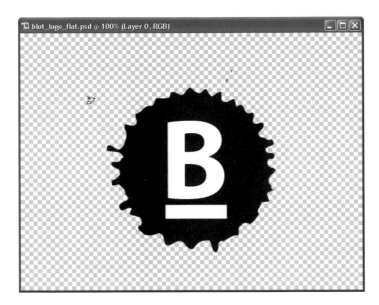

13. For now, leave the Magic Eraser tool options at their defaults: **Tolerance** is **32**, **Anti-aliased** is checked, **Contiguous** is checked, **Use All Layers** is unchecked (it's irrelevant in our case because this image has only one layer anyway), and **Opacity** is **100%**. Move your mouse cursor onto the red part of the image, and single-click.

Holey bajoley! Some of you are probably saying (to whomever is within earshot) "That jerk! Why didn't he show me this way first?!" Well…I have only my naturally sadistic nature to blame. Muahahaha.

Actually, although in this case the Magic Eraser tool (now you see why it's called the "Magic" Eraser tool, eh?) made an extremely quick and easy job of removing that flat, red background, it doesn't work that great in all situations. The Magic Eraser tool works best in removing large areas of flat color. If the background you're trying to remove is textured or patterned in any way, your results won't be this good. Modifying your Tolerance settings is how you get the Magic Eraser tool to work better in different situations. But I'll be a monkey's uncle if that nifty Magic Eraser tool didn't do a bang-up job getting rid of that red background. Now that the logo is on its own layer, and everything else except the logo is transparent, you can easily add it to the stationery and the Web site as the client requested. Everyone's happy!

Note: The Magic Eraser tool, it seems, is truly magical. Remember how, back in Step 3, you changed the Background to a normal layer so that you could work with it? Well, the Magic Eraser tool will also do that for you as well! It slices; it dices; it cuts tomatoes, tin cans; it even…well…you get the point. If you are using the Magic Eraser to remove the background from your image, you don't need to convert the Background layer into a normal layer first because the Magic Eraser will also do that task for you as well.

14. Choose **File > Save As**. Name the file **blot_logo_layered**, and save it in the **chap_06** folder that you copied to your computer earlier. After you have saved the file, don't close it—you will be using it again in the next exercise.

(3.) ─────────── **Modifying Colors**

Break out the champagne glasses 'cause it's time to work with some color, baby! In this exercise, you will learn how the Color Picker works, how to pick new colors, and how to apply those colors to your images. You should still have your image open from the last exercise. If you accidentally closed it, you can open it back up again. You should have saved it in your **chap_06** folder, and it should be titled **blot_logo_layered**. For now, leave the image open but move it off to the side of your screen or minimize it so that it's out of the way.

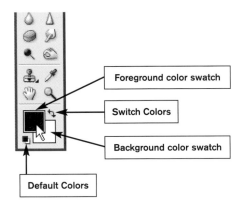

At the bottom of the Toolbox are two overlapping color swatches. By this point in the book, they might not be the default black and white, but their current color is irrelevant at the moment. The color swatch that's on the top is the **foreground color** swatch; the one behind it is the **background color** swatch. You can switch the foreground and background colors by clicking on the **Switch Colors** icon (or by pressing **X** on the keyboard), and you can always easily revert back to the default colors (black in the foreground and white in the background) by clicking the **Default Colors** icon, or by pressing **D** on your keyboard. Pretty simple, eh?

So what are the foreground and background colors used for? The foreground color is used by Elements in a variety of tasks, such as when you are painting with your paintbrush or pencil tools, and it is also used when you fill shapes, too. The background color is also used (among other things) to create fills such as gradient fills. Both the foreground and background colors are also used in some Elements filters.

Now why don't you take a look at picking colors? (This process is the same, by the way, when changing the background color as well.)

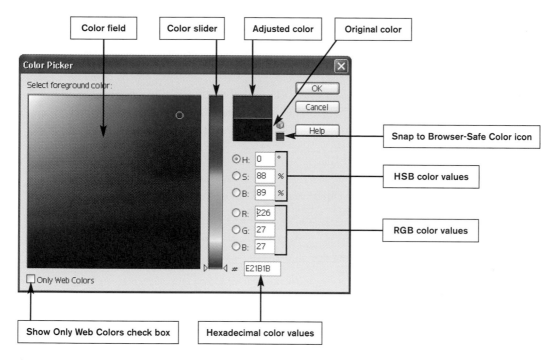

1. Single-click on the **foreground color** swatch. The Color Picker window will open. From here you can choose any color under the sun…and more.

Here is the process that you will generally want to follow when choosing a color from the Color Picker.

• *By clicking on one of the radio buttons, you can choose how you want to view and select your color, HSB (**H**ue, **S**aturation, or **B**rightness) or RGB (**Red, G**reen, or **B**lue). If you click through the HSB and RGB radio buttons, you can see how both the Color slider and Color field changes—reflecting how you're choosing to select your color. Chances are you will be spending the majority of your time in the Color Picker viewing colors in the Hue mode. So for now, leave the **H** radio button selected.*

• *After you have selected Hue as your chosen color value, drag your mouse up and down the **Color** slider until you have found the color (hue) that you want.*

• *From the Color field, you can choose (based on the color you picked from the Color slider) the saturation and brightness of the color. By dragging your mouse left and right, you determine the saturation. By dragging your mouse up and down within the **Color** field, you determine the brightness.*

• *As you are locating a new color, you can easily compare your new color with the original color (the color that was already in your foreground color swatch) by looking at the Adjusted color and Original color swatches in the Color Picker window.*

• *If you are building graphics in Elements that will be posted on a Web site, you might want to check the **Only Web Colors** check box. On some older computer monitors that cannot display thousands or millions of colors, colors in images will shift slightly. (To exacerbate the problem, the shifted colors will differ on Mac and Windows computers.) To ensure that the colors the viewer is seeing are the same as the colors you pick, check the **Only Web Colors** check box. The Color Picker will then display only "browser-safe colors," that is, certain specific colors that do not shift on these older computer monitors. Check the Only Web Colors check box only if you are creating graphics for a Web page, and you need to ensure that the colors don't shift on these older computer monitors. Otherwise, leave this check box unchecked because it will limit the colors you can pick to 216 instead of millions+. If you are interested, you can read an excellent article about browser-safe colors at **http://www.lynda.com/hex.html.***

• *If you are building graphics in Elements that will be posted on a Web site and you need to use a specific color (for instance, a color that is the same as the background color of a Web page), you can enter the hexadecimal equivalent of that color in the **Hexadecimal** color value field.*

• *Related to browser-safe colors is the **Snap to Browser-Safe Color** icon. As you are choosing a color, you might notice a small color swatch with a box icon above it appear next to the Original color swatch. Clicking on that small color swatch will snap whatever color you have currently picked to the closest browser-safe equivalent.*

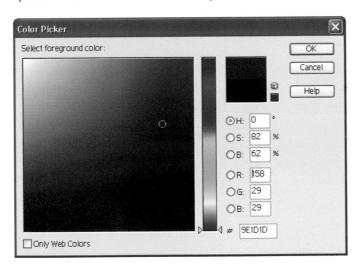

2. For now, select a **red** color. I chose a semi-dark red that is (as I can see under the saturation and brightness fields) **82%** saturated and **62%** bright. Its **RGB** value is **158, 29, 29** (respectively). If you want to use the same color values as I'm using in this example, you can just type the values into the **HSB** and **RGB** fields in your Color Picker window. Click **OK**.

You'll now notice that in the Toolbox, the foreground color swatch is now the color you picked. I chose red, so my foreground color swatch is red. Now that you've picked the color you want and it's ready in the foreground color swatch to use, you need to find a place to use it! Here is where that logo you were working on in the last exercise comes back into play.

3. At the beginning of this exercise I asked that you move the **blot_logo_layered** image off to the side so that it wouldn't get in the way while you were learning about color. Now that you've learned to pick colors, you're going to apply the color you picked to the logo. Bring that logo image back into view so you can work with it some more. (If you've accidentally closed it, you can easily open it back up again by navigating to your **chap_06** folder and double-clicking on **blot_logo_layered.**)

The goal here is to change the color of the logo to the color that you picked (in my case, red). Every part of the logo that is black you will change over to your new color, but the white parts of the logo (the letters "B" and "I") will remain white.

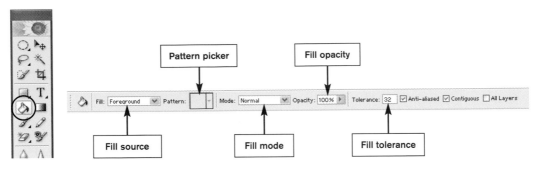

4. Start by selecting the **Paint Bucket** tool in the Toolbox.

As with many of the other tools, there are options you can set in the options bar. By now, you should also be starting to realize that many of the options you can modify are the same (or they set very similar things) across many of the tools. This is a good thing because you won't have to learn a bunch of new settings for each tool in the Toolbox. Thank goodness! Here is a breakdown of the Paint Bucket options you can set.

Paint Bucket Tool Options	
Option	**Description**
Fill source	From this pull-down menu, you can specify what you're filling with. Your two options are **Foreground** and **Pattern.** The Foreground option is pretty obvious—you can use the Paint Bucket tool to fill objects with whatever your foreground color is. Pattern allows you to fill with…yep—you made the obvious leap in logic—a pattern. If you select Pattern, you can choose a pattern to fill an object with. Which leads me to…
Pattern picker	From this pull-down menu, you can choose from a list of prebuilt patterns to fill your object with. You have choices ranging from **Wood** to **Bubbles**, and even **Tie Dye.**
Fill mode	The **Fill** mode allows you to specify how the color (and the value [the degree of lightness/darkness] of that color) you're filling with interacts with the other colors underneath it. For more information about blending modes (the same thing as Fill modes, essentially), refer back to Chapter 4, "*Layers.*"

continues on next page

Paint Bucket Tool Options *continued*

Option	Description
Fill opacity	From this slider you can specify how opaque of a color you are filling with.
Fill tolerance	Sets how similar a color must be (to the one you click on) for it to be filled with the Paint Bucket tool. The higher the number, the broader the range of colors are considered similar and the more area will be filled. The lower the number, the fewer the range of colors are considered similar and less area will be filled. In essence, when you use the Paint Bucket tool and you click on an object to fill it with your foreground color, if it doesn't fill enough of the object that you want to fill, *increase* the Tolerance and try again. If it fills too much of the object, *decrease* the Tolerance and try again.
Anti-aliased	Sets whether or not you want the edge of your fill to be smoothed (anti-aliased) or jagged (aliased). In most cases, you will want to leave the Anti-aliased check box checked.
Contiguous	Fill only the pixels that are contiguous (adjacent) to the pixel you click on with the Paint Bucket. By unchecking this check box, Elements will fill all similar colors ("similar" is defined by your Fill tolerance) over the *entire image.*
All Layers	Pretty straightforward. Do you want to use the Paint Bucket tool to fill shapes in only the layer that you currently have selected in the Layers palette or throughout all layers in your image document?

5. Make sure you have the **Paint Bucket** tool selected, and in the options bar—now that you've learned what all the options do—you need to set them up for this particular image. Set **Fill** to **Foreground**, **Mode** to **Normal**, **Opacity** to **100%**, and **Tolerance** to **32** (the default will do fine for this example). The **Anti-aliased** check box should be checked, the **Contiguous** check box should be unchecked (remember, you want to change the color of the black in the logo throughout the *entire* image), and **All Layers** should be unchecked as well (it's actually a moot point because this image document doesn't have any other layers).

6. Move your **Paint Bucket** cursor over onto the black area of the logo and single-click. If you've set up the options correctly, all the black areas of the logo should now be replaced with your chosen foreground color. Ohhh…ahhhh.

7. Save this image by pressing the keyboard shortcut **Ctrl+S** (Windows) or **Cmd+S** (Mac). Once the image has been saved, close it because you won't be needing it again in this chapter.

*Note: You can also use the menu item **Edit > Fill** to fill objects (with the foreground color). The Edit > Fill method, however, fills everything in a layer and doesn't give you the selective fill settings (based on a tolerance) like the Paint Bucket tool does. That is why you used the Paint Bucket tool for this particular example. But the Edit > Fill method is also a great and easy way to fill the contents of a layer. I'll talk a little more about using Edit > Fill in conjunction with the preserve transparency feature later in this chapter, and you will also get some experience using Edit > Fill in other chapters as well.*

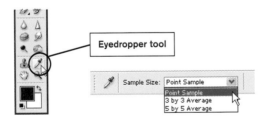

Eyedropper tool

*Also not to be overlooked in the arena of choosing and selecting colors is the Eyedropper tool. It's super simple to use. Just single-click on the **Eyedropper** tool in the Toolbox; then click on a part of an image that you want to take a color sample of. You also have one pull-down menu of options in the options bar. The pull-down menu allows you to specify if you want to take a color sample of the exact pixel color that you click on (**Point Sample**), or if you want to have Elements take an average color sample of the three pixels around that point or even five pixels around (**3 by 3 Average** and **5 by 5 Average**, respectively). The color that you pick will be inserted into your foreground color swatch. To have Elements take the color you pick and insert it into the background color swatch instead, hold down the **Alt** key (Windows) or **Option** key (Mac) when you click on an image with the Eyedropper tool.*

Note | Preserve Transparency

In the last exercise, you saw how to fill part of an image using the Paint Bucket tool. Another way to fill the contents of a layer, while at the same time preserving the transparent areas in a layer, is by using a feature called **preserve transparency**.

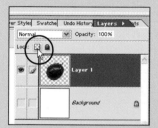

To enable the preserve transparency feature of a layer, select a layer in the Layers palette and click on the **Lock Transparency Pixels** button. This means that when you fill a particular layer with a color, Elements will preserve all the transparent areas of the layer and fill only those areas that *aren't* transparent.

By choosing **Edit > Fill** or by using the keyboard shortcut (**Alt+Backspace** [Windows] or **Option+Delete** [Mac]) to fill with the foreground color, the object will be filled with your chosen color. Thanks to the preserve transparency feature, only the contents of the layer (in this example, a ladybug) were filled. If the preserve transparency feature is turned off when you use **Edit > Fill**, the entire layer will be filled, transparent areas and all.

In this chapter you learned how to draw and paint using the Pencil, Paintbrush, and Gradient tools. You learned to use the different Eraser tools to erase portions and even entire swatches of an image based on tolerance settings. Lastly, you learned how to use the Color Picker to pick different colors and how to apply those colors to objects using the Paint Bucket tool. Wow-ee!

In the next chapter you will be expanding on your drawing/painting/graphics creation skills by learning about Elements shapes and layer styles. *Warning* Fun and cool (oh yeah…and useful, too) stuff ahead!

7.

Shapes and Layer Styles

| Bitmaps and Vectors | Creating Shapes |
| About Layer Styles | Layer Styles |

chap_07

Photoshop Elements 2
H•O•T CD-ROM

In this chapter you will learn about bitmap (raster) and vector graphics, and how Elements can work with both. You'll learn how to easily create vector shapes and then how to add a little spice to them by applying layer styles to those shapes. Layer styles are an exciting way to non-destructively add effects (such as bevels, drop shadows, glows, and so forth) to the graphics in layers. These layer styles can easily be turned on or off, or customized to your liking. So what are you waiting for? Oh right…you're waiting for me to stop babbling… ;-)

Bitmaps and Vectors

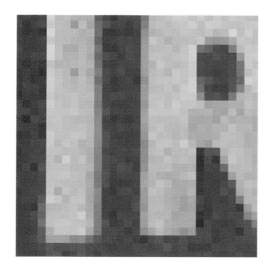 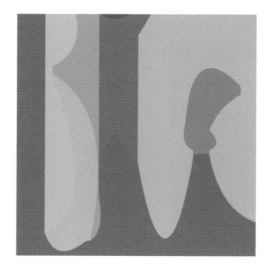

bitmap   *vector*

There are essentially two ways for graphics programs to create your graphics: bitmap (a.k.a. raster images) or vector. **Bitmap graphics** are constructed entirely of tiny squares of color (pixels). If the resolution (how many of those pixels there are per inch) is high enough, when you look at the image at its actual size you won't even see the pixels. Like a painting by Georges Seurat, the tiny points of color blend together to create a detailed image. **Vector images**, on the other hand, are created by lines and curves. These lines and curves combine to create your image.

Bitmap images are "resolution dependent," meaning that an image has a fixed number of pixels (you define how many when you create a new image). This is the primary reason why enlarging a bitmap graphic is discouraged. When you enlarge a bitmap graphic (called "resampling"), the graphics program (in this case, Elements) has to take an image that has a fixed number of pixels and find a way to make a larger image with *more* pixels. Elements does this in a process called *interpolation*, where it actually adds pixels to the image based on the color values of existing pixels. This always results in an image with lower quality. (You can't get something from nothing, eh?)

Vector images, on the other hand, are "resolution independent," meaning that vector images are *not* dependent on the resolution of an image and can be resized up or down without any loss in image quality. Here is a short list of pros and cons of bitmap and vector images.

Bitmap

Pros: Because you have complete control over every pixel that makes up an image, and because complex images can be created with those pixels, bitmap images are great for continuous-tone images (photographs). Working with a bitmap image, you can also easily add filters or effects to images to distort their appearances.

Cons: You can't increase the size of a bitmap image without losing image quality. Bitmap images also require more memory and hard drive space to work with than vector images. This is because Elements has to keep track of *every pixel* in a bitmap image, whereas with a vector image, Elements has to keep track of just the vector points that make up the lines and curves of a vector image.

Vector

Pros: You can easily increase or decrease the size of a vector image without any degradation in quality. They also require less memory and hard drive space than equivalent bitmap images.

Cons: You don't have the same level of control with a vector image as you do with a bitmap image. You can't add the same kind of specialized filters or effects to vector images that you can add to bitmap images. In vector editing programs, such as Adobe Illustrator, you *can* add some specialized effects to vector images, but not nearly the same type, variety, or quantity of effects available for bitmap images.

The reason why I bring up this discussion and a breakdown of bitmaps and vectors now (as some of you might be wondering) is because Elements uses vector graphics to create certain objects, such as type and shapes. As you'll see in this chapter, Elements can work simultaneously within one image using both bitmap and vector graphics.

I. ——————————Creating Shapes

In this exercise, you're going to learn the basics of shapes in Elements. In the next exercise, you'll spice those shapes up a bit by adding layer styles to those shapes.

1. Copy the **chap_07** folder and files from the **H•O•T CD-ROM** to your hard drive.

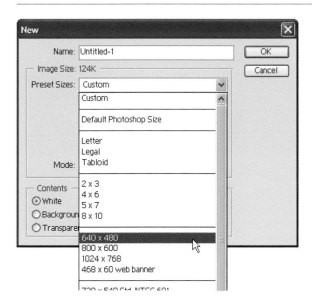

2. Create a new image by choosing **File > New**. In the New dialog box, from the **Preset Sizes** pull-down menu, choose **640 x 480**. Make sure the **Mode** is **RGB Color** and under **Contents** that the **White** radio button is selected. Click **OK**. This will create a new, blank, 640 x 480 document at 72 ppi.

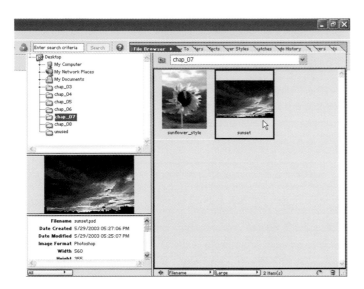

3. Open the file browser by choosing **Window > File Browser**. Within the file browser, navigate to the **chap_07** folder that you copied onto your computer in Step 1 and double-click on the **sunset** picture to open it.

In this exercise, you are going to add a little spice to a photograph by using shapes and layer styles. In the next chapter, you will also add a little bit of text to the image as well. In this hypothetical situation, you're going to email a photo to someone (or put it up on a Web site…more on both of those in Chapter 12, "Elements and the Web"), but you are going to add a little more visual interest to the photo first.

Now at this point you should have two images open: the blank 640 x 480 image that you created in Step 2 and the sunset picture that you just opened.

4. First make sure that you have the **Move** tool selected; then, with the images open so you can see both of them together, drag the **sunset** picture onto the blank, 640 x 480 image. After you've success-fully done this, you can close the **sunset** image document because you won't need it further.

5. Position the **sunset** image so that it's towards the top of the image space and roughly centered horizontally within the overall image space.

Next you are going to create a shape to go behind *the sunset photograph—visually framing it.*

6. Open the **Layers** palette by choosing **Window > Layers**. Select the **Background** layer by single-clicking on it.

7. In the Toolbox, single-click on the **Shape** tool.

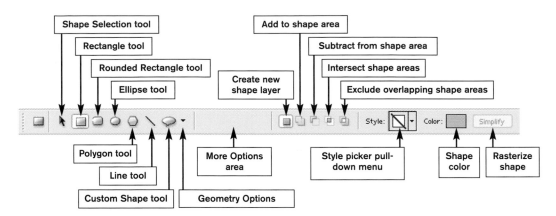

Once you click on the Shape tool, you're greeted with a variety of options in the options bar. Toward the left-hand side of the options bar, you can choose which shape you want to draw with. Your options are a rectangle, rounded rectangle (the corners are rounded), ellipse, polygon, line, or a custom shape. When you click on some of the aforementioned shapes in the options bar, you are given an option to set in the options area. For instance, when you click on the Rounded Rectangle tool, you can specify the corner radius for the curve, and when you click on the Custom Shape tool you can select, from a preset list, which shape to draw with. To the right of the Custom Shape tool is a small, downward-facing, black arrow. This is the Geometry Options button. Single-clicking on it will give you additional geometry options to set for each tool.

To the right of the More Options area is where you specify shape interaction. It's here where you control how you want the shapes to interact with each other when they are drawn. The following table outlines the options you're given and what they mean:

Shape Tool Options	
Option	**Description**
Create new shape layer (default)	Creates a new, unique layer for each shape that you draw.
Add to shape area	Adds the shape you're drawing to the same shape layer that you currently have selected. If you don't have another shape layer selected, this option is grayed-out.
Subtract from shape area	Subtracts the shape you're drawing from any other shapes in your shapes layer, wherever they overlap.
Intersect shape areas	Shows only the areas where shapes intersect (overlap). All other areas will be removed.
	continues on next page

Shape Tool Options *continued*	
Option	**Description**
Exclude overlapping shape areas	The opposite of Intersect. Removes the area where shapes intersect and shows all other areas.
Style picker pull-down menu	As you'll see in the next exercise, the Style picker pull-down menu allows you to apply a layer style to the shape you're drawing.
Shape color	Where you can choose what color to make the shape you're drawing.
Rasterize shape button	To add a filter or effect to a shape, the shape must first be rasterized (converted from a vector to a bitmap). Clicking on this button will allow you to rasterize your vector shape in preparation to add a filter or effect.

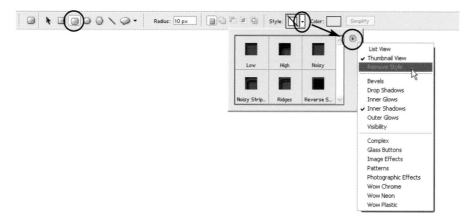

8. With the **Shape** tool selected, in the options bar single-click on the **Rounded Rectangle** tool. Leave the corner radius set to the default **10 px**. (If your corner radius is not set to 10, type **10** into the **Radius** field and press **Enter** [Windows] or **Return** [Mac].)

*Note: If you used a layer style while playing around with Elements previously, a layer style might still be selected in the Style picker pull-down menu. Because you don't want the shape you're about to draw to automatically have a layer style applied to it, make sure you single-click on the Style picker pull-down menu. From the Style picker menu that appears, single-click on the additional layer styles pull-down menu button (a circle button with a right-facing triangle in it) and choose **Remove Style**. If you already have a style selected, this will remove it.*

9. Single-click on the **shape** color swatch. In the Color Picker window that opens, choose any color you'd like. Click **OK**.

10. In the image document, drag from the top left down toward the right until you've created a shape around the sunset photograph. Give a little bit of room around the left, right, and top of the photograph, but a little extra room at the bottom.

Congratulations! You've just created a vector shape in Elements!

Note: Because this is a vector shape, you can easily scale it up or down with no loss in quality, as I described at the beginning of this chapter. Scaling up bitmaps is highly discouraged because it will slightly distort and blur the image. Vector shapes, on the other hand, can be scaled up or down without any degradation. So feel free to scale that shape around because it's a vector! Yeah, baby, yeah!

Next you're going to learn how to change the color of a vector shape. Changing the color of a shape, although very easy, is done quite differently than changing the color of objects.

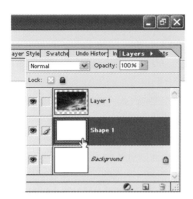

11. Open the **Layers** palette by choosing **Window > Layers**. In the Layers palette, you'll see a layer titled **Shape 1**. Notice how it is underneath the layer with the sunset photo (**Layer 1**) and above the Background layer? The reason why it's in that particular place is because before you created the shape, back in Step 6, you first selected the Background layer. So when you drew out your shape, it was automatically added above the layer you had selected (just like when you create a new layer). This is precisely what you want because this shape is supposed to be *behind* the sunset photo. Aren't you smart! ;-)

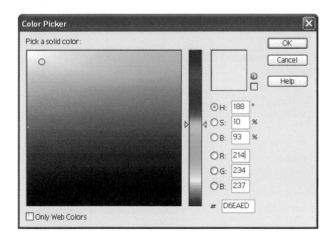

12. Double-click on the **Shape 1** layer thumbnail. When the Color Picker window appears, enter **214** in the **R** (Red) field, **234** in the **G** (Green) field, and **237** in the **B** (Blue) field. (If you need help with the Color Picker, refer back to Chapter 6, "*Painting and Colors*.") This will give you a light turquoise color. Click **OK**.

Awesome! Now in the image document, the shape that you drew is the new color you just picked! Told ya it was easy! See, I'd never lead you astray...except there was that one time with the Magic Eraser tool... ;-)

13. Leave the image open—you will be using it in the next exercise.

At this point, I would encourage you to create a new blank image document (just like you did in Step 1) and experiment with the different shapes. In this exercise, you only gained experience with the rounded rectangle shape but, as was pointed out, there are other shapes that we didn't cover. However, the process of creating the other shapes is the same as the process of creating the rounded rectangle shape.

In the next exercise, you will learn how to apply a layer style to the shape that you just created. A layer style is a great and easy way to add a little flair to the dull, flat shape that is created by the Shape tool.

About Layer Styles

Layer styles are an easy way to add a complex effect to the contents of a layer. Elements gives you many different preset effects to choose from—ranging from simple drop shadows and bevels to more complex effects such as "cactus" and "molten gold." As you'll see in this next exercise, applying and modifying layer styles to the shape that you created in the last exercise is easier than pie…or is it "simpler than cake"? Well…you get the idea. ;-)

Simply put, layer styles go back to that term I introduced in Chapter 4, "*Layers*," called "non-destructive editing." What this means is that when you add a layer style to a layer, you're not permanently altering the graphics in that layer. Layer styles can easily be applied and removed from layers with a couple clicks of the mouse. So go crazy! Experiment! You can do so knowing that if you mess up, or if you don't like the changes you have made to your image using layer styles, you can always easily delete the effect, and you're back to your original, unaltered graphic. It just doesn't get any cooler than that…

2. ——————Layer Styles

In this exercise, you will learn how to add layer styles to the shapes that you created in the last exercise.

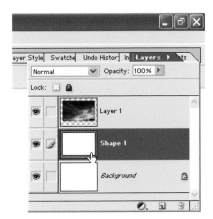

1. Open the **Layers** palette by choosing **Window > Layers** and single-click on the **Shape 1** layer to select it.

Note: If you already have the Move tool selected, you'll notice that when you select the Shape 1 layer, a bounding box (a dashed outline with boxes on the corners and sides) will appear around the shape in the image. This is how Elements tells you, visually, that the shape is selected. Now that it is selected, you can add a layer style to it.

2. Make sure that the **Move** tool is selected by single-clicking on it in the Toolbox.

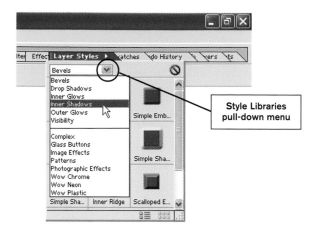

3. Open the **Layer Styles** palette by choosing **Window > Layer Styles**. In the Layer Styles palette, single-click on the **Style Libraries** pull-down menu. From this pull-down menu, you can choose from a variety of different styles (effects) to add to your shape. Select **Inner Shadows**.

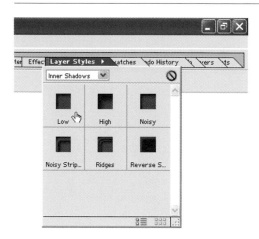

4. The Layer Styles palette will change to show you the different Inner Shadow effects you can apply to your shape. If you hover your mouse over one of the effects, a small tip will appear, telling you the full name of the effect. Single-click **Low**.

Wow! Instantly the shape behind the sunset picture now has a small, interior drop shadow.
That was easy!

Next you're going to learn how to change the settings for that effect.

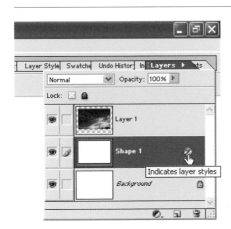

5. Open the **Layers** palette by choosing **Window > Layers** and double-click on the **Layer Styles** icon (it looks like an "**f**" inside a circle) on the **Shape 1** layer.

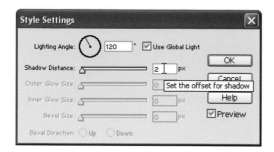

6. The **Style Settings** dialog box will open. From here, you can specify the settings for the particular style that you've applied to your shape. As you can see in this example, you can modify the **Shadow Distance.** (Unchecking the **Use Global Light** check box would enable you to modify the other settings, but all you want to modify right now is the Shadow Distance, anyway.) Drag the **Shadow Distance** slider down from the default of **5** to a more subtle **2.** If you prefer, you can also just type **2** in the Shadow Distance field. Notice that as you drag the slider around, you can see it change the effect in real time. Nifty!

7. Click **OK**.

Next you are going to draw another shape. This new shape will act as a backdrop where you can type a small description of the image.

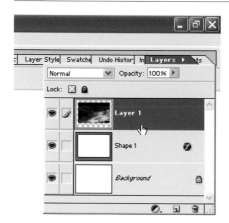

8. Open the **Layers** palette by choosing **Window > Layers**. Single-click on the layer with the sunset picture on it, **Layer 1**.

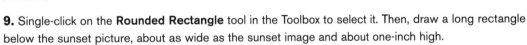

9. Single-click on the **Rounded Rectangle** tool in the Toolbox to select it. Then, draw a long rectangle below the sunset picture, about as wide as the sunset image and about one-inch high.

Note: It's normal if this second shape is a different color than the first, larger shape you drew. When you draw a shape, Elements will color that shape with the current foreground color. In this case, however, because you're about to apply a layer style to the shape that will change the shape's color, it doesn't matter what color it is.

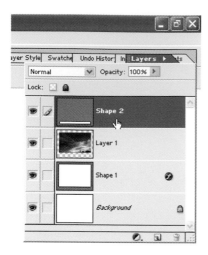

10. Checking to make sure you have the correct layer selected before you begin editing is a good practice to get into. First, open the **Layers** palette by choosing **Window > Layers**. Then, single-click on the **Shape 2** layer to double-check that it is selected.

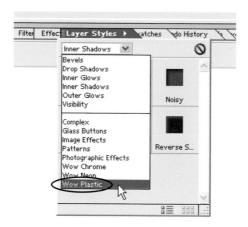

11. Single-click on the **Move** tool in the Toolbox to make sure it's selected, and then open the **Layer Styles** palette by choosing **Window > Layer Styles**. Click on the **Style Libraries** pull-down menu and choose the bottom-most option, **Wow Plastic**.

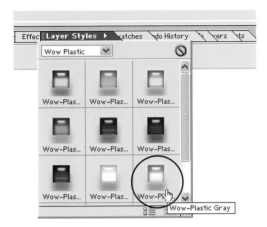

12. In the Layer Styles palette, single-click on **Wow-Plastic Gray**.

Nice! You just applied a layer style to the new shape. In the next chapter, you're going to add some text on top of that shape to give the image a short description.

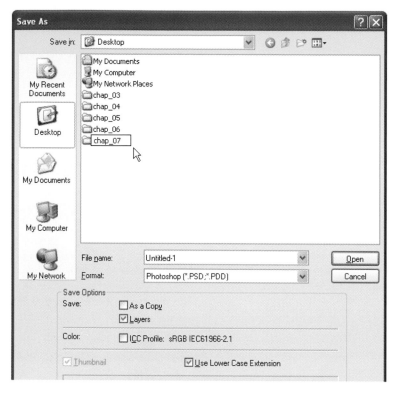

13. Save the image by choosing **File > Save**. In the **File name** field, name the image **first_shape**, make sure the **Format** is set to **Photoshop**, and save the image in the **chap_07** folder.

14. After you have saved the image, leave it open because you will be using it again in the next chapter.

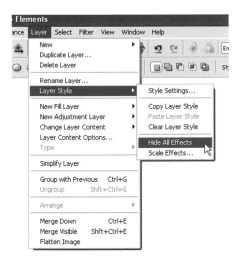

Note: *There are some very useful layer style options tucked away under **Layer > Layer Style** to be aware of. You can get access to **Style Settings** (which you already modified in Steps 5–7 by double-clicking on the Layer Styles icon on the shape layer); you can easily copy a layer style that you've added to a layer by choosing **Copy Layer Style**; and you can then apply that layer style to another layer by selecting the layer in the Layers palette that you want to apply the style to, and then choose **Paste Layer Style.** To remove a layer style, choose **Clear Layer Style**. If you want to temporarily hide the layer style you've added to a layer, simply choose **Hide All Effects**. (To show the layer style once you've hidden it, choose the **Layer > Layer Style** menu item again and select **Show All Effects** to make your layer style visible again.) Lastly, you can easily scale the layer style (independently from the graphics on that layer) by choosing **Scale Effects**.*

Tip: *If you really want to "push the envelope," you can apply a layer style on top of other layer styles. Normally, if you choose a different layer style to add to a layer, it removes the old layer style first and then applies the new one. But if you want to apply one (or more) layer style(s) on top of another, after you've applied one layer style, open the layer style picker pop-up menu again, and while holding down the Shift key, single-click on a different layer style. There you have it! Instead of having only one layer style per layer, you can now have multiple layer styles that overlap and affect each other. Be careful, though—you might go blind from some of the wacky (and extremely ugly) visual effects you can achieve using this method. ;-)*

In this chapter you learned how to create a simple shape and then how to apply and modify a layer style to that shape. Shapes and layer styles can also be used with great success to create snappy Web graphics or to easily add some nice effects to a postcard or flyer.

In the next chapter you will learn the ins and outs of working with type in Elements. You will also learn how to apply layer styles—like you learned in this chapter—to some text to give it a little more "umph" as well. I'll see you there!

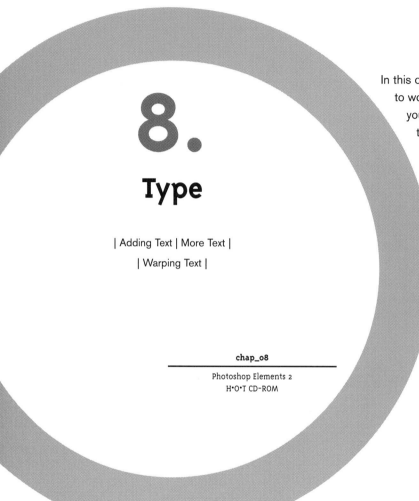

8.

Type

| Adding Text | More Text |
| Warping Text |

In this chapter, you will examine the various ways to work with type in Elements. Not only that but you will also learn how to add some appeal to the text by using layer styles and the warp text feature to distort the path of the text. So don't go anywhere…the party's just getting started!

chap_08

Photoshop Elements 2
H•O•T CD-ROM

I. ——————Adding Text

In this exercise and the next, you will learn how to add type to an image document, and how to change various type settings such as font size/face, font color, font alignment, and so forth.

1. Make sure you have the image open that you were working on in the previous chapter, **first_shape**. If you accidentally closed it, you can open it back up—assuming you followed the steps in the previous chapter and saved the document—by opening the file browser (**Window > File Browser**), navigating to the **chap_07** folder, and double-clicking on the image **first_shape**.

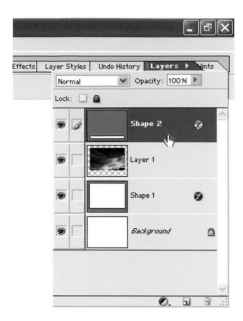

2. Open the **Layers** palette by choosing **Window > Layers**. Make sure that you have the top-most layer, **Shape 2**, selected by single-clicking on it.

3. Single-click on the **Type** tool in the Toolbox to select it.

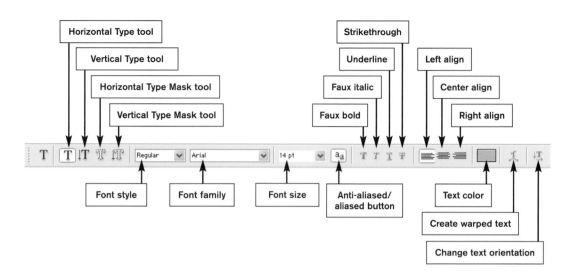

As with the other tools you have learned thus far in this book, the Type tool offers a variety of options in the options bar. Here is a chart describing what each items does.

Type Tool Options	
Option	**Description**
Horizontal Type tool	The default option. Allows you to create text along a horizontal (left-to-right) line.
Vertical Type tool	Selecting this option allows you to type text vertically (top to bottom).
Horizontal Type Mask tool	Same as the Horizontal Type tool, except the type becomes a mask (simply, a selection).
Vertical Type Mask tool	Same as the Horizontal Type Mask tool, except the type is vertical (top to bottom) instead of horizontal (left to right).
Font style	Based on whichever font is selected in the font family pull-down menu, the font style pull-down menu allows you to choose a style for the selected font (bold, italic, and so forth).
	Note: Some font families don't have any styles associated with them. If this happens to you, see (in this chart) faux bold and faux italic.
	continues on next page

Type Tool Options *continued*	
Option	**Description**
Font family	From this pull-down menu, select the font family (font face) that you want to type with.
Font size	Choose what size you want the type to be. The size is rated in points (pt). For your reference, a 72-pt font is approximately one-inch high when added to an image that is 72 ppi. Increasing the resolution of an image will make the type look smaller because in a higher-resolution image, the pixels are closer together.
Anti-aliased button	Turns anti-aliasing on or off for your type. An anti-aliased typeface will have a smoothed edge, whereas an aliased typeface will have a jagged ("stair-stepped") edge.
Faux bold	If the chosen font family does not include a bold style, you can elect to have Elements make the font look bolded for you. Most, if not all, typographers and designers cringe at faux bold—and faux italic for that matter—because they distort the typeface in a manner that the original font designer didn't construct. Although I would recommend not using faux bold or faux italic—because many printers don't like/support font families that are using faux bold/italic—it will do in a pinch.
Faux italic	Same as faux bold, except italicized instead of bolded.
Underline	Underlines the text, <u>like this</u>.
Strikethrough	Puts a line through the text, ~~like this~~.
Left align	Aligns a block of text so that each line of type is aligned together on the left.
Center align	Aligns a block of text so that each line of type is aligned, centered, to the place where you originally clicked with the Type tool.
Right align	Aligns a block of text so that each line of type is aligned together on the right.

continues on next page

Type Tool Options *continued*	
Option	**Description**
Text color	Single-clicking on this color swatch will open the Color Picker window. From here, you can choose what color your type will be. **Note:** The foreground color swatch in the Toolbox and the text color swatch are interconnected. Changing one will change the other. So another way to change your text color would be to just change the foreground color swatch color in the Toolbox.
Create warped text	After typing some text in your image document (or by clicking with the Type tool in the image document window), you can click on the Create warped text button. This will open the Warp Text dialog box, where you can choose (from a preset list) different styles to warp your text (such as Arch, Bulge, Fisheye, and so forth).
Change text orientation	Clicking on this button will change the orientation (horizontal to vertical, or vertical to horizontal) of your selected text.

4. From the **font family** pull-down menu, choose a font. In this example, I've chosen the standard font: **Arial**. Also, if the font you selected has the proper font style, choose **Bold**.

Note: The fonts that you see in the font family pull-down menu are fonts that you currently have installed on your computer.

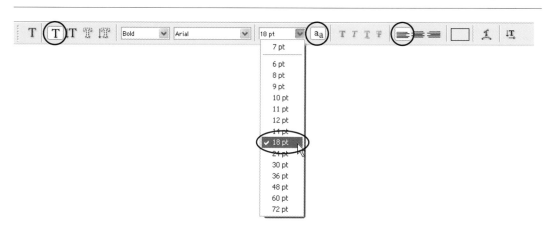

5. From the **font size** pull-down menu, choose **18 pt**. Make sure that the **Horizontal Type** tool is selected, **anti-aliased** is selected, and that the alignment is set to **left aligned**.

6. Now, you need to set the foreground and background colors to their defaults (**black** for foreground and **white** for background). You can do this by clicking the small **black/white color swatches** icon located at the bottom-left of the main foreground/background color swatches in the Toolbox. Because the text color pulls its color choice from the foreground color, this makes the text color black.

7. Then, simply single-click toward the left side of the gray bar that's underneath the picture. This creates an insertion point—the place where you will start typing your text.

You should see a blinking vertical line where you clicked. This is Element's way of telling you that it is ready for you to start entering text.

8. Type **Arizona Sunset**. As you type, you'll see the text appearing from left to right. This is much the same as working with type in a text editor, such as Microsoft Word.

9. When you're finished typing, click on the **Commit Edits** button in the options bar. This will make the blinking vertical line disappear, and now, if you'd like, you can select the **Move** tool from the Toolbox and drag the text around the document to reposition it wherever you'd like. Pretty straightforward, eh?

*Note: You can also commit the text changes by pressing **Enter** (on the keypad) for both Windows and Mac. Commit edits will also be performed automatically as soon as you select another tool, such as the Move tool.*

Note: As I mentioned in previous chapters, when you have the Move tool selected, the content in the currently selected layer will have a "bounding box" around the outside of it. This is how Elements shows you that you have content selected in the image. For more information about the bounding box, and what its uses are, refer to Chapter 3, "Opening and Importing Images" in the Place *exercise.*

*Tip: While you are typing your text, you can always quickly and easily reposition the text block without having to commit the changes first. While you're editing text, hold down the **Ctrl** key (Windows) or **Cmd** key (Mac). This will change your mouse cursor to the Move tool icon. Once you see the Move cursor, drag the text around the stage. When you have moved the text block to the correct location, simply release the **Ctrl** (Windows) or **Cmd** key (Mac) and you're back in text-editing mode. Yippee!*

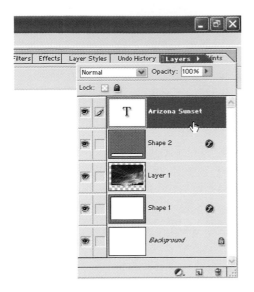

10. Open the **Layers** palette by choosing **Window > Layers**. Notice that there's now a new layer titled **Arizona Sunset**.

Where in the world did that come from? When you add text to a document, Elements will auto-matically create a new layer for you to hold that text. Very cool! Not only that but it will also automatically name that layer based on whatever text you are typing in. If you type in a paragraph of text, however, Elements will only display the first 30 characters of that text in the layer name. Ahhh...I remember back in the good ol' days when I had to create text layers and rename them all...manually! And I had to hike a mile...no, two miles...in the snow...just to get to my bus stop... ;-)

11. When you're done, save your changes and close the image.

2. ——————**More Text**

In this exercise, you're going to learn more about editing and creating text in Elements. Because this exercise is for experimenting with the different text options, you're going to start by creating a blank document to give you a place to play.

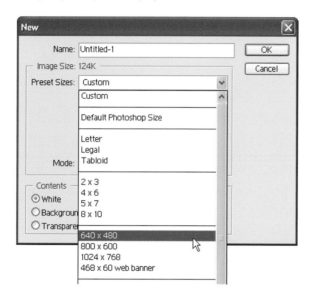

1. Create a new document by pressing the keyboard shortcut **Ctrl+N** (Windows) or **Cmd+N** (Mac). In the **New** dialog box, choose **640 x 480** from the **Preset Sizes** pull-down menu. Make sure the **Mode** is **RGB Color** and select the **White** radio button. Click **OK**. This will create a new, blank, 640 x 480 document at 72 ppi.

2. Single-click on the **Type** tool in the Toolbox.

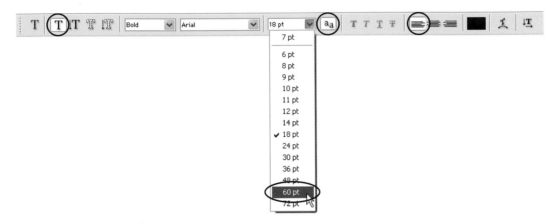

3. Before you start typing, you need to specify the font settings in the options bar. From the **font family** pull-down menu, choose a font. In this example, I've chosen the standard font **Arial**. Also, if the font you've selected has the proper font style, choose **Bold**. From the **font size** pull-down menu, choose **60 pt**. Make sure that the **Horizontal Type** tool and **anti-aliased** are selected, and that the alignment is set to **left aligned**.

4. Then, simply single-click toward the left-hand side of the image document and start typing! Type **ce n'est pas text**. After you have finished typing, click on the **Commit Edits** button in the options bar.

5. With the Type tool still selected, single-click on the **font family** pull-down menu again and choose a different font face. In this example, I chose **Book Antiqua**. Notice that the text in the image changes immediately!

As you can see, changing the font family of a block of text is quite simple. Just make sure you have the layer with the text on it selected in the Layers palette, make sure any of the Type tools are selected (Horizontal, Vertical, and so on), and then change the font from the font family pull-down menu in the options bar. The same technique applies, of course, to changing the font style, font size, text alignment, and color.

*Note: When you clicked with the Type tool, typed out some text, and clicked on the Commit Edits button, you created what is technically called a **type block** (because it's one "block" of text). Well, all of the text in a type block doesn't have to be all the same font family, size, or color. Different letters can be different font families, sizes, and colors.*

ce n′es

6. Make sure the **Type** tool is selected; then drag your mouse to select just the letter **c** in the first word.

Note: In Elements—and in other graphics programs—it's very easy to accidentally create a new text block when you actually meant to select some text in an existing text block. So be careful to click right on *the existing text. If you click too far away from a text block, Elements will think you are trying to create a new text block, and it will automatically create a new insertion point and text layer. I've seen beginner students wind up with multiple text layers with no text in them because they weren't clicking right on the text they were trying to edit and were inadvertently creating new text layers instead. Also, when editing the text in a layer, you don't have to have the layer selected first to be able to edit it. As long as you click with your Type tool right on the text block, Elements will automatically select the text layer for you. Nifty!*

Ce n′est

7. In the options bar, change the **font family**, **font style**, **font size**, and **text color** to something different. In this example, I chose **Arial**, **Bold**, **100 pt** (I typed **100** into the **font size** field), and **blue**. Because the letter **C** was the only letter in the type block that I had selected when I made those changes, it is the only letter that was modified.

As you can see, you have quite a bit of flexibility when working with type in Elements. But that's not all…

8. Single-click on the **Move** tool in the Toolbox. If you're currently editing text, this will commit the changes you've made.

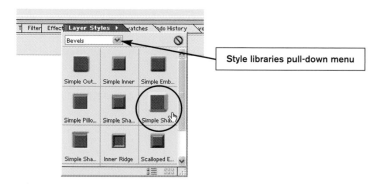

Style libraries pull-down menu

9. Open the **Layer Styles** palette by choosing **Window > Layer Styles**. From the **style libraries** pull-down menu, choose **Bevels**. Then, single-click on the **Simple Sharp Outer** style.

Wow! With just one click from the Layer Styles palette, the text now looks like it is embossed on the page. Also note that the text is still editable. If you select the Type tool and click anywhere on the text, you'll notice that you can still edit and modify the text. If you add, remove, or change the text in the layer that you just added the layer style to, the layer style will automatically change as well to fit the edits you make to the text! That definitely rates a 10 on the coolness factor! :-)

10. Leave this image open—you will be using it again in the next exercise.

Next you're going to ratchet this whole text funny business up a notch. In the next exercise, you're going to distort the text—that still has a layer style applied to it—using the built-in warp text feature. So fasten your seat belts ladies and gentlemen, 'cause this ride is about to get a whoooole lot crazier! Actually… it's really straightforward and simple, but I'm trying to get you pumped up here…play along, would ya?

Warping Text

In this exercise, you will learn how to distort the appearance of text using Element's built-in warped text feature.

1. Before you get started, make sure that you have the correct layer and tool selected. Open the Layers palette by choosing **Window > Layers**. Make sure that the "ce n'est pas text" layer is selected by single-clicking on it. Then single-click on the Type tool in the Toolbox to make sure that it is selected as well. When applying the warp text feature in this manner, you need to make sure that the layer that contains the text is selected and that the Type tool is selected.

2. Single-click on the **Create warped text** button in the options bar. This will open the **Warp Text** dialog box.

Note: You can also warp text by selecting the layer containing the text you want to warp in the Layers palette and choosing **Layer > Type > Warp Text.**

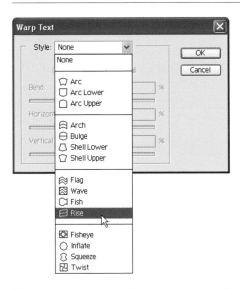

3. In the **Warp Text** dialog box, from the **Style** pull-down menu, choose **Rise**.

As you can see from this pull-down menu, there are quite a few other warp text styles to choose from. I would recommend giving them a try (later) so you can get a good idea of what each one looks like.

*As soon as you choose **Rise** from the style pull-down menu, the text in the image document will immediately show you what that style looks like. Neat!*

Tip: *With the Warp text dialog box still open, move your mouse over the text in the image and drag to easily reposition the text. This allows you to change the position of the text in case the applied style makes it run off the edge of the image document.*

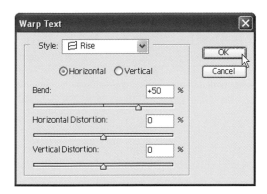

4. Leave the **Rise** style settings in the Warp Text dialog box set to their defaults. If you *were* to change the settings, however, the text in the image immediately updates to incorporate the setting changes. Click **OK**.

5. Single-click on the **Type** tool in the Toolbox, once again, to make sure you have it selected. Then move your mouse onto the image document, and drag to select just the letter **C** at the beginning of the phrase.

6. From the **font family** pull-down menu in the options bar, select the same font family that you chose for the rest of the phrase. In this example, I selected **Book Antiqua**–the same font family as the rest of the text in the phrase.

7. Single-click on the **Commit Edits** button in the options bar to commit the changes that you made to this text.

Ce n'est pas text

So, as you can see from this example, even after *applying a layer style to this text, and even* after *warp-ing the text, it is still editable. I remember quite clearly when I first saw this feature…I was blown away.*

At this point, feel free to play around some more, using this text, with different warp text styles, differ-ent type settings, or even different layer styles. When you're finished experimenting, close the image and don't save the changes—you won't need this image again.

In this chapter, you learned how to add type to a document, how to apply a layer style to the text, and even how to warp it using the warp text feature. Although the text options in Elements are limited—by Adobe Photoshop standards—there is still a lot you can do with type in Elements.

In the next chapter, you will depart from the more "basic" features of Elements you have been learn-ing thus far and will delve more into the photo correcting features that Elements provides. You will learn how to adjust the value and hue of your photographs, using various methods, to fix a poor image or to enhance its good qualities. There's lots of information to cover in the next chapter so make sure you take a bathroom break, grab a cup of tea, and meet me back here in 10 minutes, mmm k? I'm starting the timer……now! ;-)

9.
Correcting Photos

| Adjusting the Value of a Photo |
Bringing Out Details in Shadows	Correcting Overexposed Areas
Automatic Value Adjustments	Dodge and Burn
Color Adjustments	Automatic Color Adjustments
The Sponge Tool	Transforming Your Image

chap_09

Photoshop Elements 2
H·O·T CD-ROM

Just arriving back from a six-week vacation in Italy, Greece, China, Russia, and the Isle of Man, you can't wait to get those photos developed. After dropping them off at the photo developers, you return later to pick them up. Opening up the photo packages as you head back to your car, you stop dead in your tracks—some of the photos look horrible! Some are grayish because the contrast is all off, some have horrible color, and others are either under- or overexposed!! What'll you do? Throw them all away?! How can you when in that stack of horrible photos are hundreds of memories of Rome, Moscow, the Great Wall of China, and who could forget the fine city of Peel on the Isle of Man? *Sigh*

In this chapter, you will learn the skills to fix those photos. You will learn how to adjust the value (darkness/lightness) and color (hue) of photos by using a variety of different techniques—everything from one-click adjustments to using precise, manual methods. So grab the IV coffee drip and lock your office door because there's lots to cover in this chapter.

It Starts with the Source

If at all possible, you should try to make every attempt to take good photos. Sure, in this chapter, I will show you how to correct photos with bad contrast and color. In later chapters, I will even show you how to remove scratches, dust, and stains from photos. Elements can do a lot to a photo after it has been taken. But why spend hours trying to fix a photo when you could spend a couple minutes taking a few precautions to make sure you end up with a good photo? Although many digital cameras do a bang-up job of automatically correcting for different lighting and color situations, it's still a wise idea to make sure you are taking photographs under the best possible situations. Here is a short and simple list of tips for taking good photographs:

• Buy a tripod or monopod. This will stabilize the photos you take and will yield sharper photos. Tripods are essential if you are going to be taking photographs in low-light situations. A good brand to go with is Bogen (**http://www.bogenphoto.com**). Of course, for the budget-conscious, there's always the local WalMart or Target–I'm no tripod snob.

• Make sure you have proper lighting. Too much light and your photos could be overexposed– too much light in the image washes out all the detail; too little light and your image could be underexposed (too dark), of course. If you're shooting photos in low-light situations, a flash will help to illuminate the nearby area and give you instant sufficient light. Beware though, using a flash tends to overexpose anything that is too close to the flash itself.

• If you are using a film-based camera (nondigital), make sure that you have appropriate film speed for what you will be shooting. Film is rated by its sensitivity to light, called its ASA (or ISO) rating. The higher the ASA rating, the more sensitive the film is to light. So if you were taking photos of you and the family at the beach on a sunny day, 100 ASA film would work fine. On the other hand, if you were taking pictures on a cloudy day at dusk, you would need film with a higher ASA rating, like 400 or higher. A good all-purpose film is ASA 200. Be aware though, because higher ASA film can pick up low-light images better, they also have the unfortunate side effect of giving images a grainy or "soft" look.

I. ——————Adjusting the Value of a Photo

In this exercise, you will learn to adjust the value (darkness/lightness) of a photograph by using a few different methods—each with its own strengths.

1. Copy the **chap_09** folder and files from the **H•O•T CD-ROM** to your hard drive.

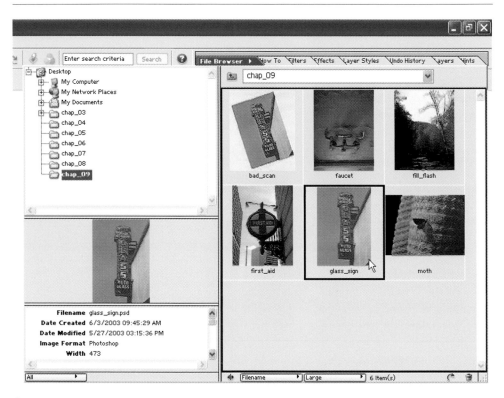

2. Open the File Browser by choosing **Window > File Browser**. Navigate to where you copied the **chap_09** folder and single-click on it. In it, you should see six images. Double-click on the image **glass_sign** to open it.

Note: If you don't see your chap_09 folder in the File Browser window, right-click (Windows) or Ctrl+click (Mac) anywhere on the file listing portion of the File Browser window. A pop-up menu appears with one option that says Refresh. Select that option to refresh the file listing, displaying your chap_09 folder. Elements keeps a cache of the location of your files, and if you've added something—such as copying the chap_09 folder off of the H•O•T CD-ROM—since the last time you used the File Browser, it might not display your new files. Using the Refresh option, however, forces Elements to update its cache.

As you can see, here is a good example of an image that needs its values adjusted. (No…it doesn't need to go to counseling…the other *kind* of value adjusting.) One element that makes up good imagery is strong lights and darks. In this image, the darkest point is a dark gray color, and the lightest point is a light gray color. What this image is lacking is a black-point (some part of the image that is black) and a white-point (some part of the image that is white). You can achieve this by increasing the contrast of the image, which you can do in a few different ways.

---

3. First, you are going to adjust the brightness/contrast of this image. Choose **Enhance > Adjust Brightness/Contrast > Brightness/Contrast**.

This menu command will open a rather unassuming dialog box. By dragging the Brightness slider up and down, you can increase or decrease the total amount of light in the image. This is essentially like adding white or black to your picture. Conversely, by dragging the Contrast slider up and down, you are either increasing or decreasing the intensity of the lights and darks in the image. The higher the contrast, the greater the intensity of the lights and darks in the image. The lower the contrast, the lesser the intensity of lights and darks. You can also adjust the values by entering a number in the fields above the sliders.

---

4. Because this image is a little dark, and its contrast is a little too low—see how the image looks a little faded?—you're going to increase both the brightness and contrast. Drag the **Brightness** slider (or type in this number in the **Brightness** field) up to **+8**. Then drag the **Contrast** slider up to **+52**. As long as you have the **Preview** check box checked, you should see these changes occur as you drag the sliders.

Note: The gamma value (the value of the middle tones of colors) that Mac and Windows computers use to display their graphics onscreen will differ. What this simply means is that Windows computers will display images a little darker than Mac computers will. A brightness adjustment of +8 and a contrast adjustment of +52 might look good on a Windows computer, but an image with those same settings will look a little too light on a Mac computer. The reason I'm mentioning this is because this exercise, and the accompanying screen shots, were done on a Windows XP system. As such, you may need to compensate the brightness and contrast settings if you are using a Mac. On a Mac, set the brightness to be the same (+8), but set the contrast to be +58. Keep this in mind as you work with the exercises throughout the remainder of this book. If you're using a Mac, you may need to slightly adjust any value changes in the exercises to compensate.

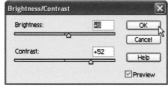

5. Once you have your brightness and contrast values set, click **OK**.

Now, doesn't that image look much better? Because you increased the contrast of the image, the lights and darks of the image are more intense. This gives the image some zest…some panache… a certain…je ne sais quoi…you get the idea. ;-)

*Next, you're going to adjust the values of the image again, but this time using a different method. Why do it again, you ask? Although the method you just learned (**Enhance > Adjust Brightness/Contrast > Brightness/Contrast**) works well, your options are fairly limited. In this next method, as you'll see, you have more options and control over adjusting the values of an image.*

6. Revert back to the unaltered, original image by choosing **File > Revert**. Your image should then revert back to its boring ol' self.

---

7. Choose **Enhance > Adjust Brightness/Contrast > Levels**.

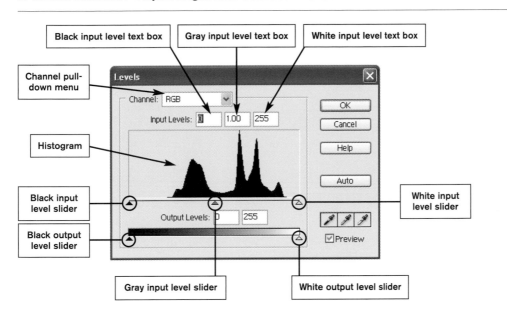

The Levels dialog box will open. Don't worry about all those buttons and sliders—you're only going to focus on a few in this exercise.

---

8. Start by increasing the intensity of the highlights in the image. Drag the **white input level** slider toward the left. Technically, you're supposed to drag the white input level slider to the left until it reaches the point where the black histogram starts to rise. From an aesthetical point of view, however, I sometimes like to drag the white input level slider farther to the left, past that point. Sometimes I may want more a more intense highlight—it all depends on the image. For this image, drag the **white input level** slider until the **white input level** text box reads **210**.

Note: *In case you're wondering what the numbers (0–255) correspond to, here it is. Each channel of color—Red, Green, and Blue in this case—can have 256 (0 also counts as a value) different shades of value intensity (brightness/darkness). By dragging the black, gray, and white input sliders back and forth, you're essentially specifying how intense you want the image's shadows, midtones, and highlights to be.*

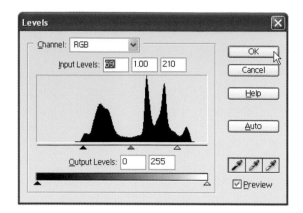

9. Drag the **black input level** slider until the **black input level** text box reads **69**.

Note: Here are a few other items in the Levels dialog box you might find interesting:

• *The **Channel** pull-down menu. From this pull-down menu, you can choose which channel's levels you want to modify. By default, you modify all three channels simultaneously (RGB). But by clicking on the pull-down menu, you can choose to modify either the Red, Green, or Blue channels—independently from the others. Simply select the channel from the pull-down menu, and drag the black, gray, and white sliders around to suit your needs. Why would you want to do this? Maybe you have a picture you took of a bunch of roses, and you want to modify the levels of just the red in the flowers. Simply select the Red channel and adjust the levels accordingly.*

• *The **black output level** and **white output level** sliders. By adjusting these sliders, you can effectively lighten the shadow range or darken the highlight range. By dragging the white output level slider to the left, you are essentially instructing Elements to lower the value of the highlight range in the image, which means the image will get darker overall. Alternatively, by dragging the black output level slider to the right, you are telling Elements to lighten the value of the shadow range of the image, which means the image will get lighter overall.*

10. Click **OK**.

As you can see, the resulting corrected image is similar to what **Enhance > Adjust Brightness/ Contrast > Brightness/Contrast** yielded starting on Step 3. But when you use **Enhance > Adjust Brightness/Contrast > Levels**, you have much more control over the shadow, midpoint, and highlight tonal range (the lights and darks) of an image. You even have the option of adjusting the tonal range of each channel (Red, Green, or Blue) independently of one another! The more you work with adjusting the values of your images, the more I think you'll learn to appreciate the power that Levels gives you.

11. Close this image and don't save the changes. You'll be using this image again in an exercise later in this chapter, and you'll need to keep the original image as is—uncorrected.

MOVIE | Bringing Out Details in Shadows

Included on the **H•O•T CD-ROM** in the **movies** folder is a movie titled **shadow_details.mov**. In this movie, I demonstrate, using the file **fill_flash.psd** file in the **chap_09** folder on the **H•O•T CD-ROM**, how to lighten an image and to bring out details that are hidden in the shadows.

Note: Some operating systems, particularly Windows systems, hide the file extensions (.psd, .mov, and so forth) from you. So although I may reference a file titled **fill_flash.psd**, your computer may only display a file titled **fill_flash**. Rest assured that it is the same file.

You will open the **fill_flash.psd** file and use the **Enhance > Adjust Lighting > Fill Flash** command to bring detail into the shadowed area of the image. As you can see, the **fill_flash.psd** image foreground is heavily in shadow.

But by using the **Fill Flash** command, you can easily and quickly bring some detail into the shadowed areas of the image.

MOVIE | Correcting Overexposed Areas

Included on the **H•O•T CD-ROM** in the **movies** folder is a movie titled **overexposed.mov**. In this movie, I demonstrate, using the file **first_aid.psd** file in the **chap_09** folder on the **H•O•T CD-ROM**, how to correct overexposed (too bright) areas of a photograph and how to bring some more detail into those areas.

You will open the **first_aid.psd** file and use the **Enhance > Adjust Lighting > Adjust Backlighting** command to bring detail into and darken the overexposed areas of the image. Backlighting happens when the subject matter that is the focus of the picture—in this case, the First Aid sign—has a strong light source behind it. In this shot, the bright background gets washed out and loses detail.

The **Adjust Backlighting** command is designed to bring detail back into the overexposed places by darkening those areas. **Adjust Backlighting**, unfortunately, also has the tendency to lighten parts of the image you don't necessarily want lightened. To fix this, you will learn to use layers in combination with a layer blending mode to darken only the overexposed areas while leaving the other areas of the photograph relatively untouched.

2. ———————————Automatic Value Adjustments

In a rush? Can't be bothered with correcting the value of your image by noodling with all of the sliders in the Levels dialog box? Then the automatic value adjustment commands may be just what you're looking for. In this exercise, you will learn how to use the **Auto Levels** and **Auto Contrast** commands to have Elements automatically correct the values of an image for you.

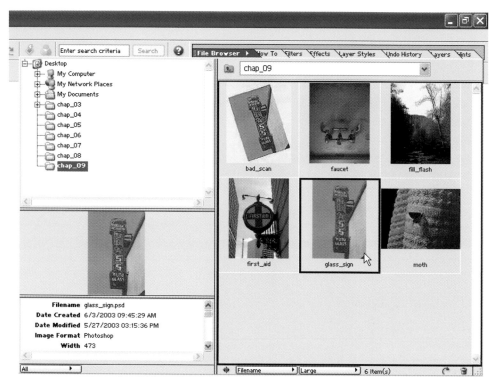

1. Open the **File Browser** by choosing **Window > File Browser**. Navigate to where you copied the **chap_09** folder and single-click on it. In the File Browser window, double-click on the file **glass_sign** to open it.

---

2. First, you're going to have Elements automatically guess what the best contrast settings are for this image. Choose **Enhance > Auto Contrast**.

Presto! Now go take a break because that was hard work! Just kidding, of course. ;-) As you can see, Elements did a decent job automatically adjusting the contrast of the image. It takes the darkest parts of the image and sets them to black, and takes the lightest parts of the image and sets them to white. This obviously increases the contrast of the image. An image with strong contrast almost always is more engaging and interesting to look at than an image with weak contrast. Next, you're going to revert the image back to its original, uncorrected state, and check out the Auto Levels feature.

3. Revert back to the unaltered, original image by choosing **File > Revert**. Your image should then return to the way it was when you first opened it.

4. Choose **Enhance > Auto Levels**.

Great! As you can see, Auto Levels did a bang-up job correcting that ugly, grayish photo for you. Similar to Auto Contrast, Auto Levels sets the darkest parts of the image to black, and the lightest parts to white. At this point, some of you may be asking, "Geez…what's the difference? They both look the same to me!" The main difference between Auto Levels and Auto Contrast is that Auto Contrast adjusts the values in an image to all the channels (Red, Green, and Blue) simultaneously. Auto Levels, on the other hand, also adjusts the values of an image on each channel, but it does so one channel at a time. Because Auto Levels adjusts the channel values one at a time, it has the added side effect of possibly adding or removing color tints (where the image appears to have a subtle tint to it). You can see this if you compare the results of the Auto Contrast and Auto Levels images. The Auto Contrast image will have a slight greenish tinge to it that the Auto Levels image is lacking. This is because the Auto Levels feature automatically removed that green color tint by applying value adjustments to each channel of the image, one at a time. Although this may sound like a good thing, Auto Levels might also inadvertently add a color tint to the image. If Auto Levels gives your image a slightly tinted color, undo Auto Levels and try applying Auto Contrast instead.

5. When you are finished with this image, close it and don't save any changes.

3. ―――――――――Dodge and Burn Tools

With the adjustment techniques I've shown you thus far, the entire image is adjusted. But what if you wanted to lighten or darken only a specific part of your image—not the whole caboodle? One way is to use selections—as demonstrated in Chapter 5, "*Selecting*"—to select only part of an image, and then use the techniques you've learned so far to adjust just that area. Another method is to use two specific tools—the **Dodge** and **Burn** tools—to selectively lighten and darken (respectively) portions of an image. Because you have already learned how to use and make selections, in this exercise, you will learn how to adjust the value of specific parts of an image by using those two tools.

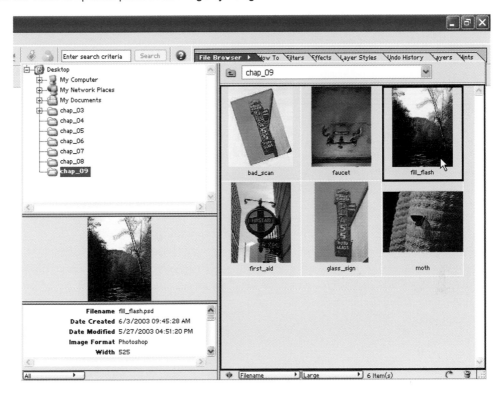

1. Open the **File Browser** by choosing **Window > File Browser**. Navigate to where you copied the **chap_09** folder and single-click on it. In the File Browser window, double-click on the **fill_flash** file to open it.

As you can see, the trees and rocks in the foreground/middleground are so dark that much of the detail has been lost. In the movie **shadow_details.mov** on the **H•O•T CD-ROM**, I demonstrate how to lighten this image by using the Fill Flash feature. The only problem with Fill Flash is that it lightens the entire image, not just the dark areas. Yes, you could use selections in combination with Fill Flash to lighten only certain areas of the image. In this case, however, why go through the hassle of making a decent selection and then utilizing Fill Flash when you can do it faster and easier with the Dodge and Burn tools?

2. Select the **Dodge** tool by single-clicking on it in the Toolbox.

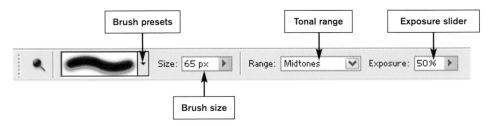

As with most tools, there are a few options you will need to look over before you actually dig in and start using the tool. The following table describes those options and their meanings:

Dodge Tool Options	
Option	**Description**
Brush presets	From this pull-down menu, you can choose from a preset list of brush sizes and styles—everything from hard-edged brushes to soft-edged brushes, and a circular-shaped brush to a grass-shaped brush (and more). It's all inside this pull-down menu.
Brush size slider	Dragging this slider (or typing a value in the Size field) allows you to specify the size of the brush you will be using to lighten the image.
Tonal range	Choose which tonal range you want to lighten. Do you want to lighten the Midtones, Shadows, or Highlights in the image?
Exposure slider	Essentially, this is how much you want to lighten the image per stroke of the brush. Is it lightening the image too much for your liking when you drag the brush across the image? Lower the exposure percentage. Not lightening the image enough? Raise the exposure percentage. Nuf said. ;-)

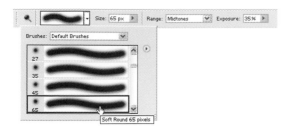

3. From the **brush presets** pull-down menu, choose the **Soft Round 65 pixels** brush. (Remember, if you hover your mouse over one of the brush preset images, it will show you the name of that brush preset.) When you select that brush preset, the **Size** should automatically set itself to **65 px**. Also, set the **Range** to **Midtones** and the **Exposure** to **35%**. You may think that the tonal range should be set to Shadow (after all, you want to lighten the shadows), but in this case, you don't want to lighten just the shadows, but the midtones of the image as well.

4. Then, just like you're painting with a paintbrush, drag the **Dodge** tool brush around the tree in the left middleground of the image to lighten it up.

Note: If you paint over the same area more than once, it will lighten even further. This is because the Exposure is set to 35%, so every time you paint with the Dodge tool over a previously painted area, it lightens an additional 35 percent. To make sure I'm lightening the image consistently, I usually make one pass with the Dodge tool over everything I want to lighten without letting go of the mouse button. I also try to make sure that I don't go over the same area more than once. Then I know that all of these areas should be lightened by 35 percent.

5. Press the **[** (left bracket) key on your keyboard about three times to reduce the size of the brush to **40 px**. Now drag over the smaller areas you want to lighten, such as the rocks in the stream foreground, the tree that's hanging over the stream, and so forth. Be careful that you don't go Dodge-tool crazy and lighten everything though! Remember, strong lights and darks makes for an interesting image. If you remove all of the strong darks with the Dodge tool, the image will become boring and dull to look at.

*Note: If you want to go one step further, feel free to set the **Range** to **Highlights** and drag over some of the highlights in the stream. This will bring some more light into the lower half of the image, increasing the overall contrast, and also helping to visually balance out the light area in the top half of the image.*

At the moment, the sky is somewhat of a white blob at the top of the image and could use a little darkening in places. You're going to use the Burn tool to give it a little dimension.

6. Single-click on the **Burn** tool in the Toolbox.

Just like the Dodge tool, the Burn tool also has options you can set in the options bar. I won't outline what each option does—the options are identical to those of the Dodge tool, except the Burn tool options apply to burning (darkening) the image, not dodging (lightening) it.

7. From the **brush presets** pull-down menu, choose **Soft Round 65 pixels**. Set the **Range** pull-down menu to **Midtones** and set **Exposure** to **75%**.

8. Drag around the sky to darken parts of it.

The Burn tool can't really do much with some parts of the sky where it is really bright (such as between the dead tree in the middle of the image and the green tress on the left). But at the top left of the image and around the branches of the dead tree, you'll notice that the Burn tool will darken the sky a little and will bring some detail back into those overexposed areas.

9. Close the image and don't save the changes.

From this exercise, I hope you learned how the manual tools, in some ways, can give you more control and yield better results than their menu counterparts, such as the Fill Flash command. In this case, the resulting adjusted image looks more balanced, and no details get lost in shadows.

Color Adjustments

Now that you have learned how to adjust the value of an image, it's time to look at adjusting the color of an image. In this exercise, you will learn a variety (variety? heck…a smorgasbord!) of different techniques to adjust the color of an image. You can do everything—change the saturation (how "bright" or "dull" a color is), remove colors, and even replace colors. When you get pictures developed from a film-based camera (that is, non digital), many different factors can determine how the colors in the photographs look. How old the film is, how clean (or dirty) the developing chemicals are at the photo lab, how well trained the staff is, and even the quality of the paper that the photos are printed on will all play a part in the quality of the photos. The techniques you will learn in this exercise—combined with what you learned earlier in this chapter—will enable you to bring home those sometimes poorly printed photographs and correct them so they look like they were printed by a professional. Of course, I can't help you if you took a picture with your thumb in the frame, or if you accidentally cropped off everyone's head.

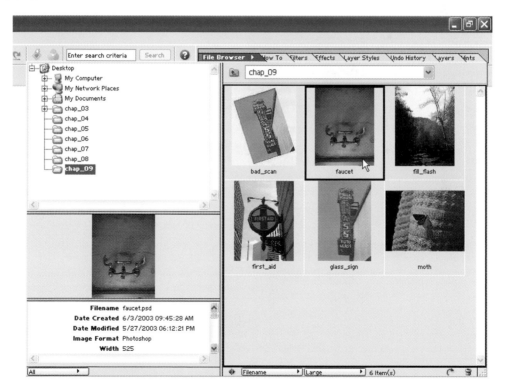

1. Open the **File Browser** by choosing **Window > File Browser**. Navigate to where you copied the **chap_09** folder and single-click on it. In the File Browser window, double-click on the file **faucet** to open it.

*Because you weren't "on location" when this photograph was taken, you can't tell that the actual scene didn't have a blue tint to it like this photograph does. The wall is actually supposed to be a semi-desaturated (dull) green color. My digital camera performed an automatic white balance when I shot this photo, which gave this image a blue tint. Using the **Color Cast** feature of Elements, however, you're going to remove that blue color tint.*

---

2. Choose **Enhance > Adjust Color > Color Cast**.

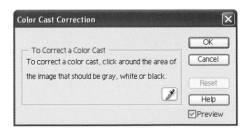

*The **Color Cast Correction** dialog box appears, and it kindly informs you that to correct a color cast (the blue tint in the **faucet** image), click around the area of the image that should be gray, white, or black. Pretty simple concept, eh? Don't click **OK** just yet.*

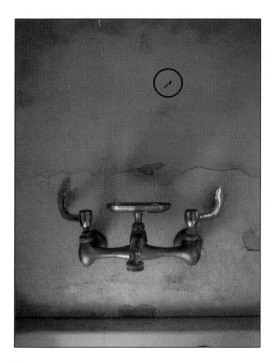

3. Leave the Color Cast Correction dialog box open and simply move your mouse over onto the image until your cursor turns into an **eyedropper**. Then, click on an area of the image. In this case, I clicked on a middle tone (gray value) area of the image.

*As if by magic (poof!), the blue color cast is gone! Now the image color looks great, and the wall is the color it should be—a desaturated green. One of the nice features of the **Color Cast** command is if you don't like the results you get the first time, you can continue to click with the eyedropper in different parts of the image until the color cast has been corrected to your liking. Nice!*

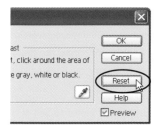

Note: *After clicking around with the eyedropper for awhile, if you feel you need to revert back to the original, uncorrected image so you can start over again, simply click on the **Reset** button in the Color Cast Correction dialog box. Your image will then reset to the way it was before you started making color cast changes.*

4. When you have the image looking the way you want it, click **OK** to accept the changes.

Next, you're going to learn how to adjust the overall hue and saturation (color and color intensity) of this image. This technique is very useful when you want to add a little extra color to dull images, or when you want to tint an image a certain color.

5. Choose **Enhance > Adjust Color > Hue/Saturation**.

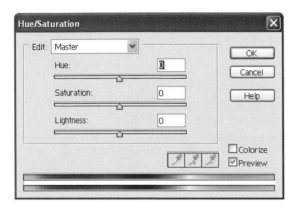

*The **Hue/Saturation** dialog box will open. From here, you can adjust the **Hue** (color), **Saturation** (color intensity), and **Lightness** (similar to Brightness, which you saw earlier in this chapter when you learned the Brightness/Contrast feature) of an image. By dragging these sliders around, you can modify the entire image, or by choosing a color from the **Edit** pull-down menu, you can make adjustments to one specific color while leaving the other colors untouched. You can also check the **Colorize** check box to add a color tint to the image. By dragging the **Hue**, **Saturation**, and **Lightness** sliders back and forth, you can adjust the settings of that color tint.*

6. Experiment with the sliders by dragging them around and noticing the changes it makes to your image. You can always reset the image back to the way it was by dragging the sliders to the middle (0) point. Notice that the colors in the image change as you drag the **Hue** slider to the left and right. Now try dragging the **Saturation** slider. Notice that when you drag it to the left, the colors in the image start to fade until it is completely black and white. Dragging it to the right, on the other hand, increases the intensity of the colors. Lastly, try dragging the **Lightness** slider, which simply increases how light or dark the image is.

Next, you're going to use the Hue/Saturation feature to tint the image. This is a great effect to utilize when you want an image to look like a duotone because you are simply limiting the image's color palette to one hue.

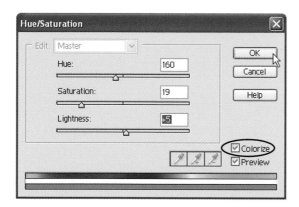

7. Click on the **Colorize** check box. This instructs Elements to display the image using only one color—well, two colors if you count black, hence the name "duotone." Drag the **Hue** slider to determine the color you want to use to display the image. As I just discussed, you can also adjust the saturation and lightness of that color by dragging the **Saturation** and **Lightness** sliders. Remember, you can also type numbers into the **Hue**, **Saturation**, and **Lightness** fields if you happen to know the exact numbers you want to use. Set **Hue** to **160**, **Saturation** to **19**, and **Lightness** to **+5**. Click **OK**.

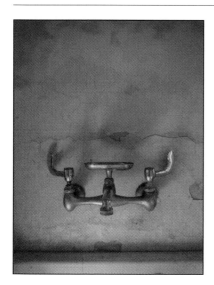

As you can see, this will tint the picture with a green hue. Cool!

But after presenting this image to the (hypothetical) client, he comes back with "Yeah. That's…nice. But try making the image black and white…let's see what that looks like." So back to the drawing board you go…muttering about clients who can't make up their minds. ;-) Luckily for you, converting an image to black and white is a snap.

8. Choose **Enhance > Adjust Color > Remove Color**.

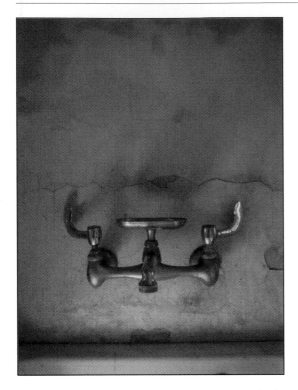

Voilà! Instant, no-fuss, black-and-white image. It doesn't get any easier than that.

Tip: Converting an image into black and white is a great way to look at just the values (the darks and lights) of an image without getting distracted by the hues (the colors). If you would rather not go through the process of converting an image to black and white, you can always use your built-in converter—your very own eyeballs! If you squint at an image, so that your eyes are barely open, you can quickly see the lights and darks in an image. I've said it before, and I'll say it again: One of the major keys to making an image look good is contrast. If you have strong lights and darks in an image—especially if they're right next to each other—the image will appear more interesting and dynamic. The preceding image looks a little washed out because it doesn't have strong lights and darks. Luckily, you've already learned how to adjust the values of an image by using Levels, so you know how to "fix" this image. :-)

9. Close this image and don't save the changes. You won't be needing this image again in this exercise.

5. ──────────More Color Adjustments

In this exercise, you are going to replace the sky color with a different color by using the **Replace Color** feature in Elements.

1. Open the **File Browser** by choosing **Window > File Browser**. Navigate to where you copied the **chap_09** folder and single-click on it. In the File Browser window, double-click on the file **glass_sign** to open it.

2. Choose **Enhance > Adjust Color > Replace Color**.

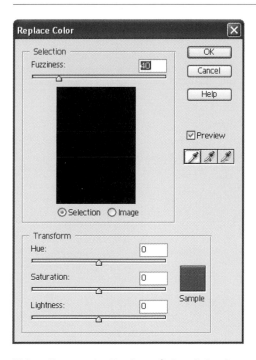

*This will open the **Replace Color** dialog box, which is broken up into two main sections. **Selection**, at the top, displays the color you have picked to replace, and **Transform**, at the bottom, is essentially the same as the Hue/Saturation dialog box.*

3. With the **Replace Color** dialog box still open, move your mouse over onto the **glass_sign** image. When your cursor passes over the image, it should turn into an **eyedropper** icon. Move your mouse onto the color you want to replace—in this example, the blue sky—and single-click.

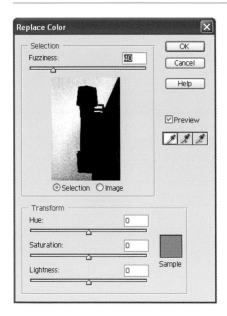

*Now look at the Replace Color dialog box. You should see a small, black-and-white silhouette of the glass sign, which represents your image. Everything that is colored black won't be replaced, and everything that is colored white will be replaced. You can change the range of colors that Elements considers similar to the one you clicked on by dragging the **Fuzziness** slider to the left or right. Dragging it to the right tells Elements to consider more colors similar to the one you first clicked on. Dragging it to the left tells Elements to consider fewer colors similar. Your goal with the **Fuzziness** setting is finding the right balance between selecting the colors you want to replace versus those you want to leave alone.*

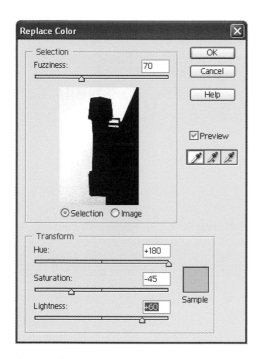

4. Drag the **Fuzziness** slider to **70**, or just type **70** in the **Fuzziness** field. As you can see in the black-and-white thumbnail image, this highlights the majority of the sky in white and leaves the rest of the image as black. Remember, when you select a new color, it will replace the parts of the image that are highlighted white, while leaving the highlighted black parts untouched. In the **Transform** section, choose a color to replace the blue sky with by setting the **Hue** to **+180**, the **Saturation** to **−45**, and the **Lightness** to **+60**. Click **OK**.

Neat! Now every place in the image that had a blue sky color has been replaced with the new color. All too easy…

*Next, you're going to learn about a really easy and intuitive way to change the hue, saturation, and lightness of an image. Yes, you already learned how to do that using the Hue/Saturation dialog box, but this method does it a little differently, as you'll see. Using **Color Variations**, you are going to make the **glass_sign** image look somewhat like an old photograph by modifying the colors.*

5. Choose **Enhance > Adjust Color > Color Variations**.

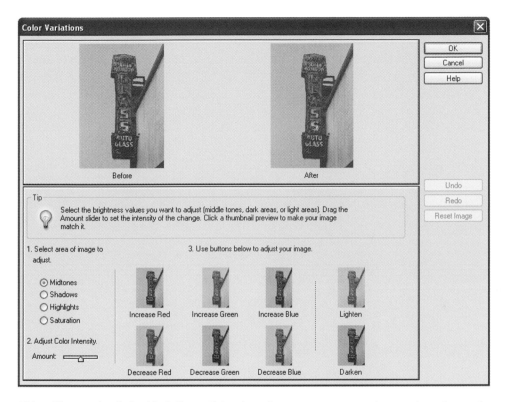

This will open the **Color Variations** dialog box. As you can see, you have quite a few options. Luckily, Adobe has made it very intuitive to use. At the top of the window are two thumbnails of the **glass_sign** image. The one on the left is the Before image, and the one on the right is the After image. As you adjust the color of the image, you'll see the After image update to reflect the changes you're making. On the bottom half of the Color Variations window, you have some numbered options:

• **Step 1: Select area of image to adjust.** From here, you can choose whether to adjust the **Midtones**, **Shadows**, **Highlights**, or the **Saturation** of this image.

• **Step 2: Adjust Color Intensity.** By dragging the **Amount** slider to the left or right, you can decrease or increase (respectively) the amount that the color variations will be applied to the image. A low amount means that a color variation of **Lighten**, for example, will only lighten the image a little, whereas a high amount will lighten the image a lot.

• **Step 3: Use buttons below to adjust your image.** From here, all you need to do is click on the image that represents what you want to do to the image. If you want to darken it, click on the **Darken** graphic. Pretty straightforward, eh? You can also easily undo or redo the last color variation you applied, or even reset the image back to the way it was before you opened the Color Variations window by clicking on the self-explanatory buttons at the right side of the window.

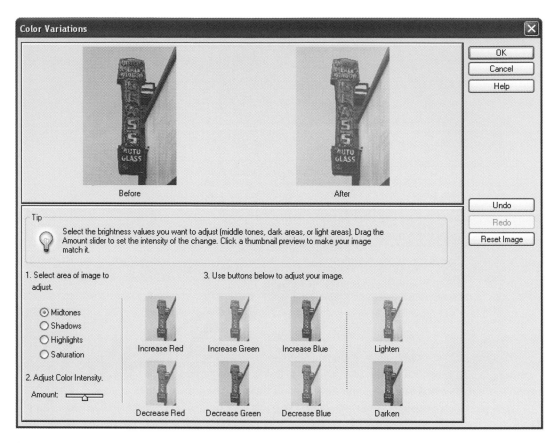

6. Select the **Midtones** radio button and make sure the **Amount** slider is in the middle. Then, make the image look a little faded and yellowish. To do that, click on the **Decrease Blue** graphic three times and the **Decrease Red** graphic once.

This has the effect of making the image look like an old, yellowed photograph. The image is a little too saturated, though. In the next step, you will use Color Variations to lower the saturation of the image a little.

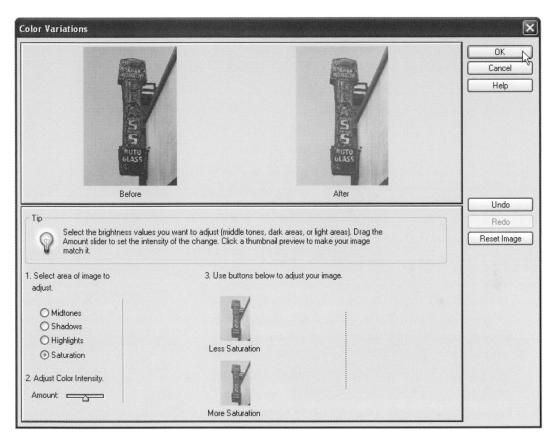

7. Click on the **Saturation** radio button. Then, Step 3 will change to display only two options: **Less Saturation** or **More Saturation**. Because you want to decrease the image saturation, click on the **Less Saturation** graphic once. You're all done! Click **OK**.

Now, thanks to Color Variations, the **glass_sign** image looks like a 30-year-old photograph pulled out of an old box in the attic.

Color Variations is also a great way to subtly modify the hue, saturation, and lightness of an image. It's similar to the Hue/Saturation window, but it is unique because it allows you to make these modifications piecemeal. This allows you to easily make small, incremental changes to your images in a step-by-step fashion.

---

8. Leave this image open–you will be using it in the next exercise.

In this exercise, you learned a variety of different ways to modify, remove, and replace colors in an image–each with its own strengths. In the remainder of the chapter, you will learn a few more methods to modify the colors in your images, as well as how to fix poorly scanned photographs.

---

6. 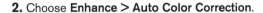 Automatic Color Adjustments

Now that you've seen some more "manual" ways of adjusting the color of an image in Elements, you're going to sit back and let Elements do the work for you.

1. Choose **File > Revert** to revert back to the previously saved version of **glass_sign**. If you accidentally closed the **glass_sign** image between this exercise and the last, you can reopen it again by opening the **File Browser** (**Window > File Browser**), navigating to the **chap_09** folder, and double-clicking on the file **glass_sign**.

2. Choose **Enhance > Auto Color Correction**.

*As always, my sadistic nature shines through. I wait until after I've shown you all the "hard" ways before I show you the one-click, "easy" way. MUAHAHAHAHA!!! (cue evil cackle) ;-) The **Auto Color Correction** command, as its name implies, automatically adjusts the contrast and color of an image. It often is a little too aggressive for my taste, but it certainly wins a blue ribbon in doing a bang-up job in an extremely short amount of time with minimal effort. Modifying the color of images using the manual methods, as you have seen thus far in this chapter, have their obvious advantages, however. By using Levels in combination with the Hue/Saturation window, I have full and complete control over all of the values and hues in my image. Although Auto Color Correction does a great job, there's something to be said for manually tweaking your images to get the exact look you want.*

3. Close this image and don't save the changes.

7. ——————————**The Sponge Tool**

In Exercise 4 of this chapter, you learned how to change the saturation of an image using the Hue/ Saturation window. Unless you selected only a portion of the image first, changing the saturation affected the whole image. The **Sponge** tool, however, allows you to selectively modify the saturation of an image.

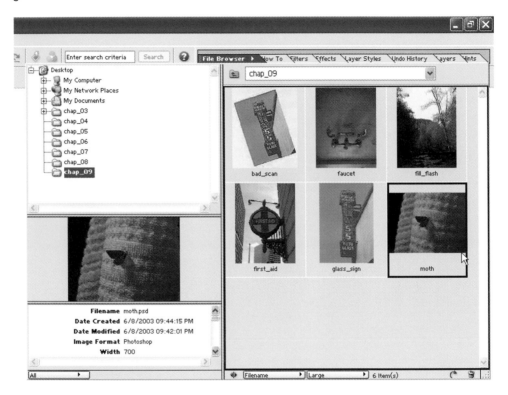

1. Open the **File Browser** by choosing **Window > File Browser**. Navigate to where you copied the **chap_09** folder and single-click on it. In the File Browser window, double-click on the **moth** file to open it.

In this exercise, you are going to bring attention to the moth by decreasing the saturation on everything but *the moth, and then slightly increasing the saturation on the moth itself.*

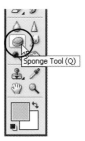

2. Single-click on the **Sponge** tool in the Toolbox. It looks like…well…a sponge.

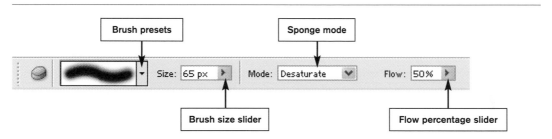

The Sponge tool has a few options you can set before you begin working with it. Here is a breakdown of the different options and what they mean:

Sponge Tool Options	
Option	**Description**
Brush presets	From this pull-down menu, you can choose from a list of preset brush sizes and styles to work with.
Brush size slider	This allows you to choose what size brush you want to use for the Sponge tool.
Sponge mode	Choose whether you want the Sponge tool to saturate or desaturate the image as you are painting with it.
Flow percentage slider	This allows you to set the rate at which the image's saturation changes. A low Flow percentage will change the saturation of the image more slowly than will a high Flow percentage. Set the Flow percentage to a low number for a subtle effect or to a high number for a more dramatic effect.

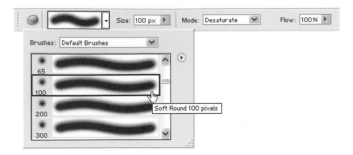

3. From the **brush presets** pull-down menu, choose a fairly large, **Soft Round 100 pixels** brush. Make sure the **Mode** is set to **Desaturate** and the **Flow** is set to **100%**. The first thing you are going to do is to desaturate the area around the moth.

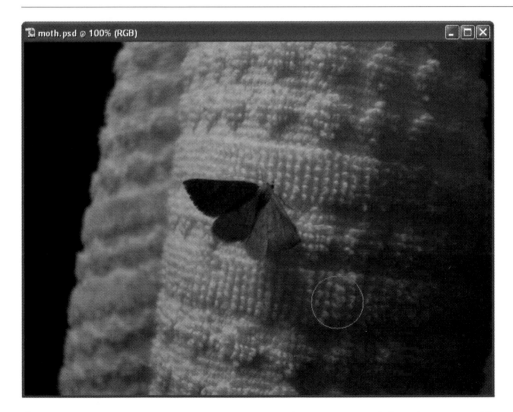

4. Move your brush onto the moth image, and start dragging it around. Drag it over everything *except* the moth. Notice how I didn't desaturate the image right up to the moth. I gave myself a little bit of room. The 100-pixel round brush is just a little too big to get all the detailed areas.

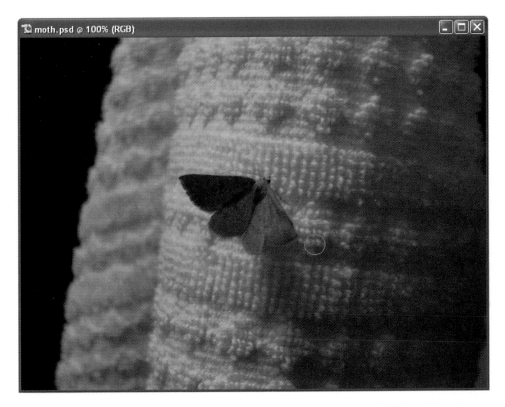

5. Press the [(left bracket) key five times to reduce the size of the brush. Then, drag closer around the outside of the moth to desaturate any of the area that's left over. Remember, don't desaturate the moth itself.

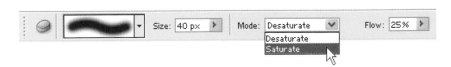

6. Click on the **Mode** pull-down menu and choose **Saturate**. Now the Sponge brush will saturate (increase the color intensity) whatever it paints over instead of desaturating. Also, set **Flow** to **25%** so that the saturation effects are more subtle.

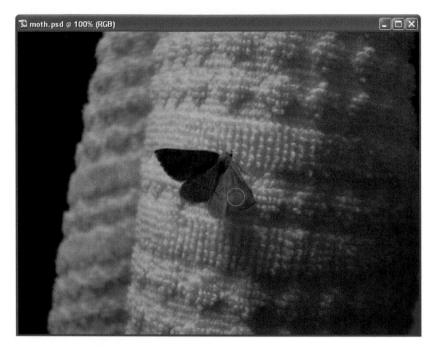

7. Drag around the moth—being careful not to stray outside the moth—to slightly increase the saturation.

before   *after*

By simply changing the saturation, you've given more interest and attention to the moth, which is what you want the focus of the image to be. You did this, quite easily, by using the Sponge tool to saturate and desaturate portions of the image. Great job!

8. Close this image and don't save the changes.

MOVIE | Transforming Your Image

Included on the **H•O•T CD-ROM** in the **movies** folder is a movie titled **transforming.mov**. In this movie, I demonstrate how to correct a poorly scanned image.

The **transforming.mov** movie opens the image **bad_scan.psd** in the **chap_09** folder on the **H•O•T CD-ROM**.

By using a command under the **Image** menu and the **Crop** tool, you will learn to straighten and crop the image.

In this chapter, you covered a huge amount of information. You learned how to take a poor photograph and improve its quality by adjusting its value and hue. As you saw, there were a variety of ways to go about adjusting those two simple things. Each method had its own strengths and weaknesses. Some were simple, and others required a little more work to master. As you work with more images, you'll learn which methods work best for you, and under which circumstances.

In the next chapter, you will delve into the image-editing universe of retouching photos. You will learn how to remove "red eye," wrinkles, and dust and scratches. You will also learn how to sharpen and blur photos to draw the viewer's interest to where you want it. There's a lot of new and exciting information coming your way. Now would probably be a good time to take that bathroom break you've been holding out on... ;-)

10.

Retouching Photos

| Removing "Red Eye" | Removing Wrinkles |
| Removing Dust, Scratches, and Imperfections |
| Sharpening a Photo | Blurring a Photo |
| Colorizing a Black-and-White Photo |

chap_10

Photoshop Elements 2
H·O·T CD-ROM

In the last chapter, you learned how to correct a photo that has bad value or color. In this chapter, it's all about the details. You will learn how to easily remove the annoying "red eye" (that makes your kind uncle Bob look like a homicidal maniac), how to subtly remove wrinkles from a face (better than botox injections—and less painful, too!), how to remove dust, scratches, and imperfections from a photo, how to sharpen/blur areas selectively, and how to colorize a black-and-white photo. So, as you can see, there are lots of new and really fun things to cover in this chapter. Read on, good friend, read on.

I. _____**Removing Red Eye**

In this exercise, you will learn how to easily remove red eye from a photograph. The dreaded red eye is caused when light–from the flash on your camera, for instance–is reflected off of the back of someone's eye(s). Although many digital cameras do a good job at filtering out red eye, some photos with red eye will invariably slip through, especially if you take pictures with a standard film-based camera.

1. Copy the **chap_10** folder and files from the **H•O•T CD-ROM** to your hard drive.

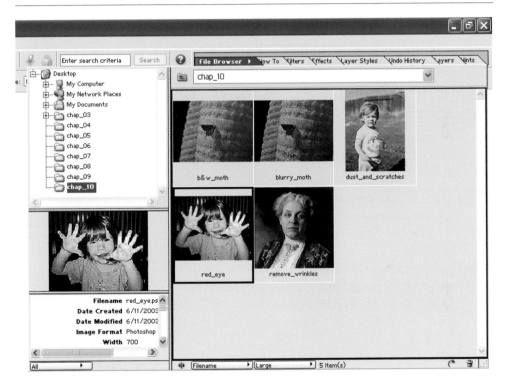

2. Open the **File Browser** by choosing **Window > File Browser**. Navigate to the **chap_10** folder you copied onto your computer in Step 1, and double-click on the **red_eye** picture to open it.

As you can see in the photograph, not only are her hands filthy, but she's got a bad case of the red eye. Luckily, it's easily corrected in Elements using the **Red Eye Brush** tool. The Red Eye Brush tool is essentially the Eyedropper tool and the Clone stamp tool, which you'll learn later in this chapter, mixed together into one tool…but in a very smart way. The Red Eye Brush tool allows you to quickly sample a color you want to replace in an image (the red pupils in the sample image) and replace it with a color of your choosing (in this case, you'll replace the red with black). Not only that, but the Red Eye Brush tool leaves the texture in the image intact while changing only the color. Pretty spiffy, eh?

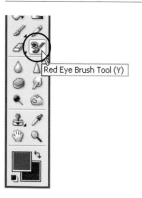

3. Single-click on the **Red Eye Brush** tool in the Toolbox.

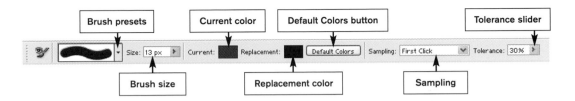

And what would a tool be if there weren't some options to set? The following table outlines the options you're given and what they mean:

Red Eye Brush Tool Options	
Option	**Description**
Brush presets	Allows you to choose different brush sizes, styles, and shapes.
Brush size	Allows you to choose what size brush you want to use. When removing red eye, you optimally want the brush size to be a little larger than the pupil.
Current color	Displays the color that the Red Eye Brush tool is currently hovering over. You can use the feedback you get from the current color swatch to make sure you are targeting (for replacement) the exact color you want.
Replacement color	Here you set which color you want to use to replace the color you're sampling with the Red Eye Brush tool. The default replacement color is black—fitting for the pupil of the eye. However, you can choose whichever color you want for replacement. Click on the Replacement color swatch to get the Color Picker where you can choose any replacement color you'd like.
Default Colors button	Sets the Current and Replacement colors back to their defaults: red for the Current color and black for the Replacement color.
Sampling pull-down menu	Allows you to choose how the target color (the color you're choosing to replace) is chosen. **First Click** means that the first color you click on with the Red Eye Brush tool will be the targeted color that will be replaced. If you select Current Color, on the other hand, you can then click on the Current color swatch, and from the Color Picker, pick a specific target color you want replaced. In most cases, leave it set to First Click so you can easily sample the exact color you want to remove in an image.
Tolerance slider	Sets how similar a color in the image must be (to your Current color) for it to be replaced. The higher the number, the more similar colors will be replaced. The lower the number, the fewer similar colors will be replaced.

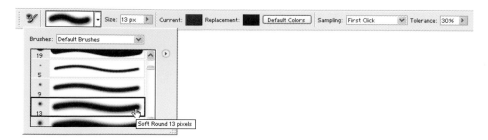

4. With the **Red Eye Brush** tool selected, you need to set a few of those options in the options bar before you start. Single-click on the **brush presets** pull-down menu, and choose the **Soft Round 13 pixels** brush. Click on the **Default Colors** button to set the **Current** and **Replacement** colors to their defaults (the **Current** color will change when you move the **Red Eye Brush** tool over the image), set **Sampling** to **First Click**, and set **Tolerance** to **30%**.

Note: The Tolerance setting is one of the more important settings for the Red Eye Brush tool because it determines how much of the target color (the red in the red eye) will be replaced as you drag the Red Eye Brush tool over the image. I'd recommend starting with the default Tolerance of 30% to see if it removes enough of the red eye in your image. If the Red Eye Brush tool is not removing enough of the red at that Tolerance level, increase it a little and try again. Conversely, if you see some areas in the image that are being affected by the Red Eye Brush—such as the pink color of the eyelid or surrounding areas—try lowering the Tolerance so that the Red Eye Brush tool is removing only the red in the red eye.

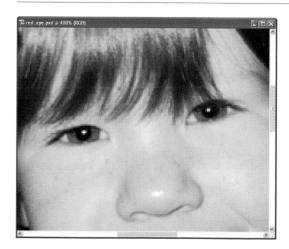

5. Zoom into the image by using the keyboard shortcut **Ctrl++** (the Ctrl key and the plus sign key—on Windows) or **Cmd++** (the Cmd key and the plus sign key—on the Mac) three times. This will zoom you closer into the image at 400 percent. Alternatively, you can also select the **Zoom** tool (the magnifying glass) in the Toolbox and click repeatedly on the image to zoom into it.

6. Make sure you have the **Red Eye Brush** tool selected first. Then, position the tool over the pupil on one of her eyes so that the small plus sign in the middle of the tool icon (a circle) is over the red color. Next, simply drag—press and hold the mouse button while you drag—around the pupil of her eye, making sure to drag over all the areas that are red. The **Red Eye Brush** tool might miss a few spots initially— because of the **Tolerance** setting of **30%**, those left-out colors are out of range. To get rid of any left-over red areas, simply click on them with the crosshairs in the center of the **Red Eye Brush** tool.

7. Repeat this process for the other eye until all of the red eye has been removed.

8. When you're done, zoom out of the image, back to 100 percent. One easy way to do that is to simply double-click on the **Zoom** tool (magnifying glass icon) in the Toolbox.

before   *after*

9. Choose **File > Save As**. Save this image in the **chap_10** folder with a title of **no_red_eye**, and then close it.

So as you can see, removing the dreaded red eye with the Red Eye Brush tool is not only quick and easy, it also does an awesome job as well! As I mentioned earlier in this exercise, one of the nifty things about the Red Eye Brush tool is that it just replaces colors and won't modify the texture in an image. Because of this, anyone would be hard pressed to tell that the "after" image had ever been modified at all. Now...if they could only come out with a Finger Cleaning Brush tool...;-)

MOVIE | Removing Wrinkles

Included on the **H•O•T CD-ROM** in the **movies** folder is a movie titled **wrinkles.mov**. In this movie, I demonstrate how to remove wrinkles from a face in the **remove_wrinkles.psd** file in the **chap_10** folder on the **H•O•T CD-ROM**.

In the **wrinkles.mov** movie, you will first open the file **remove_wrinkles.psd**. This is a picture of someone who has a few wrinkles you can touch up.

Note: Removing wrinkles, using the method that I demonstrate in the movie, is not intended to make an 80-year-old man appear like he's in his 20s. (You'll need much more than Elements for that—instead do a search on Google for "Plastic Surgery.") This technique of covering up wrinkles is better suited for a face that has a few wrinkles around the eyes, mouth, or forehead that can be easily touched up without altering the overall appearance of the face. Wrinkles give a face character, so you need to be careful which ones to remove and how many. You'll learn this, over time, with practice.

You'll then use the Clone Stamp tool coupled with a blending mode to carefully, and subtly, cover up some of the wrinkles around the eyes. The end result should be like applying makeup—you shouldn't notice it.

2.————————**Removing Dust, Scratches, and Imperfections**

In this exercise, you will learn how to remove dust, scratches, and other imperfections from a photograph. This is the same method you would use, by the way, to fix up an old, torn, and stained family photo. In this case, we're going to use a photo—for learning purposes—that has a few imperfections and scratches, and could do with a color overhaul.

1. Open the **File Browser** by choosing **Window > File Browser**. In the File Browser, navigate to the **chap_10** folder you copied onto your computer earlier, and double-click on the **dust_and_scratches** file.

2. When the image opens, double-click on the **Zoom** tool (the magnifying glass icon) in the Toolbox. This sets the image so that you're viewing it at 100 percent its actual size. When adjusting the details of an image (as you're about to do), it's always best to work with the image when it's at 100 percent, or even closer, like 200 or 400 percent. It's just easier to see the details that way.

Tip: Hold down the spacebar on your keyboard to change whatever tool you're currently using into the ***Hand*** *tool, which enables you to drag the image around. This is very helpful when you zoom close into an image but want to change the part of the image you're currently looking at. Keep in mind that you're not actually moving the image itself, you're just choosing what part of the image to look at in the image window. To return to whichever tool you were using, simply release the spacebar.*

3. Use the **Hand** tool (remember, you can just hold down the spacebar to temporarily activate the Hand tool) or the scrollbars on the sides of the image window to position the image so that you can see the top-right corner of the image.

(And yes, as you can see by my t-shirt in this image, even at the age of three, I was already the "World's Greatest Baseball Player." I was the envy of all of the other three-year-olds on my block.) Notice how the top-right corner of the image is scratched and contains a few "lumps." In this exercise, you're going to use a few techniques and tools that will make it look like those imperfections were never there. You're even going to slightly adjust the saturation and levels in this image so that it looks like it was photographed yesterday!

First, you're going to get rid of those scratches…

4. Zoom out one tick by pressing **Ctrl+–** (Ctrl key and the minus [or hyphen] key on Windows) or the **Cmd+–** (Cmd key and the minus [or hyphen] key on the Mac) once. This will zoom the image out to 66.67 percent.

I know, I know, I just told you that it's best to edit images at 100 percent or greater. So why are you zooming out then? Because first you need to select the area that has the scratches on it. These scratches cover such a large part of the image that it's best to zoom out a little so you can see the whole area without having to scroll around. If you're one of those people who is blessed with a large monitor, you probably won't need to zoom out because you'll have plenty of monitor space (often called "screen real estate") to see the whole image, even while viewing it at 100 percent. For the rest of you, though, you'll need to zoom out once to see all of the area you want to select.

5. Select the **Lasso** tool by single-clicking on it in the Toolbox.

6. In the options bar, make sure that the standard **Lasso** tool is selected and not the **Polygonal** or **Magnetic Lasso** tool. Set **Feather** to **15 px**, which will make the edge of the selection–and whatever you do to the image in that selection–softer. Make sure that the **Anti-aliased** check box is checked.

7. Then, simply drag—press the mouse button down while you move the mouse—around the right side of the image, making sure to end back where you started drawing. Avoid the "lumps" on the middle right and top right of the image because you will deal with those in a different way. Also give yourself a little bit of room next to the boy (yes, I'm referring to myself in third person). You don't want the selection to be touching, or directly next to him.

*Note: At this point, some of you might be wondering "The selection that I made with my Lasso tool is very…rough. Isn't that going to make whatever I do to that part of the image look horrible?" Remember, waaay back in Step 6, when you added a **Feather** of **15 px** to the **Lasso** tool? What this will do (even though your selection looks jagged or rough) is make a nice, smooth transition between what is selected, and what isn't. That way, when you do anything to the image within that selection, you won't see a jagged or rough line where the image was selected. Instead, it will be a nice, smooth transition. This also relates to why I had you give a little bit of room between the boy and the area you were selecting. If you had made the selection too close to the boy, because the selection is feathered 15 pixels, the cleanup you perform on that selection might have crossed over a little and been partially applied to the boy as well.*

*Note: If you make a mistake while creating your selection, it's easy to clear what you've done and start over again. To do that, choose **Select > Deselect**. This will clear your selection, and you can start over again.*

8. After you finish your selection, choose **Filter > Noise > Dust & Scratches**.

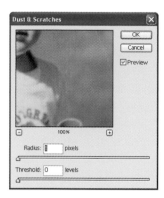

*This will open the **Dust & Scratches** dialog box. This filter works by changing pixels in the image that are different from those surrounding it—thereby concealing the dust and scratches on an image. From this window, you can set the **Radius** (how far the **Dust & Scratches** filter will search outside of your selection for dissimilar pixels), and the **Threshold** (how dissimilar a pixel must be from those surrounding it before it gets eliminated). I recommend starting off with both **Radius** and **Threshold** at their lowest settings. Then slowly start dragging up the **Radius** slider until the dust and scratches disappear. (You can see how the filter is working in the thumbnail image above the sliders.) Because increasing the **Radius** tends to blur the image, you can somewhat counteract the blurriness by slowly dragging up the **Threshold** slider. You're looking for the point right before the dust and scratches become visible.*

***Tip:** You can easily see a before/after image by clicking on the thumbnail preview in the **Dust & Scratches** window. When you click and hold on the thumbnail image, it temporarily reverts back to the original. Releasing the mouse button changes the thumbnail image back to a preview of what it will look like with the current filter settings applied. You can also view different parts of the thumbnail image by dragging it around with your mouse.*

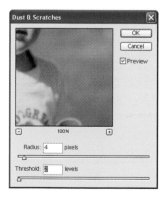

9. Set the **Radius** to **4** and the **Threshold** to **2**. This seems to be the best overall setting for this particular image. Click **OK**.

10. Get rid of the current selection by choosing **Select** > **Deselect**.

11. Zoom back to 100 percent by double-clicking on the **Zoom** tool in the Toolbox. Wow! It's hard to tell there were ever any scratches there. Because the **Dust & Scratches** filter slightly blurs the image when it removes dust and scratches, it is best used on images that are already slightly blurry, much like the background is in this sample image.

*In the next steps, you're going to learn how to get rid of those lumps on the right side of the image. To do that, you're going to learn how to use the totally awesome **Clone Stamp** tool, which, in its bare essence, allows you to take a sample of an image and paint with that sample someplace else on the image. This is great when you want to cover up parts of an image you don't like—such as the lumps in this image. You can simply sample part of the image and paint with that sample on top of the lumps, thereby covering them up.*

12. Single-click on the **Clone Stamp** tool in the Toolbox to select it.

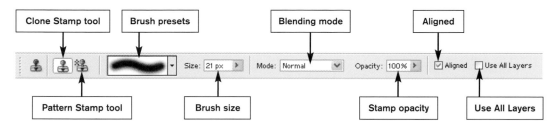

There are, of course, some Clone Stamp tool options you should be aware of before continuing:

Clone Stamp Tool Options	
Option	**Description**
Clone Stamp tool	Selects the Clone Stamp tool. The Clone Stamp tool allows you to take a sample of a portion of your image, and uses that to paint with on other areas in the image.
Pattern Stamp tool	Selects the Pattern Stamp tool. The Pattern Stamp tool allows you to paint with a pattern you've selected from the Pattern Picker pop-up menu. (Try saying *that* fast 10 times.) The Pattern Picker pop-up menu will appear next to the Opacity slider when you select the Pattern Stamp tool.
Brush presets	Allows you to choose different brush sizes, styles, and shapes.
Size	Allows you to choose what size brush you want to use.
Mode	Allows you to choose what blending mode you want applied to the Clone Stamp or Pattern Stamp tool as you work with them. For more information on blending modes, refer to Chapter 4, "*Layers.*"
Opacity	Allows you to set the opacity the Clone Stamp and Pattern Stamp tools paint with.
Aligned	If checked, when you first sample part of the image, that sampling stays at that relative distance but will follow the Stamp tool around the image as you stop and resume painting. If unchecked, each time you stop and resume painting, the sampling point will go back to the original spot you sampled.
Use All Layers	If checked, when you sample a spot in your image with one of the Stamp tools, it will use all of your layers (much as if the layers were flattened into one) to take a sample from. If unchecked, when you sample a spot, it will sample only from the layer that is currently selected.

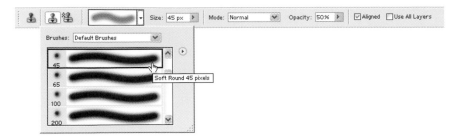

13. Select the **Clone Stamp** tool, and from the **brush presets** pull-down menu, choose the **Soft Round 45 pixels** brush. Set **Mode** to **Normal** and **Opacity** to **50%**. The **Aligned** check box should be checked, and **Use All Layers** should be unchecked.

The first thing you need to do is look at the image and figure out which imperfections you want to get rid of. Then decide what other parts of the image you can borrow (sample) from to cover up those imperfections. Circled in the preceding screen shot are the two main imperfections—those "lumps" I was referring to earlier—you need to cover up. The top lump is sitting half on the sky and half on the fence (the brown shape in the background). The bottom lump is sitting on top of the grass in the middle ground. The bottom lump is easy to cover up—you can just sample some of the blurry grass to its left, and use that sample to cover up the lump. On the other hand, the top lump is a little more difficult because it sits half on, half off of two different backgrounds—sky and fence. But you should be able to easily sample a portion of the sky to the left of the top lump and use that to paint over the part of the lump sitting over the sky. Sampling part of the fence will allow you to paint over the other half of the lump that is over the fence background. It's a snap! Give it a try by starting with the easy, lower imperfection.

14. Move the **Clone Stamp** tool onto the image, and position it to the left of the bottom imperfection so that it's over the grass but not over the imperfection itself. Then, hold down the **Alt** key (Windows) or the **Option** key (Mac). When you do, you'll see the **Clone Stamp** tool icon (a circle) turn into a small circle with crosshairs in the middle. Those crosshairs represent where you are taking your image sample from. Once you see those crosshairs, make sure they're positioned over the correct spot and then click. After you've clicked, you can release the **Alt** or **Option** key.

Congratulations! You've successfully taken a sample of that image. Now, you need to use it.

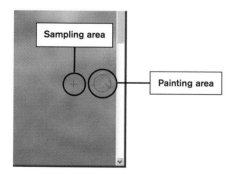

15. Move the **Clone Stamp** tool (the circle) over onto the imperfection. Then, simply drag—press and hold the mouse button while you drag—over the imperfection.

As you do, you'll see it start to fade a little. As you drag the Clone Stamp tool around, you'll notice a little plus sign that follows your movements. That plus sign represents what part of the image is being sampled, and therefore what part of the image you're currently painting with. "How did it know to start there?" you ask? Back in Step 14, you Alt-clicked (Windows) or Option-clicked (Mac) on the area to the left of the imperfection. By doing that, you instructed Elements where you wanted to take the sample from. Now, as you drag the Clone Stamp tool around, that sampling point (represented by the plus sign) follows the Clone Stamp tool around. It continually samples the part of the image beneath the plus sign, and funnels that into the Clone Stamp brush you're painting over the imperfections with. If it sounds complicated at this point, I'm sure it will become clearer to you as you get more experience working with it.

*Note: Make sure that the sampling point (the plus sign) never crosses over the imperfect area. If it does, you will be painting with that imperfection, and that's just plain counterproductive. If you're sampling point is getting too close to what you're trying to paint over, simply take a new sample (**Alt-click** or **Option-click**) of an area farther away from the imperfection and keep painting!*

16. Because back in Step 13 you set the **Clone Stamp** tool **Opacity** to **50%**, you will need to make a few passes to completely cover up the imperfection. Drag over the imperfection until it's not fading any more, and then release the mouse button, take a new sample, and drag over the imperfection again. Repeat as many times as necessary. When you're done, it should look awesome! Anyone would be hard-pressed to tell that there was ever a big lump in that spot.

Next, you're going to repeat those steps for the top imperfection.

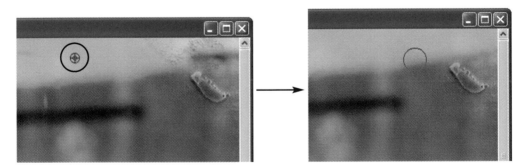

17. At the top of the image, with the **Clone Stamp** tool still selected, **Alt-click** (Windows) or **Option-click** (Mac) on part of the sky to the left of the imperfection. Then, just like you did in Steps 15 and 16, drag the **Clone Stamp** brush over the part of the imperfection that is atop the sky to paint over it.

Like magic it disappears! The first time I saw the Clone Stamp tool being used, I was amazed.

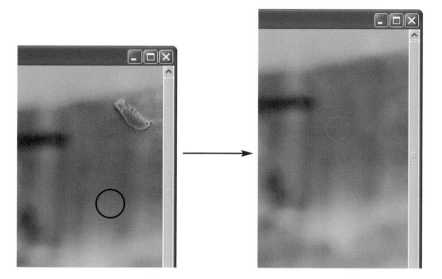

18. To get rid of the lump on the fence (kind of sounds like a bad horror movie title), first take a sample of another piece of the fence. (I chose to take a sample below the imperfection because the fence to the left has different patterns/values than the part of the fence that I want to paint over.) Then just drag the **Clone Stamp** brush around to paint over the imperfection. Again, you may need to retake the sample if the sample point strays too close to the imperfection, and you will need to paint over the imperfection a few times. This is because the **Clone Stamp** brush is set to **50% Opacity** (so that you can get some nice subtlety when cloning), which will require you to make a couple passes to fully cover the imperfection.

19. Zoom out one tick by pressing **Ctrl+–** (Ctrl key and the minus [or hyphen] key on Windows) or the **Cmd+–** (Cmd key and the minus key [or hyphen] on the Mac) once. This will zoom the image out to 66.67 percent. You should be able to see the whole image at this point. If you have a small monitor, you may need to zoom out once more to be able to see the image in its entirety.

The (nearly) finished image! It is now almost completely devoid of scratches and imperfections. For an old photo, it's starting to look almost new. But what image makeover would be complete without adjusting the levels and saturation of the image?

20. Open the **Layers** palette (**Window > Layers**) and add a **Hue/Saturation** adjustment layer by clicking on the **Adjustment Layer** icon (a circle that's half black, half white) and choosing **Hue/Saturation**. Increase the saturation of the colors in the image by dragging the **Saturation** slider until it reads **+20**. Click **OK**.

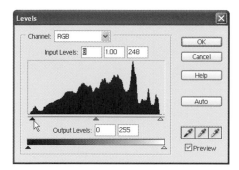

21. Open the **Layers** palette again (**Window > Layers**), and this time, add a **Levels** adjustment layer to the image by clicking on the **Adjustment Layer** icon and choosing **Levels**. In the **Levels** window, set the **black input level** (the left-most Input Levels field) to **8**, leave the **gray input level** (the middle Input Levels field) set to **1.00**, and change the **white input level** (the right-most Input Levels field) to **248**. Click **OK**.

before   after

As you can see in the before and after images, there is a huge improvement in the after image. Thanks to the Dust & Scratches filter, and thanks to the Clone Stamp tool, you've made short work of the dust, scratches, and imperfections that marred this image. You also utilized Hue/Saturation and Levels Adjustment layers to improve the hue and value of the finished image. Give yourself a big pat on the back because you covered a lot of material in this exercise and learned how to take an old photo and manipulate it until it looks like it was taken a few weeks ago instead of 25 years ago!

22. Choose **File > Save As**. Name this file **no_dust_or_scratches**, and save it in the **chap_10** folder. After the image has saved, close it.

3. ────────────**Sharpening a Photo**

Don't you hate those photos that would be perfect if they weren't just a little blurry? In this exercise, you will learn how to fix those blurry photos by sharpening them. You will see not only how to sharpen an entire photo, but also how to use the Sharpen tool to sharpen specific areas of an image. Now don't expect to be able to take a super blurry photo—one that looks like it was taken on a foggy day, or in a car wash, or underwater—and expect to run it through Elements' Sharpen filter, and have it come out the other side all crispy sharp. The techniques you're about to learn are best used when sharpening a photo that is a little blurry. If it's *too* blurry, sharpening it is only going to make it look weird.

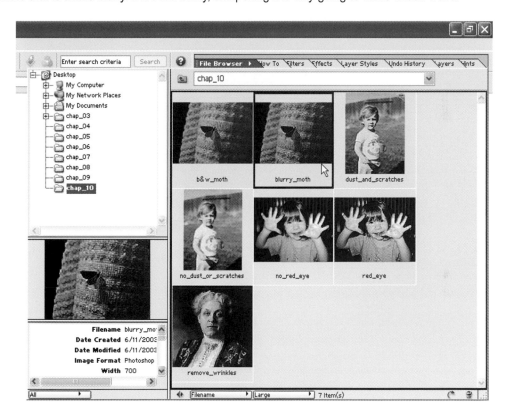

1. Open the **File Browser** by choosing **Window > File Browser**. Navigate to the **chap_10** folder, and double-click on the file **blurry_moth**.

As you can see, this image is a little blurry. First, try sharpening the whole image by using
a **Sharpen** filter.

2. Choose **Filter** > **Sharpen** > **Unsharp Mask**.

*"Why choose Unsharp Mask?" you ask? "What about the other sharpen filters that I saw under that
menu?" you say?* **Sharpen**, **Sharpen Edges**, *and* **Sharpen More** *will sharpen the image, but they don't
give you options to set for* how much *to sharpen the image.* **Unsharp Mask***, however, allows you to
specify various options when sharpening an image. This ultimately gives you more control over how
much, or how little, to sharpen an image.*

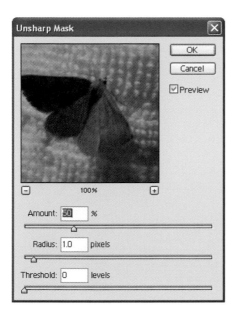

The Unsharp Mask filter window has three fields/sliders:

- **Amount:** A percentage of how much you want to increase the contrast of the pixels in the image. Adobe recommends setting the Amount slider to **150%** to **200%** for high-resolution (200ppi or higher) images you are going to print.

- **Radius:** The number of pixels to sharpen around edges. A low Radius sharpens only the pixels right near edges, whereas a high Radius sharpens a wider area around edges. Adobe recommends a Radius between **1** and **2** for high-resolution images you are going to print.

- **Threshold:** Sets how different a pixel must be from the other pixels surrounding it before it is considered an "edge pixel" and sharpened. A Threshold of 0, the default, sharpens all the pixels in the image. Essentially, the lower the threshold, the more pixels will be sharpened; the higher the threshold, the fewer pixels will be sharpened. To avoid reducing visual "noise" in the image, Adobe recommends setting the Threshold somewhere between **2** and **20.**

When I sharpen images, I usually start by setting the **Amount** to **100%** (it's a good starting spot), and then slowly increase the **Radius** amount until the image has the sharpness I want. If there's too much of an "edge" around shapes, I can fine-tune it with the **Threshold** slider.

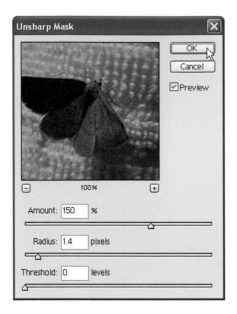

3. For this particular image, set the **Amount** to **150%**, the **Radius** to **1.4** pixels, and leave the **Threshold** set to **0** levels.

*Note: An easy way to see a quick preview of how the image looked before your current filter settings, and how it looks after the filter will be applied, is to simply click on the image thumbnail in the **Unsharp Mask** window. By holding the mouse button down on the image thumbnail, you can see how the image looked before any filter settings were applied to it. When you release the mouse button, you will see a preview of how the image will look (based on the current filter settings) after the filter has been applied.*

4. After you enter the Unsharp Mask settings, click **OK**.

before (detail)   *after (detail)*

As you can see in the before/after images, there's quite a big difference. The before image (although nice artistically because of its blurry, dreamlike quality) is quite blurry when compared to the sharpened after image.

But what if you didn't intend to sharpen the whole image? What if you like the blurry qualities of the before image, and you just want to make the moth itself sharper? At this point you would have two options. You can either use your various selection tools to first select the moth, and then apply a Sharpen filter to that selection, or you can use the Sharpen tool to selectively sharpen only the areas you want. You have already learned the skills necessary to select and sharpen images, so now you're going to learn how to sharpen areas of an image by using the Sharpen tool.

5. Choose **File > Save As**. Check the **As a Copy** check box, name the image **sharp_moth**, and click the **Save** button to save it in the **chap_10** folder.

*The As a Copy check box tells Elements to save this image as…well…a copy. This allows you to save the current state of the image, while leaving the image you're currently working with alone. The reason you're doing this is because you want to continue to work with and modify this image, but in the next exercise you will work with the sharpened image—**sharp_moth**. If you look at the title bar of the image you're currently working with, you'll notice that it still has the same name, **blurry_moth**.*

6. Revert to the saved, blurry version of this moth image by choosing **File > Revert**.

7. Single-click on the **Sharpen** tool in the Toolbox.

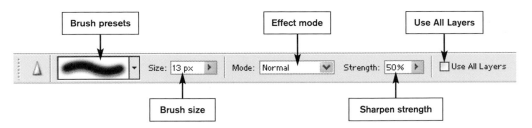

There are, of course, some options for the Sharpen tool. Here's what they all mean:

Sharpen Tool Options	
Option	**Description**
Brush presets	Allows you to choose different brush sizes, styles, and shapes.
Brush size	Allows you to choose what size brush you want to use.
Effect mode	From this pull-down menu, you can choose a blending mode to be applied to the areas you're sharpening. Note that only a few blending modes are available. This is because the Sharpen tool just sharpens images, and cannot affect the image in ways that would allow the use of the other blending modes. Most of the time, you will probably want to leave this set to **Normal.**
Sharpen strength	Specify the amount that you want to sharpen the image, 0% to 100%. The greater the percentage, the more it will sharpen the image.
Use All Layers	With this checked, the Sharpen tool will sharpen images that are in all of the layers in an image. With this option unchecked (the default), the Sharpen tool will only sharpen the image that is in the currently selected layer.

8. With the **Sharpen** tool selected, in the options bar, choose the **Soft Round 100 pixels** brush from the **brush presets** pull-down menu. Set the **Mode** to **Normal** and set **Strength** to **50%**. **Use All Layers** should be unchecked.

9. Move the **Sharpen** tool onto the image, and drag over the moth, as well as a little of the area around the moth—so that it doesn't appear as if the moth, while in focus, is floating on this unfocused background.

I find it helpful to "dab" when I use the Sharpen tool. I'll drag a small area with the tool, and then release the mouse button. Drag, release. Drag, release. That way I can make sure that I don't go too far and over-sharpen the image. You'll know when you have over-sharpened the image when you start to see some "noise" (small, multi-colored dots) being introduced into the image. Your goal is to sharpen the image to the point you want it, but not to sharpen it so much that you see noise. Dabbing helps to make sure that you don't overdo the sharpening. If you dab, and start to see noise appear, you can always undo the last command. At that point, you know the image is as sharp as it's going to get.

10. Close this image and don't save the changes.

In this exercise you saw how to sharpen the entire image using the Sharpen filter, and you saw how to sharpen specific areas of an image—while leaving the other areas untouched—by using the Sharpen tool. In the next exercise, you will switch from learning how to sharpen an image to learning how to blur an image.

Blurring a Photo

You've seen it in magazine pictures, and you've seen it in your own pictures (but probably due to an accident). Now it's time to learn how to blur your photos! *Cue echo machine* At this point, you're probably wondering why you are going to learn how to blur photos. "Sharpening a photo I can understand, but making a photo blurry?" you say. "Are you nuts?" Yes I am. But that doesn't have anything to do with blurring images! Blurring photographs can be used for a variety of purposes. The most common is to draw the viewer's eyes toward specific areas of the image by blurring areas that you want to draw their attention away from. The viewers eyes will inherently stray away from blurry areas and will be drawn towards areas of contrast and areas that are in focus.

1. Open the **File Browser** by choosing **Window > File Browser**. Navigate to the **chap_10** folder and double-click on the image **sharp_moth** to open it.

This is the image you applied the Sharpen filter to, and saved, in the preceding exercise. For the sake of this exercise, suppose you want to add that blurry, dream-like quality back to this moth image. Luckily for you, Elements not only sharpens, it blurs as well. (Elements is better than a Ginsu® knife, I tell ya!)

2. Choose **Filter > Blur > Gaussian Blur,** which enables you to add a nice, hazy blur to an image.

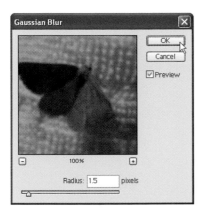

3. The Gaussian Blur filter is super straightforward. The **Radius** slider is the only setting you can modify. Essentially, the higher the **Radius**, the more the image is blurred. As you can see in the thumbnail preview, as you drag the slider farther to the right, it will eventually become an unintelligible, blurry mess. (That's what my computer screen looks like at 4:00 a.m.) For this example, however, you just want to blur the image a little, so drag the Radius slider to the right until it reads **1.5**. Click **OK**.

before (detail)   after (detail)

As you can clearly see in the before and after images, the Gaussian Blur filter certainly does its job. The after image now has that same blurry look back again—you've gone full circle. ;-)

Although the Gaussian Blur filter did a good job at blurring the entire image, sometimes you don't want the entire image blurred. Elements has a Blur tool that will allow you to selectively blur portions of the image. Because blurring an already blurred image won't do much good, you first need to revert this image back to its saved, sharp state.

4. Choose **File** > **Revert**.

5. Single-click on the **Blur** tool in the Toolbox.

In the options bar, there are options you can set. I won't go over them because they are the same as the options for the Sharpen tool (which I covered in the last exercise). Just keep in mind that these options refer to blurring *an image, not* sharpening *it.*

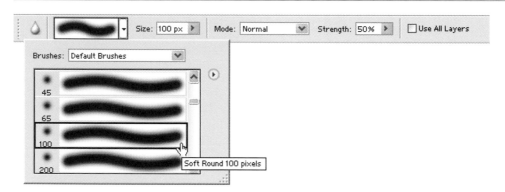

6. From the **brush presets** pull-down menu, choose **Soft Round 100 pixels**. Set the **Mode** to **Normal** and the **Strength** to **50%**, and make sure that **Use All Layers** is unchecked.

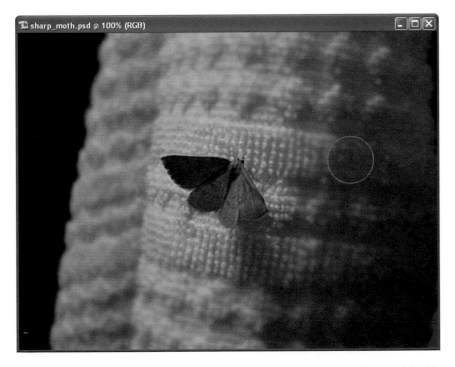

sharp_moth.psd @ 100% (RGB)

7. Move the **Blur** tool onto the image, and start dragging it around. The goal, in this example, is to blur everything but the moth and the area directly around it. You can blur some areas more than others by repeatedly dragging the **Blur** tool across the area multiple times. Be sure to release the mouse button after each pass. Releasing the mouse button, and then dragging over an area again, adds more blur to that part of the image.

When you're done, you have effectively brought the viewer's eye, and thereby the point of focus of the image, to the moth. Because everything is blurry except for the moth, the viewer's eye will continually be drawn back to that area. That's one practical reason to selectively use sharpening and blurring—it will allow you to draw attention to certain areas or objects in an image.

8. Close this image and don't save the changes. You won't need the image again in this chapter.

MOVIE | Colorizing a Black-and-White Photo

Included on the **H•O•T CD-ROM** in the **movies** folder is a movie titled **colorizing.mov**. In this movie, I demonstrate how to take a black-and-white image and colorize it using a combination of layers, blending modes, and the Paintbrush tool. You will learn how to do this using the **b&w_moth.psd** file included in the **chap_10** folder on the **H•O•T CD-ROM**.

In the **colorizing.mov** movie, you will start by opening a black-and-white image.

Then, by using layers, blending modes, and the Paintbrush tool, you will add color to selective portions of the image. This is a great and beautiful way to add some new life to an old image. You'll be surprised at how easy it is to colorize an old photo, and how simple it is to easily change the colors to anything you want.

In this chapter, you learned some very powerful and very important image-editing techniques. You learned how to remove the dreaded red eye, how to subtly remove wrinkles from a face, how to remove dust, scratches, and imperfections from an old(ish) picture, how to selectively sharpen and blur a photograph, and how to colorize a black-and-white image. You're on your way to creating your own "image restoration" business with just the techniques you learned in this chapter!

In the next chapter, you will learn the intricate ins and outs of photo manipulation. Everything from creating a panoramic photo using a series of stitched-together photographs, to photo compositing (creating one photo "composition" using a series of separate photos), to some fun and useful experimentation with the Smudge tool and Liquify filter. Turn the page...you can do it! :-)

11.

Photo Manipulation

| Photomerge | Photo Compositing |
| Smudge Tool | Liquify |

chap_11

Photoshop Elements 2
H•O•T CD-ROM

This is it. This is the chapter where you finally learn how to add giant hairy moles to a picture of your sister's face. This is where you learn how to make it look like her eyes are about to pop out of her head, and her nose is dripping down her face. This is where, sorry, I forgot where I was for a moment. Although you *could* do all those things with the skills you learn in this chapter (if you are so inclined), you will instead learn by using more practical examples. In this chapter, you will learn how to create a panoramic photo, how to take multiple photos and combine them together into one image composition, how to utilize the Smudge tool, and how to use the Liquify filter. This chapter is a mix of both serious and important learning material (photo compositing) as well as more fun and playful examples (Liquify). I'm ready. Are you?

Photomerge

Ever gone on vacation to a scenic area, where you have a wide-open view and every direction you look is beautiful? A common thing to do under those circumstances is to whip out the camera and start taking pictures. You'll take a picture and turn a little, take another picture and turn a little, and so on and so forth. Then when you get the pictures developed (if you're using a film-based camera), you'll tape them all together to create a Frankenstein poster of images in a desperate attempt to recapture that moment. *Sigh.* Well now, using Elements, you can combine all those separate photos together to create one, seamless, panoramic photo. This feature is called **Photomerge**.

1. Copy the **chap_11** folder and files from the **H•O•T CD-ROM** to your hard drive.

2. Choose **File > Create Photomerge**. This will open the **Photomerge** window.

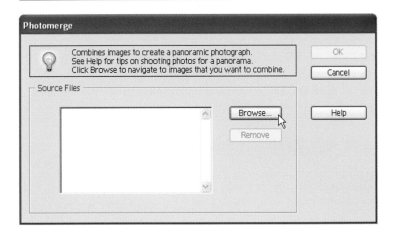

3. From here, you choose which files you want to merge together into a panoramic photo. Click **Browse**.

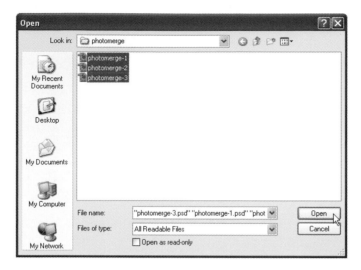

4. From the **Open** window, navigate to where you copied the **chap_11** folder, and open the folder **photomerge**. In that folder, you will see three images: **photomerge-1**, **photomerge-2**, and **photomerge-3**. These are the three photographs you will be merging. Single-click on **photomerge-1**, hold down the **Shift** key, and single-click on **photomerge-3**. This will select all three images. Click **Open**.

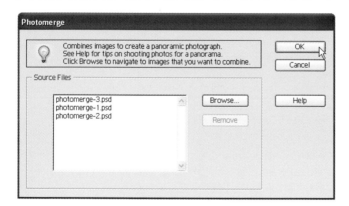

5. Now you'll see that Elements has placed the three images you want to merge together in the **Source Files** list. Click **OK**.

Then just sit back and watch Elements go crazy. All by itself, Elements will open the three images, shuffle them around, open the Photomerge window, and stitch the three photos together by making its best guess. That process right there is probably one of the more impressive features that Elements has. All you had to do was select the images you want to merge, and Elements goes and does the rest. Very, very cool!

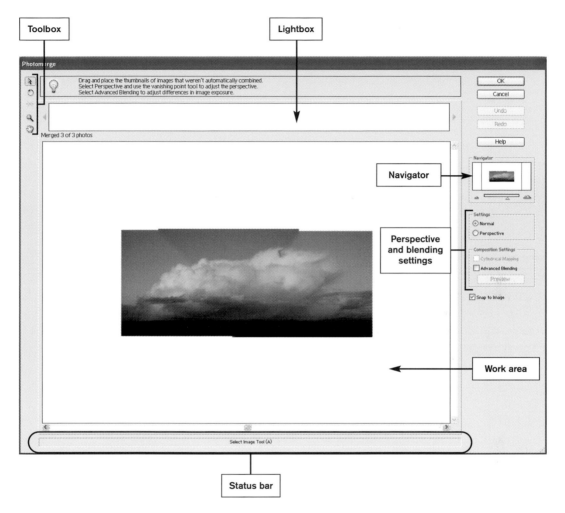

Note: *Sometimes, Elements doesn't understand how to place one of the photos you've chosen in the panorama. If it can't automatically place all the images, it will kindly inform you that it "could not automatically arrange the images." Any images that Elements could not automatically place in the panorama are placed in the Lightbox area. All you'd need to do is drag them from the Lightbox to the work area, and position them in the panoramic photo.*

As you can see in the Photomerge window, Elements did a fantastic job of merging those three photos to create one panoramic shot.

6. Zoom into the panorama a little by selecting the **Zoom** tool (magnifying glass icon) in the Toolbox, moving your mouse onto the panorama, and clicking a couple times.

*Note: These three photos combine together to create a nice panoramic photo, but that's not always the case. Sometimes, when Elements tries to automatically place the images in the panorama, it might place them a little off from where you want them to be. To change the position of a photo in the panorama, simply select the Arrow tool in the Photomerge Toolbox and drag the image you want to reposition. You'll also notice that as you drag an image around, it becomes partially transparent. This is to help you to align the images together properly. If you need to, you can also rotate the image by selecting the Rotate tool and dragging the image to adjust its rotation. Easy! As you're attempting to reposition an image in the panorama, you will notice that it has a tendency to snap to the other images. The **Snap to Image** check box, on the right side of the Photomerge window, causes an image that is being repositioned to snap to the other images in the panorama. Uncheck the **Snap to Image** check box to turn off that feature.*

Notice the darkened, diagonal lines that extend toward the center of the image? Those darkened lines are where Elements is blending the images together. To get a smoother transition between the images, follow these steps:

7. Click on the **Advanced Blending** check box so that it's checked, and click on the **Preview** button.

Elements takes a few seconds to think about it, and then shows you the same panoramic photo. If you look closely, however, you'll notice that now those diagonal, darkened lines are much less notice-able. You can still see a little bit of that darkened area towards the top of the image, but most of that will be cropped out when you trim the image at the end of this exercise.

8. When you're done marveling at what an excellent job Elements does at blending those photos, click on the **Exit Preview** button.

*Note: Under the Settings section, the **Perspective** radio button will add—you guessed it—perspective to the image. This will change the position of the images in the panorama so they all point towards a vanishing point in the image. (By default, the vanishing point is the center-most image.) When you have **Perspective** selected, you can change which image is the default vanishing point by selecting the **Vanishing Point** tool in the Toolbox (underneath the **Rotate** tool) and then click on the image you want to be the vanishing point. The other images in the panorama will adjust themselves accordingly. This option is useful if you want the image to look as if it actually has perspective—that the panoramic photos all point towards a singular vanishing point. When using perspective, you can also check the **Cylindrical Mapping** check box to counteract the bending and warping that occurs when perspective is applied. I don't like the image distortion that occurs when perspective is applied to a panorama, so I usually don't turn it on.*

9. If you like the way the panoramic photo looks, and you don't need to do any adjusting, click **OK**.

Elements takes a few seconds to stitch all those photos together, and then voilà! As you can see, Elements does a fantastic job stitching those separate photos together to create one panoramic photo. You'll also notice, however, that some small transparent areas are visible at the top right and bottom left of the image. This is space left over from when Elements automatically repositioned some of the images to make sure that they all lined up. No worries, though, you can just crop them out.

10. Single-click on the **Crop** tool in the Toolbox to select it.

11. With the **Crop** tool, drag around the entire image. Then, by dragging the resize handles on the sides of the crop area (the animated, dashed line), resize the crop area so that the transparent areas (checkerboard pattern) at the top right and bottom left of the image are on the *outside* of the crop area.

Note: *When trying to drag a side of the crop area close to the edge of an image, the crop area might snap to the edge of the image. This is really annoying if you are trying to crop off just a little bit around the outside of the image. Luckily, it's easy to turn off that snapping feature. Just choose **View > Snap to Grid** to uncheck it. Then you should be able to easily drag the crop edge right next to the image edge without it snapping. Yay!*

12. Once you have the crop area where you want it, press **Enter** (Windows) or **Return** (Mac) to have Elements crop the image.

Now you're left with a beautiful panoramic photo. It's hard to tell that this photo actually started off as three separate photos!

13. Choose **File > Save** (or if you're feeling adventurous, use the keyboard shortcut to save the file: **Ctrl+S** [Windows] or **Cmd+S** [Mac]). Title this image **photomerged** and save it in the **photomerge** folder in the **chap_11** folder you copied onto your computer at the beginning of the exercise. After the image has finished saving, close it.

Here are some suggestions from Adobe to make sure the Photomerge feature will work the best it can with your images:

- *When you're taking photos of a scene, make sure to overlap the photos about 15 to 45 percent. In other words, don't take a picture, and then take the next picture where you think the last one got cut off—overlap the photos by about a third. Elements needs the pictures to overlap a little to give you the best results.*

- *As you're taking photographs of a scene you are going to turn into a panorama, make sure that you keep the camera level. Using a tripod makes that super simple.*

- *Stay in the same place as you take the photographs. Don't walk around when you're shooting the photos because if you do, parts of the image will shift and change perspective. This will make the final panorama look blurry, and you'll be able to more easily see the seams between the photographs.*

- *Don't zoom in or out between photographs. Pick whatever zoom level you want, but keep it the same as you take all the photographs for the panorama.*

- *Don't use any distortion lenses, such as Fisheye. Elements will have a harder time attempting to create a seamless panoramic photo if the image is distorted.*

- *Don't use the flash for one photo in the panorama and not for others. Try to keep the exposure for each photo the same. If the lighting is the same throughout all the photos in the panorama, you'll have better success with making the final image look seamless.*

Now get out there, snap away, and capture the moment!

 MOVIE | Photo Compositing

Included on the **H•O•T CD-ROM** in the **movies** folder is a movie titled **composite.mov**. In this movie, I demonstrate how to combine multiple photographs, using a variety of techniques, to create a singular image composition.

You will work with images provided for you on the CD-ROM. You will edit, combine, and modify them to create one image composition.

In the end, you're left with one, beautiful image composition.

2. _____Smudge Tool

In this exercise, you will learn how to use the **Smudge** tool to add a little distortion to an image. Although I find the Smudge tool quite useful to distort and warp areas of my illustrations, it's also fun to just play around with.

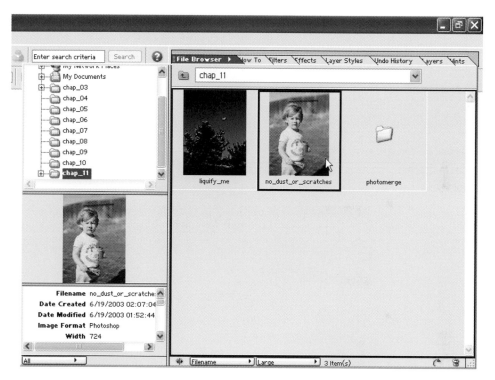

1. Open the **File Browser** by choosing **Window > File Browser**. Navigate to the **chap_11** folder and double-click on the file titled **no_dust_or_scratches** to open it.

---

2. Make sure you're viewing the image at 100 percent by double-clicking on the **Zoom** tool (the magnifying glass icon) in the Toolbox.

*In this exercise, you're going to use the **Smudge** tool to make it look like this boy's hair is being blown around by the wind.*

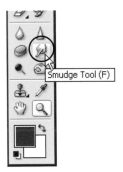

3. Single-click on the **Smudge** tool in the Toolbox.

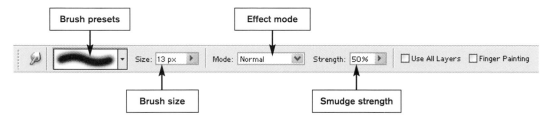

Brush presets

Effect mode

Brush size

Smudge strength

The options (in the options bar) for the Smudge tool are pretty standard. The following table outlines the options and what they mean:

Smudge Tool Options	
Option	**Description**
Brush presets	Allows you to choose different brush sizes, styles, and shapes.
Brush size	Allows you to choose what size brush you want to use.
Effect mode	From this pull-down menu, you can choose a blending mode to be applied to the areas you're smudging. Note that only a few blending modes are available. This is because the Smudge tool smudges only images and cannot affect the image in ways that would allow the use of the other blending modes. Most of the time, you will probably want to leave this set to Normal.
Smudge strength	Specify the amount you want to smudge the image, from 0 to 100 percent. The greater the percentage, the more it will smudge the image.
Use All Layers	With this checked, the Smudge tool will affect parts of the image that are in all of the layers. With this option unchecked (the default), the Smudge tool will only affect the part of the image that is in the currently selected layer.
Finger Painting	With this check box unchecked (the default), the Smudge tool smudges the image using the color in the image you initially click on. If checked, the Smudge tool will smudge the image using the current foreground color.

4. Click on the **brush presets** pull-down menu, and choose the brush **Soft Round 17 pixels**. Set **Mode** to **Normal** and **Strength** to **50%**, and **Use All Layers** and **Finger Painting** should both be unchecked.

5. Move your cursor over the image, and then starting from on the hair, drag to the left. The effect is subtle, so you'll probably need to do it a few times before you start seeing results. Just make sure that after you've dragged the mouse a little to the left, release the mouse button, and then drag again from the hair, off to the left a little.

As you'll start to see, the Smudge tool smudges the pixels in the image! It's almost like the image is made of wet paint, and you're running your finger through it. So cool!

6. Continue doing this on different spots on the left side (your left side) of his head until it looks like the hair is being blown in the wind.

Tip: If you want to make it look more realistic, vary the size of the brush you're smudging with. Remember, it's really easy to change the size of the brush. Just press the [(left bracket) or] (right bracket) keys to decrease or increase, respectively, the size of the brush. That way, you'll make some thick smudges and some thin smudges, creating a more realistic effect. Neat!

This is just a small and subtle example of the Smudge tool. The Smudge tool, very simply, smudges pixels in an image. Think of the possibilities!

7. When you're finished smudging, close this image and don't save the changes.

3. ——————Liquify

Admittedly, Liquify is just fun to play around with. Liquify allows you to, for example, take a picture of your third-grade teacher who used to smack your hands with her ruler when you weren't paying attention, and turn her face into silly putty. You can stretch out her nose, make her eyes bug out, or give her gopher teeth. Ahhh—modern technology. In this exercise, you won't be doing anything so immature. (I mean, what kind of guy do you think I am?) But seriously, the Liquify filter can be used to create some really neat effects in your imagery. It's all up to you. Should you use it for good, or for…muah… muaaha…MUAHAHAH…evil? ;-)

1. Open the **File Browser** by choosing **Window > File Browser**. Then navigate to the **chap_11** folder and double-click on the **liquify_me** image.

*This will open up the **liquify_me** image. As you can see, it's a tranquil night scene with a crescent moon hovering in the sky. Using Liquify, however, you're going to add a little twist to this image.*

2. Choose **Filter > Distort > Liquify**.

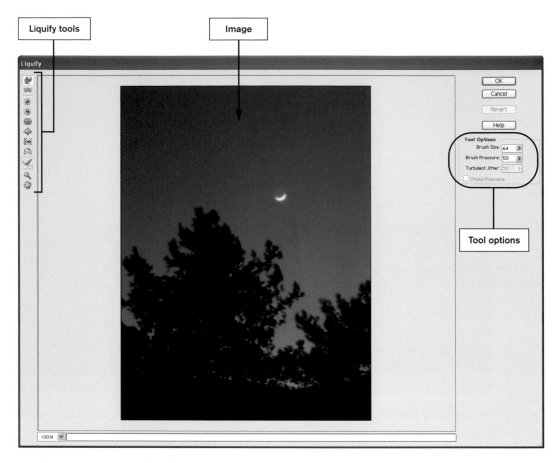

On the surface, the Liquify window is pretty harmless. But if you look closer at the Liquify tools, you'll notice that you have quite a variety of tools to choose from. From Turbulence, to Twirl, to Pucker, to Bloat, you can construct a wide variety of effects from this one, unassuming window. First, you're going to make the moon a little bigger.

3. Single-click on the **Bloat** tool in the Liquify Toolbox.

4. Set the **Brush Size** to **52** and the **Brush Pressure** to **50**.

5. Position the cursor so that the moon is in the middle of it. Then, hold the mouse button down until the moon has nearly filled the brush cursor.

Neat! You've just used the Bloat tool to increase the size of the moon. How's that for wielding ultimate power!! Next you're going to add a little something extra to give the moon a twist—quite literally.

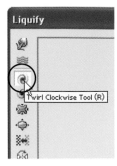

6. Single-click on the **Twirl Clockwise** tool in the Liquify Toolbox.

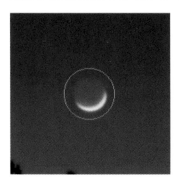 

7. Position the mouse cursor so that the moon is in the center, and then hold the mouse button down until the moon starts to twist around itself a little. The longer you hold the mouse button down, the more the moon will twist. Say—this image is starting to look a little like a Van Gogh painting! ;-)

That twist effect is so neat, why don't you apply a little of it to the tree branches to give them a stylized look.

8. Just like you did with the moon, press and hold the mouse button on a few of the ends of the tree branches to make them twirl a bit, too.

Note: You can also get some neat effects by moving the brush slightly while you hold down the mouse button. This will continue to twirl the image as you drag across it.

9. Mix it up a little by single-clicking on the **Twirl Counter Clockwise** tool in the Liquify Toolbox.

10. Just like what you did with the **Twirl Clockwise** tool, use the **Twirl Counter Clockwise** tool to twirl some of the branches in the opposite direction. Oooh—spooky.

11. When you're finished warping, twisting, bulging, and puckering the image, click **OK**.

There you have it. A spooky, stylized night scene—complete with a twisted, crescent moon.

12. Close this image and don't save the changes.

By playing around with the Liquify filter, you got a glimpse of how easy it was to use the Liquify tools to twist and bulge an image like it's clay. There are many other Liquify tools that weren't covered in this exercise, but they're all really straightforward and easy to use, so I encourage you to experiment with them at your leisure. I don't know about you, but I think the Liquify filter is a really fun and playful way to distort your pictures, and it gives you great freedom to manipulate images.

In the next chapter, you will be departing from learning how to adjust, correct, manipulate, and composite images, and instead will learn how Elements can work with the Web. You'll learn how to easily send your images via email, create an animated GIF (an animated image to put on a Web page), create a gallery of images to put up on the Internet, and create a PDF slideshow of images. The next chapter is one you definitely don't want to skip over.

I2.

Elements
and the Web

| Image Sizes, Resolutions, and the Web |
Attach to Email	Web Photo Gallery
Save for the Web	Creating an Animated GIF
What Is PDF?	PDF Slideshow

Photoshop Elements 2
H•O•T CD-ROM

This chapter is a slight departure from the others that came before it. Rather than focus on adjusting the value or hue of your photographs, or on how to replace your date in your prom photo with a picture of someone else, you will instead learn how Elements can create content for Web and email delivery. Coming from an image-editing program, it may be somewhat surprising to you that Elements can easily (and I mean *easily*) attach photos to an email, create a Web photo gallery, create an animated GIF, and even assemble a PDF slideshow you can send to friends and family. By this point, you may be asking yourself, "Geez. What does this program *not* do? Can it do my dishes, take out the trash, and mow the lawn?" My answer would be yes, it can…err…I mean…not yet it can't. ;-)

Image Sizes, Resolutions, and the Web

Now that you are going to be learning how to put your images on a Web page, and how to email them to people, it's important that you revisit, and have a good understanding of, the topic of image size and image resolution.

When posting an image to a Web site, or emailing photos to someone, you should be aware of image size. A common error that beginners make when emailing photos to a friend, or when posting images on a Web site, is using an image that is much too large for the job at hand. In a hypothetical situation, you are going to email a photo of a flower to your mom for Mother's Day (awwww). So you go out to the garden with your digital camera, snap a photo, load it onto your computer, attach it to an email, and click Send. After waiting 10 minutes, and the image still hasn't finished uploading, you start to wonder what the problem is. So you cancel the email, open the image in Elements, and choose **Image > Resize > Image Size**. It's then that you see this:

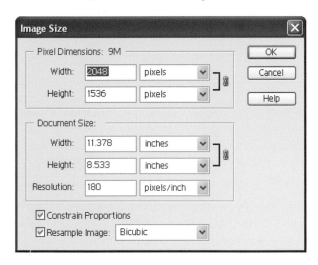

From this **Image Size** window, you can see that the **Document Size** is 11.4 inches wide by 8.5 inches high, and the Resolution is 180 pixels/inch (ppi)! No wonder that image was taking a long time to send over an email; the file size (how much "space" it takes up on your hard drive) of the image must be huge! Essentially, the larger the image, the larger the file size, and the longer it will take to send and receive the picture on the Web or via email. Although there are no hard and fast rules for sizes and resolutions for specific purposes, here are my suggestions:

Image Size and Resolution Suggestions	
Target	**Image Size and Resolution setting**
Image to send via email to someone who will view it on her computer screen	640 pixels wide by 480 pixels tall (or thereabouts) 72 ppi
Image to send via email to someone who will view it on his computer screen *and* print it out	5 inches high by 7 inches wide (or thereabouts) 300 ppi
Image to post on a Web site	Whatever pixel dimensions you require 72 ppi
Image to give to a professional printer for printing.	Whatever size is required 300 to 350 ppi

When preparing an image that someone will only view on her computer screen (on a Web site, or sent via email), the pixel dimensions are what you want to pay close attention to. Whatever dimensions you have entered for the image under **Pixels Dimensions** will dictate how large (or small) the image will appear on the viewer's computer screen. Remember, the larger the image, the bigger the file size, and the longer it will take to upload or download from your computer.

On the other hand, when preparing an image for printing, you want to pay close attention not only to the document size (how many inches wide or high it is), but to the resolution as well. A standard photograph size is 4 inches high by 6 inches wide, or 5 inches high by 7 inches wide. And if you're going to print the image, you will want the **Resolution** around 300 to 350 ppi.

Fortunately, in many cases, you won't have to deal with resolution and image size. Elements knows that it can be a confusing topic, so in many cases it does much of the resizing work for you automatically. Whew!

I. ————————Attach to Email

In this exercise, you'll learn the process of attaching a photo to an email so that it can be easily sent to whomever you'd like.

1. Copy the **chap_12** folder and files from the **H•O•T CD-ROM** to your hard drive.

2. Open the **File Browser** by choosing **Window > File Browser**. Navigate to where you copied the **chap_12** folder, and within that folder, double-click on the **sunflower_detail** image to open it. This is an image straight from my digital camera, and as yet has not been resized or optimized for Web or email delivery.

When the **sunflower_detail** image opens up, you can see that it's quite large. If you look at the title bar of the image, you'll also notice that it says **33.3%**. (If you have a large monitor, it might have a different value, such as **50%**.) As I've mentioned previously, this value symbolizes how far zoomed in or out you are to the image. This image is so large, that you're currently viewing it at only 33.3 percent of its actual size. But what is the actual size of this image?

3. Choose **Image > Resize > Image Size**.

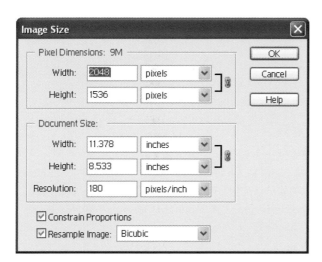

In the **Image Size** window, you can see that this image is 2048 pixels wide by 1536 pixels high, and its resolution is 180 ppi. Because you are just emailing this photo to a friend to look at, this image certainly doesn't need to be that large with that high of a resolution. Luckily, you don't have to worry about changing a thing. Elements is going to do it all automatically for you.

4. Click **Cancel** to exit the Image Size window.

5. Single-click on the **Attach to E-mail** button in the shortcuts bar.

Elements also recognizes that you probably don't want to email such a large photograph, so it offers to automatically convert the image to a smaller size for you. Of course, if your intent is to email this large image as is, you can just click on the **Send As Is** button. In this case, however, you definitely want Elements to resize the image to something more appropriate for email delivery.

6. Single-click on the button **Auto Convert**.

At this point, you'll see Elements going crazy! Windows will start opening up, resizing, and closing. What Elements is actually doing is resizing your image and compressing it for you—all to get ready to send it via email.

Note: Element's Attach to Email feature works with your default email program and your existing Internet connection. Unfortunately, it can't get you an Internet connection, install an email program, and send itself off with the click of a button. To use the Attach to Email feature, you need to have an active Internet account as well as an installed email program. (You should already be able to send/receive emails through it.) If you haven't yet set up your email program, your operating system (Windows, Mac, and so on) might prompt you to do so. Also, some email programs (especially the myriad fantastic email programs available for Mac OS X) aren't compatible with the Attach to Email feature. If your chosen email client isn't compatible, Elements will let you know. If your email client isn't compatible, and you really want to use the Attach to Email feature, you'll need to change your preferred email program to one that is compatible with Elements. Good choices would be Mail on Mac OS X and Outlook on Windows.

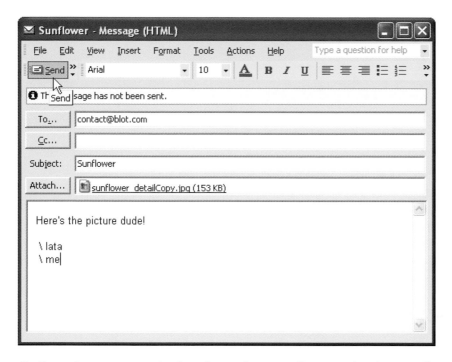

So if your Internet connection is active, and your email program has been configured and set up, you should see a new email message open with your image already attached! All you have to do is enter the recipient's email address, add a subject line, type a message, and click **Send**. Was that super easy or what?! As long as you have Internet access and an email program, attaching an image to an email is only a couple clicks away.

MOVIE | Web Photo Gallery

Included on the **H•O•T CD-ROM** in the **movies** folder is a movie titled **photo_gallery.mov**, which shows you how to take a folder of images (also provided on the **H•O•T CD-ROM**) and use Element's Web Photo Gallery feature to create an interactive photo gallery you can easily upload to the Web. Most ISPs (**I**nternet **S**ervice **P**roviders–the people that give you Internet access) give you a small amount of free Web space. Make use of that free Web space by putting your Web photo galleries there and then give the URL (http://www.mywebpage.com, for example) to family and friends. The Web Photo Gallery is a great feature to use when you have a lot of images you want to show friends and family, and you don't want to have to email the images to a whole bunch of people. With the Web Photo Gallery, you just build it, upload it, and pass out the URL to whomever you want to see the photos. (For more information about uploading your Web Photo Gallery, contact your ISP.)

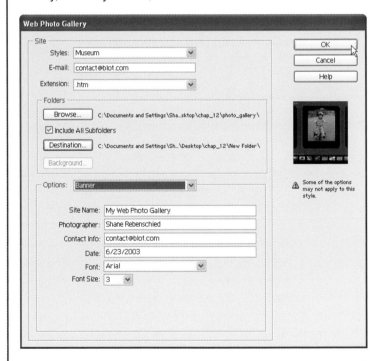

In the **photo_gallery.mov** movie, you will start by choosing **File > Create Web Photo Gallery**. You will then tell Elements where the photos (included on the **H•O•T CD-ROM**) are located on your computer, specify where you want the finished Web photo gallery to go, and select a few different options such as how big to make the small, medium, and large images. Then, you just click **OK** and watch Elements do the rest.

continues on next page

MOVIE | Web Photo Gallery *continued*

Elements will then go through your images, process them, build an interactive Web page, and open it in Internet Explorer where you can scroll through your images and click on the thumbnails to see larger versions. One word: Wow. Actually, one more: Simple.

GIF or JPEG?

When an image gets compressed (as either a GIF or a JPEG), the compression program (in this case, Elements) actually removes data from the image to lower the file size. That way, when you send the photo via email or post it on a Web site, it can be sent and received faster. Depending on whether you choose GIF or JPEG, some information in the image will be removed in different ways. GIF removes visual information from your image in a way that favors large areas of flat color, whereas JPEG removes information in a way that is more friendly towards photographs (a.k.a. "continuous tone images"). Also note that whereas an image saved as a JPEG can be comprised of millions of colors, a GIF image can have only 256 colors at the most—yet another reason why JPEG is best if used to compress photographs, and GIF is best if used to compress flat color graphics.

2. _____**Save for the Web**

In this exercise, you will learn how to "manually" open an image (that you—in a hypothetical situation—imported from your digital camera or scanner), resize it, and compress it using Elements' Save for Web feature. Knowing this technique is very important if you plan to send your images via email or put them on a Web site. Before you do either of those things, you need to make sure you're saving your images at a proper size and compressing them properly for email or Web delivery. Why should you learn how to resize and optimize an image manually when Elements can do it for you in the click of a button? Good question. When you use the Attach to Email feature, Elements will optimize and resize the image without any input from you. But what if you want to save the image at a different size? What if you want to spend a little extra time trying to optimize the image as much as you possibly can so it uploads and downloads faster? Although the Attach to Email feature does a great job at quickly optimizing and resizing your image for email delivery, it gives you absolutely no control over how the image is either resized or optimized. What you will learn in this exercise will allow you to do both.

1. First, you obviously need to open the image. Open the **File Browser** by choosing **Window > File Browser**. Navigate to the **chap_12** folder, and within that folder, double-click on the **sunflower_detail** file (the same image you used in Exercise 1).

As you saw in the first exercise, this image is very large. It's 2048 pixels wide by 1536 pixels high (in this case, that's approximately 11.4 inches wide by 8.5 inches high) at 180 ppi. Because you just want to email this photo to a friend and post it to your Web site, it doesn't need to be nearly that large. A size that fits neatly onscreen would do much better. Not only is a large-sized image overkill, but it also makes for an image that takes up more room on your hard drive. (That is, it has a large file size.) The only time I would recommend emailing someone an image with large pixel dimensions is if the recipient wants to print it. Remember, you want a high-resolution (more pixels) image when you want to print. That way the printed image will have more detail and will look better.

2. Click on the **Save for Web** button in the options bar.

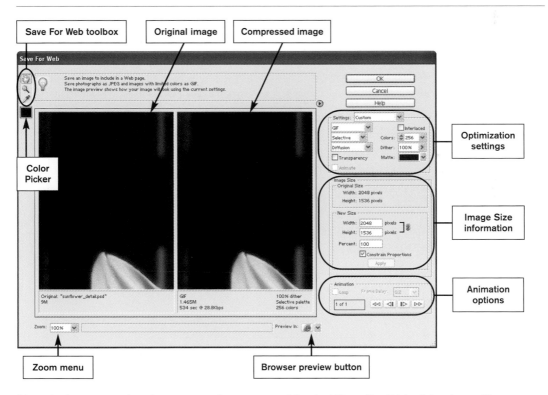

Now don't get scared and run away when you see this giant Save For Web dialog box with many different fields, buttons, and pull-down menus for you to click on. It's actually quite simple and straightforward. Here's a short description of what everything does:

Save for Web Options

Option/Setting	Description
Save for Web toolbox	The **Hand** tool allows you to pan around the image in either the original image or compressed image window. This functions the same way as the hand in the Elements Toolbox. The **Zoom** tool (magnifying glass icon) allows you to zoom in and out of the image. (Hold down the **Alt** [Windows] or **Option** [Macintosh] key to zoom out.) Double-clicking on the **Zoom** tool will also zoom the image to 100%. The **Eyedropper** tool allows you to take a sample of color in the image, which is useful if you're creating a GIF image that you want to contain transparency.
Color Picker	Clicking on this color swatch will open the standard Color Picker you have seen in earlier exercises. From here, you can pick a color that will be used, for instance, when creating a GIF image.
Optimization settings	From this set of pull-down menus and options, you specify how you want to compress your image. Two main forms of image compression are used: JPEG and GIF. (You will also see PNG under one of the pull-down menus in the **Optimization** settings, but they are another matter entirely.) To put it very simply, use JPEG image compression if you are compressing a continuous tone image (a photograph), and use GIF image compression if you are compressing a flat-color image (such as text, a business logo, and so on).
Image Size information	Here you can view and change the size of your image. One thing you'll notice missing is the ppi of the image. When posting images on a Web page, the ppi of the image doesn't matter, only the pixel dimensions of the image does. Elements knows this, so it doesn't even bother displaying the ppi of the image in the Save For Web dialog box. It displays only the pixel dimensions.
Animation options	When creating an animated GIF (as is demonstrated in a movie on the **H•O•T CD-ROM**), you can specify various options as to how the animated GIF will perform.
Zoom menu	From this pull-down menu, you can choose how far to zoom in or out of the image.
Browser preview button	By clicking on this button, you can preview your image in a Web browser. (The default, as it is in many other places throughout Elements, is Internet Explorer.) You can change the preview browser by clicking on the pull-down menu to the right of the button, choosing **Other**, and then locating a different browser. This button is useful to see how your compressed image will look in a Web browser, but more importantly, it will allow you to preview an animated GIF while you're still working on it. Neato.

The first thing you should do is change the size of the image to something more appropriate for email/Web delivery.

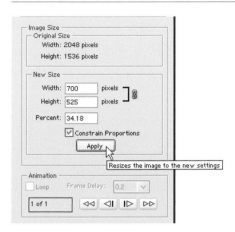

3. In the **New Size** area, change the **Width** to **700**. Because the **Constrain Proportions** check box is checked (it is by default), changing the width will also automatically scale the height as well. It does this so your image doesn't scale out of proportion. Click **Apply**.

4. Click on the pull-down menu in the **Settings** area and choose **JPEG**.

Because this image you're optimizing (the sunflower) is a continuous-tone image (a photograph), a compression format of JPEG will work the best.

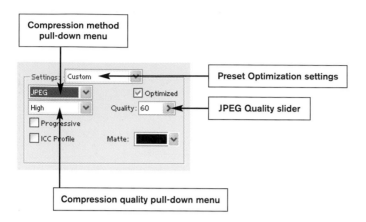

When you select JPEG from the Compression method pull-down menu, you are given a few options to set:

JPEG Compression Options	
Option	**Description**
JPEG Quality slider	When compressing an image as a JPEG, this is probably the setting you will want to pay the most attention to. The higher the **Quality** value, the higher the quality of the image, but the larger the file size. (Remember, larger file sizes take longer to email or upload to a Web site.) A lower **Quality** value gives you a lower-quality image, but will also yield an image with a smaller file size.
Optimized check box	Leaving this check box checked will create an image with a smaller file size, but might not be compatible (viewable) with older computers.
Compression quality pull-down menu	If you don't want to bother with dragging the **Quality** slider around, click on this pull-down menu and select a preset quality from **Low** to **Maximum.**
	continues on next page

JPEG Compression Options *continued*	
Option	**Description**
Progressive check box	Checking this check box will enable the **Progressive** option, which means that your JPEG, when viewed in a Web browser, doesn't display all at once. The browser first displays the image at low quality, and then as the image is downloaded over the Internet to the viewer's computer, it draws in a successively higher quality image until the final image is displayed. Almost immediately, viewers see the "first pass," low-quality image, but from that they can get a sense of whether or not they want to hang around for the entire image to download. Leaving this check box unchecked will allow you to save the image as a standard JPEG, which will download the image to the viewer's computer, at the quality you specify, from top to bottom. Although it sounds neat, I recommend leaving the **Progressive** check box unchecked because **Progressive** JPEGs aren't supported by some Web browsers.
ICC Profile check box	ICC stands for **I**nternational **C**olor **C**onsortium, which is essentially a group of companies who are attempting to standardize color management on the computer screen and in print. Clicking on this check box will embed the ICC color profile for your computer into the JPEG image. Theoretically, when a JPEG image with an embedded ICC color profile is viewed in someone's Web browser, the image will actually shift its color to compensate for the viewer's monitor color calibration. Translation? The image will change itself on the viewer's computer so the colors look the same as the ones you saw on your monitor. Because each computer monitor displays colors differently (even with the same image), **ICC Profile** is a great way to try to standardize how colors are displayed across different computer monitors. Unfortunately, not all Web browsers support JPEG images with embedded ICC Profiles, and not all computer users have taken the time to calibrate their monitors.
Matte color	JPEG images cannot have transparency in them. So if the image you are compressing contains transparent areas, Elements will need to make those transparent areas some opaque color. Whichever color you pick for the Matte color will be used to fill in any transparent areas in your image. Usually, if your image has any transparent areas, you would want to pick the same color that is going to be on the background of your Web page. That way the image will blend in better with the Web page itself.

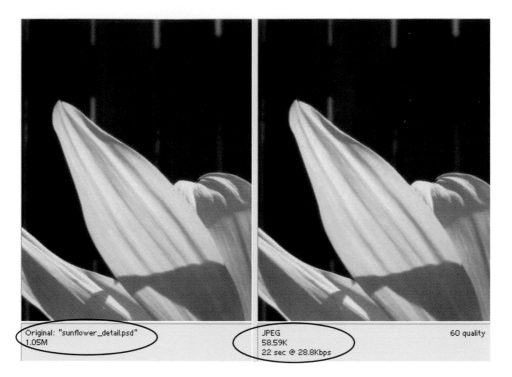

Note: As you are compressing an image and changing the compression settings, you can see how the compression you're applying is affecting the image. In the original and compressed image previews in the middle of the Save For Web dialog box, right underneath the images, Elements will show you what the original file size of the image is—in this case, 1.05 MB. (Hint: That's quite a large file size to be emailing to someone.) Many ISPs put a cap of 3 to 5 MB on each email. If you try to send an email with more than the allotted limit, the email will get bounced back to you and won't be delivered. You'll also see the file size of the compressed image—in this case, a measly 58.6 Kb. Elements will also tell you how long it will take for you to email this image (and also, how long it will take the recipient of your email to receive it) on a 28.8 Kbps modem. So as you are changing the compression settings for your image, keep your eye on the file size of your compressed image. The goal is to get the file size the smallest while still keeping the image looking decent.

Original: "sunflower_detail.psd"
1.05M

JPEG
58.59K
22 sec @ 28.8Kbps

60 quality

5. Make sure the **Hand** tool is selected in the Save For Web dialog box Toolbox and drag the sunflower image around to get a better view of it. (It doesn't matter which image you drag from—they will drag together.)

By looking at different parts of the image, you can get a better idea what the image looks like with the selected compression. In this case, you can hardly tell the image has been compressed at all. Why don't you try a lower JPEG quality and see what that gives you?

Original: "sunflower_detail.psd"
1.05M

JPEG
22.75K
9 sec @ 28.8Kbps

20 quality

6. Drag the JPEG **Quality** slider down to **20**, and then look at the optimized image again.

*At a compression quality of 20, you can clearly see heavy JPEG compression having an adverse affect on the quality of the image. Especially towards the center of the sunflower, you can see how the image is starting to get blurry and clumpy. This is even more evident at a lower quality, such as 10 or even 5. Yuck! But look at that file size!! It's a paltry 22.75 Kb. Elements also tells you that even on a slow 28.8 Kbps modem, this image will take only nine seconds to download. Zowee! The question that I always ask myself at this point is, "Is that file size worth that image quality?" In other words, yeah, the file size of the image is small, but is the loss in image quality worth having that smaller file size? To really answer that question, I'll usually raise the JPEG **Quality** slider until the image looks just good enough to where I'd consider it "acceptable." I'll then look at that file size, compare it to this low image quality file size, and* then *decide if the loss in image quality is worth the smaller file size.*

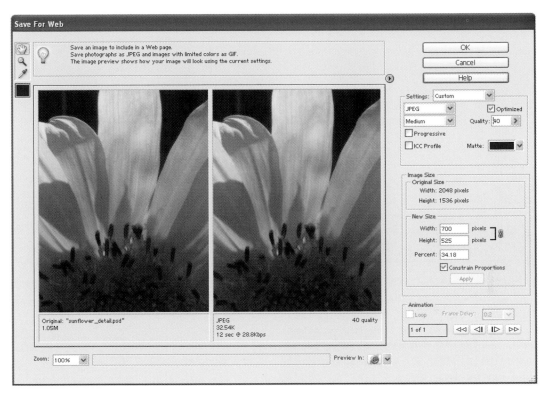

7. Set your JPEG **Quality** to **40**. After looking at the image at different quality settings, this middle value seems to be the best combination of image compression and small file size. Click **OK**.

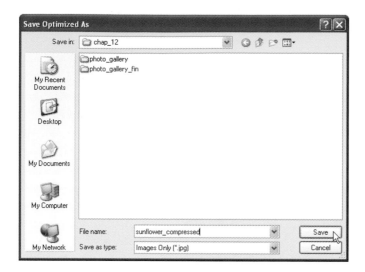

8. The **Save Optimized As** dialog box appears. From here, you can choose what name to give this file and where to save it. Name the file **sunflower_compressed**, navigate to the **chap_12** folder you copied onto your computer at the beginning of this exercise, and click **Save**.

*Note: After you click Save, the compressed image will be saved into the **chap_12** folder. The Save Optimized As window will automatically close, the Save For Web window will also automatically close, and you'll then be back in the Elements interface with the original **sunflower_detail** image. Now remember, when you saved the optimized image, you performed a Save As. This means that the optimized image was saved without making any changes or modifications to the original image (which you see in front of you now).*

9. Close the image and don't save any changes.

*Note: If you are a Mac OS X user, and you like the idea of putting your images on a Web page, you might want to consider signing up for Apple's .mac service. .Mac (not to sound like an Apple advertisement or anything) gives you the ability to easily put your photos online for the world to see—plus many, many other nifty goodies. .Mac is integrated with iPhoto (Apple's photo organizing program), which allows you to easily take a collection of photos and put them on your own .mac Web site as a photo gallery, or you can also use the .mac Web space to take your own Elements-generated photo gallery or optimized images and put them online as well. For more information about this service, check out **http://www.mac.com.***

*Congratulations! You just took a large, medium resolution image and scaled it, optimized (compressed) it as a JPEG image, and saved it into your **chap_12** folder. Now if you wanted to attach it to an email, or upload it to your Web site, the image is all ready to go. You just need to follow the directions that came with your email program to attach the image to an email, or follow the directions your ISP gives on how to upload the image to your Web site.*

MOVIE | Creating an Animated GIF

In the **movies** folder of the **H•O•T CD-ROM** is a movie titled **anim_gif.mov**, which shows you how to take a layered Elements file and turn it into an animated GIF. An animated GIF (as I'm sure you've seen many, many times all over the Internet) is a single GIF image file that is actually composed of multiple images within it. When this image is displayed in a browser, it animates. It's a great, quick, and easy way to add a little bit of animation to your Web page(s).

You will start by opening the file **sunflower_anim** image from the **chap_12** folder. This file is actually just a standard Elements PSD file that is composed of a series of layers. On each layer, the image is a little different from the one before it.

continues on next page

MOVIE | **Creating an Animated GIF** *continued*

Then, by using the **Save For Web** dialog box, you will set up the compression options to create, optimize, and save an animated GIF.

What Is PDF?

(from the upcoming *Learning Adobe Acrobat 6 H•O•T* book by Garrick Chow):

Adobe Acrobat and the **P**ortable **D**ocument **F**ormat (PDF) were developed out of a need for a universal file format that could be opened on any computer, regardless of platform or operating system. The PDF format allows you to create exact copies of your documents for the purpose of electronic distribution. With Acrobat installed on your computer, you can create PDF files from any application that has a print function, and remain confident that your users will see the document exactly as you intended it to be viewed. PDF files preserve a document's layout, formatting, fonts, colors, and graphics and can be opened and accurately printed by anyone who has Acrobat or the free Adobe Reader installed on his or her computer.

3. _____**PDF Slideshow**

In the first exercise in this chapter, you saw how to open a photo and, by using the Attach to Email feature that Elements provides, easily attach a photo to an email. But what if you had a series of photos you wanted a friend to see, and what if you didn't want her to have to worry about how to open the photos, or even if they're in the right format? Along comes Elements 2 with the sparklin' new PDF Slideshow feature. Elements allows you to take a series of images and use those to create an interactive PDF slideshow. Because many computers and software come with Adobe Reader, you're nearly guaranteed that whomever you're sending your PDF slideshow to will already have the software installed to view it. In the off chance that the person you emailed the PDF slideshow to doesn't have Adobe Reader installed on her computer, she can always download it for free from Adobe's Web site.

1. Choose **File > Automation Tools > PDF Slideshow**.

2. This will open the **PDF Slideshow** dialog box. The first thing you need to do is tell Elements what images you want to put in the slideshow. Click on the **Browse** button.

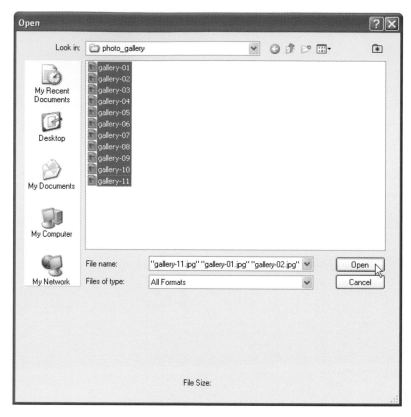

3. In turn, this will open the **Open** dialog box. Navigate to the **chap_12** folder you copied onto your computer back in Exercise 1, and then into the **photo_gallery** folder. These images are the images you want to make into a PDF slideshow. Single-click on the top-most image, **gallery-01**, and then hold down the **Shift** key and click on the bottom-most image in the list, **gallery-11**. This will select all of the images in the **photo_gallery** folder. Click **Open**.

4. Back in the **PDF Slideshow** dialog box, click on the **Advanced** button.

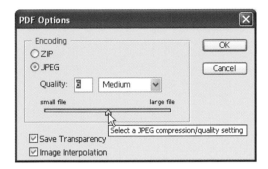

5. From here, you can specify how the images will be compressed when they are built into the PDF Slideshow. Because they're photographs, JPEG will do just fine. But a **Quality** setting of 10 (the default) is a little too high in my opinion. Drag the slider down until the **Quality** is **6**. (You can always go back and change it later if you'd like by repeating this exercise.) Click **OK**.

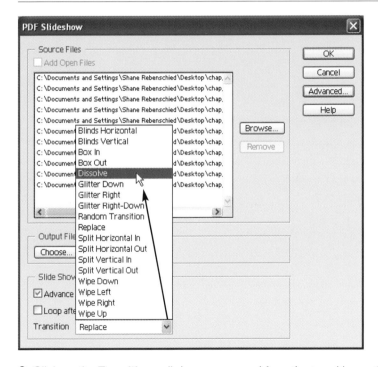

6. Click on the **Transition** pull-down menu, and from the transition options that appear, choose **Dissolve**. These different options all allow you to choose how you want the slideshow to transition between each slide. As you can see, there are quite a few to choose from.

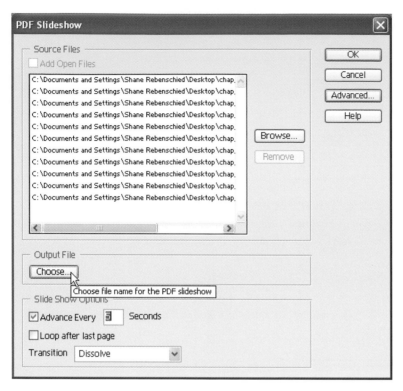

7. Now that you have selected which images you want to make into a PDF slideshow, you've chosen how to compress those images, and you've specified how each slide will transition into one another (the **Advance Every** _____ **Seconds** is self-explanatory), you now need to tell Elements where to save the slideshow PDF. Click on the **Choose** button.

8. In the **Save** window that appears, navigate to the **chap_12** folder, name the file **my_slideshow**, and click **Save**. Now even though you clicked **Save**, the file hasn't actually been saved yet. Not until the next step, that is.

9. In the **PDF Slideshow** dialog box, click **OK**. Elements will then go to work, automatically opening and closing images as it creates your slideshow for you. Boy, this is *hard* work. *whew* ;-) When the construction of the slideshow is complete, Elements will open a window telling you that "PDF slideshow was successful." Just click **OK** to exit out of that message.

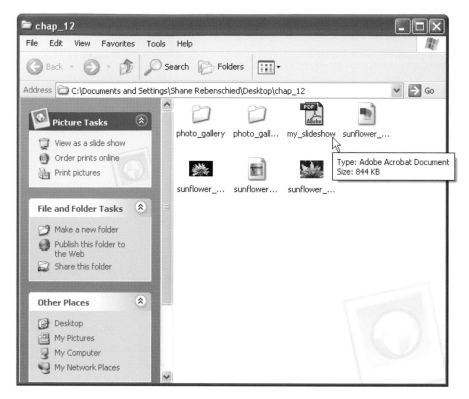

10. Minimize Elements (or hide it on the Mac), and open the **chap_12** folder where you have been saving all your work in this chapter. In there, you should see the PDF slideshow you just created, **my_slideshow**. However, sometimes on Mac OS X and in Windows XP, if you were to double-click on the slideshow PDF to open it, it would not open in Adobe Reader. Mac OS X prefers to open PDF files using its built-in Preview program, and Windows XP prefers to open PDF files using Windows Picture and Fax Viewer. To see the slideshow, you need to open it in Adobe Reader.

11. Right-click (Windows) or Ctrl-click (Mac) on the **my_slideshow** file, select **Open With**, and from there you should see an option to open the file with Acrobat Reader.

After performing these steps, if you don't see the Acrobat Reader from this list, first make sure that you have it installed. There's a free Acrobat Reader installer on your Adobe Elements 2 CD-ROM and on the H•O•T CD-ROM. After you've installed Acrobat Reader, go back and perform this step again.

Once the file opens in Acrobat Reader, you'll notice that the screen will fill with black, and the first slide will "dissolve" in. The slide will stay on the screen for five seconds (this is based on the setting in the PDF Slideshow dialog box), at which point it will dissolve into the next slide. It continues doing this until it reaches the end of the slideshow, where it stops. Very, very neat! You can also go back and forth through the slides in the slideshow by pressing the right arrow and left arrow keys. So as you can see, creating a PDF slideshow is a more stylish way of presenting a group of images than just sending someone a folder of images. If you know more about Adobe Acrobat (the professional version, not the free Acrobat Reader), at this point you could also add voiceover audio files, movies, music, and more PDF pages to make this a fully interactive presentation. Groovin' baby…groovin'.

Tip: *To exit out of the slideshow (because there is no "exit" or "quit" button), press the* ***Escape*** *key. This will exit you out of the slideshow and back into Acrobat Reader.*

In this chapter, you learned how Elements can create Web content—everything from easily sending images via email to creating an online, interactive Web photo gallery to creating an interactive PDF slideshow. Not only can Elements create these things for you, but it also does most of the work, leaving you to kick back, surf the Web, and check out prices on that new digital camera you've been dreaming about. ;-)

In the next chapter, you will learn how to print your images. Elements has a few cool features (of course it does!) when printing out a batch of images, including printing out a contact sheet and printing out a professional-style picture package. So go grab some ink and paper and warm up that printer because it's time to get down and dirty with printing in Elements!

I3.
Printing

| Print Preview | Contact Sheet |
| Picture Package |

_chap_13_

Photoshop Elements 2
H•O•T CD-ROM

If you've followed the exercises in this book from the beginning (or from close to the beginning anyway), you should congratulate yourself. You've covered a large amount of information that will only begin to sink in if you continue to work with it and experiment with your own imagery. But something is strangely lacking. Ah-ha—printing! You haven't yet learned how to print your images. Printing your images is something that will vary widely from Mac to Windows, and from printer to printer. Each printer manufacturer develops their own, unique software to enable you to print out images. Some of that software is really good, and some of it is really bad. This chapter, however, will focus on the different print options that Elements provides you.

I. ——————————Print Preview

Have you ever printed an image, only to realize—after waiting 10 minutes for the high-quality printout on glossy paper to finish printing—that the image was too small? Too big? Not in the right place on the paper? In this exercise, you will learn about an Elements feature called Print Preview, which allows you to preview (imagine that!) your image document before you print it. Although I wouldn't recommend using the Print Preview feature to test how the color will look when it's printed (you, unfortunately, actually have to print the image to see that), you can still use it to test what the image size and position on the paper will be when it is printed.

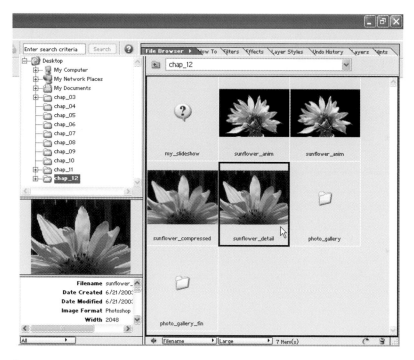

1. Open the **File Browser** by choosing **Window > File Browser**. Navigate to the **chap_12** folder you copied onto your computer in Chapter 12, and double-click on the **sunflower_detail** image to open it.

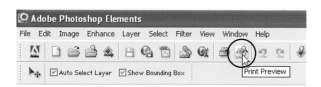

2. After the image opens, click on the **Print Preview** button in the options bar.

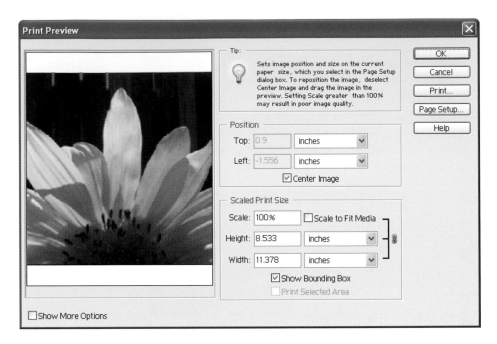

As you can see in the Print Preview dialog box, you have quite a few options to choose from. You can also see that if you had just printed the image without previewing it first, the image would have run right off of the paper. This sunflower image has a "landscape" orientation, meaning that it is longer than it is wide. If it was the other way around–wider than it was long–the image would have a "portrait" orientation. So because this sunflower image is landscape, it would stand to reason that the paper should be rotated to be landscape as well. (By default, the printer will print out portrait unless you tell it otherwise.) The place to change the orientation to landscape or portrait is in Page Setup, which you will learn to access next.

3. On the right side of the Print Preview window, click on **Page Setup**.

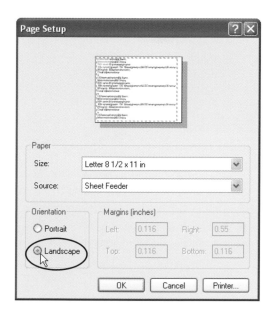

4. Although this Page Setup window will look different depending on the brand/model of your printer and which operating system you're running, the essence is still the same. Change the **Orientation** from **Portrait** to **Landscape**. Click **OK**.

As you can see in the Print Preview thumbnail image, the image fits better once the printer has been told to print the image using landscape orientation instead of portrait. The image is still a little too big for this paper size, however.

5. Resize the image in the thumbnail image by moving your mouse over the top edge of the image. Your mouse cursor will then change to an up/down arrow. When you see that icon, drag your mouse down. As you drag your mouse, the image will resize! Remember, the white box in this thumbnail image represents a sheet of paper in your printer, and the image thumbnail represents your actual photograph, where it will be placed on the paper, and how large it will be. Resize the image so there's a little room around all four sides.

Note: *You can also scale the printed image's size by changing the scale percentage or the height and width values directly in the **Scaled Print Size** area of the Print Preview dialog box. By clicking on the **Scale to Fit Media** check box, you can also have Elements scale your image (I would only recommend checking this checkbox if your image is larger than the paper size, not smaller) to fit inside your paper dimensions.*

6. Under the **Position** section, uncheck the check box **Center Image**. Then, by dragging the image thumbnail, you can drag the image around the paper area, thereby changing where that image will be placed on paper when it is printed. Keep in mind, this is all done *before* any actual printing is done. Neat-o! If you want the image to snap back to the center of the paper area, recheck the **Center Image** check box.

Note: *By clicking on the **Show More Options** check box at the bottom of the Print Preview window, you can set some more options such as creating crop marks and color calibration. Due to their advanced nature, these topics aren't covered in this book.*

7. Once you've positioned the image thumbnail where you want it, click **OK**.

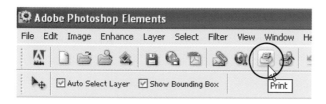

8. Then, all you have to do to print your image is click on the **Print** icon in the options bar. Your image will then print out just the way you specified in the Print Preview dialog box.

Print Preview is a fantastic way, as you just saw, to check your image before you print it. It enables you to make sure that when the image is actually printed, it gets printed at the correct size and location on paper. When you're first getting started in Elements, I highly suggest going through Print Preview first to make sure your image is set up correctly for printing.

9. Close the image and don't save the changes.

Note: *If you were to save the image, the modifications you've made to the print settings would be saved along with the image. So the next time you opened the image and printed it, it would have all the same customizations you specified.*

2. _____Contact Sheet

When I illustrate a book cover that requires a model, I contract out the photo shoot to a photographer in New York. A couple of days after the photo shoot, I receive the photos, copied onto a CD-ROM, with a couple of prints in the package as well. On the prints are small, thumbnail images of all of the photographs, with the name of the file printed underneath each image. This saves me a great deal of time because by looking at the printout, I can pick which photos I like. Then, I can just look at the file-name, and easily find that exact file on the CD-ROM; I don't have to open each file (or wait while the File Browser tries to preview 50 high-resolution images) to find the ones I want. In this exercise, you're going to learn to create that same printout. It's called a contact sheet, and it essentially allows you to take a batch of photos and print small thumbnails, each labeled with the filename of that photograph. This is *invaluable* if you have a collection of photographs on your computer, and you don't want to have to open each photo to find the exact one you're looking for. Printing a contact sheet, for example, is also a great way to visualize a series of photos you've backed up onto a CD-ROM.

1. Choose **File > Print Layouts > Contact Sheet**.

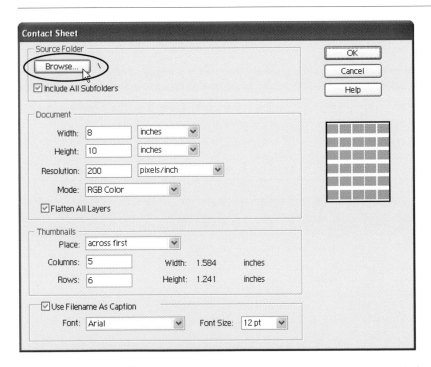

2. This will open the **Contact Sheet** dialog box, where you can specify myriad options for how the photos will be arranged when they're printed. First, choose the photos you want to make a contact sheet with by clicking **Browse** (or **Choose** on the Mac).

3. In the **Browse For Folder** dialog box, browse to the **chap_12** folder and maximize it by clicking on the small plus sign to the left of the **chap_12** folder. Then, single-click on **photo_gallery** to select it, and click **OK**. (See the following screen shot and accompanying text for the Mac steps.)

You've just picked a folder of images (the same folder of images you used in the Web Photo Gallery exercise in the last chapter) for Elements to create the contact sheet with.

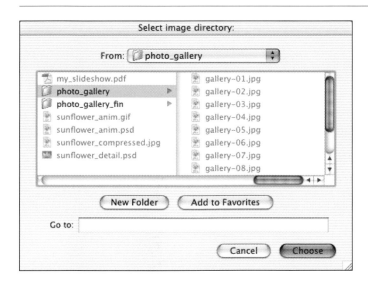

*Note: On the Mac, the Browse For Folder dialog box is titled **Select image directory**, and it looks quite different from the Windows dialog box. On the Mac, browse to the same **chap_12** folder, single-click on the **photo_gallery** folder, and click **Choose**.*

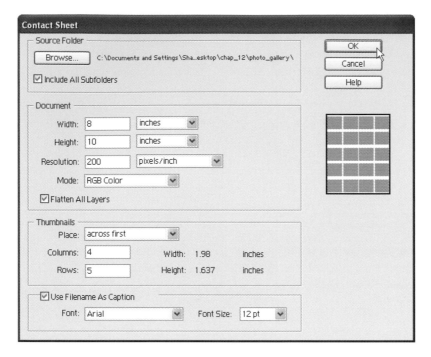

4. The rest of the options are pretty self-explanatory. Under **Document**, set the **Width** and **Height** of the paper you're printing on, minus about half an inch for the margins (a standard, consumer printer can't print all the way to the edge of a piece of paper), as well as the **Resolution**. If you want to print the contact sheet in black and white, just select **Grayscale** from the **Mode** pull-down menu. For my printer (and the same settings might work for your printer as well), I chose a **Width** of **8 inches**, a **Height** of **10 inches**, and set the **Resolution** to **200 pixels/inch**. Leave **Mode** set to **RGB Color**, and leave the **Flatten All Layers** check box checked.

Note: The Contact Sheet feature is best if used to print out a folder of high- to medium-resolution images. In other words, your results aren't going to be very good if you instruct Elements to print out a contact sheet of a bunch of 72-ppi images. When printing, make sure the ppi of the image is around 200 or higher (preferably 300) for the best results.

5. Under **Thumbnails**, choose **across first** from the **Place** pull-down menu (which means that the images will be printed sequentially from left to right instead of top to bottom), set the **Columns** to **4**, and the **Rows** to **5**. The fewer columns and rows you have, the larger the thumbnails will be on the contact sheet. Conversely, the more columns and rows you have, the smaller the thumbnails will be.

6. Check the **Use Filename As Caption** check box, and choose a font from the **Font** pull-down menu and a font size from the **Font Size** pull-down menu. On the Mac, the font defaults to **Helvetica**; on Windows, the font defaults to **Arial**.

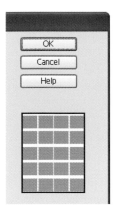

You'll notice that on the right side of the dialog box is a layout preview of the contact sheet. As you modify the settings in the Contact Sheet dialog box, this preview will update to reflect your changes. Sweet!

7. Click **OK**. Then just kick back, relax, and marvel at the beauty of this automated task. It's fun to watch as Elements opens each image in the folder you chose, resizes it, places it into a new document, and types the filename under each image. And you hardly had to lift a finger!

When Elements finishes, you're left with a sheet of thumbnail images that are all nicely labeled for you and ready to print out. Elements places this grouping of thumbnail images, by default, at the top left of this image. If you'd like, you can drag that thumbnail image grouping down toward the center of the image space.

As you just witnessed, very little effort is involved to print out a contact sheet such as this. Just point Elements to a directory of images, set a few options, click **OK**, and off it goes! Again, this feature works great if you're backing up your photo collection to a CD-ROM. After you've burned the CD-ROM, just point the Contact Sheet feature at the CD-ROM, click **OK**, and presto! You have a nice, labeled print-out of all the images on the CD-ROM.

8. Feel free to print this image if you want. After you're finished with it, however, close the image and don't save the changes.

MOVIE | Picture Package

When I was in elementary school, they would have a photo shoot day, once a year. Every year they would line up the whole class, take a group photo, and then you would go to another room to get individual photos taken. About a month later, they would hand out manila envelopes with the photos inside. To save costs, the photo companies would place as many photos as they could on a single sheet of photo paper—some large, some small, some medium, and some "wallet sized." Most photography studios still do this. In the movie **picture_package.mov** on the **H•O•T CD-ROM**, I will show you how to use Elements' Picture Package feature to print out the same kind of image layout that professional photography studios use.

In the movie, you will use the Picture Package feature to have Elements automatically arrange a photo on a standard 8.5 x 11-inch sheet of paper. This is a great feature to utilize, for example, if you want to send out a picture to a large group of people. By using Picture Package, you don't have to worry about trying to squeeze as many pictures onto the page as possible (*whew*—try saying that fast 10 times!). Elements will do that for you.

In this chapter, you learned about some of the features that Elements provides to make printing images a little easier. The Print Preview feature is a great paper-saver because it allows you to catch mistakes by simulating a print before you actually click the Print button. The Contact Sheet and Picture Package features are also extremely valuable and useful—not to mention that their automation makes for some good entertainment for those days when there's nothing good on TV. ;-)

A.
Online Resources

Thanks to the Internet, and to a few individuals with some spare time, there are some great online resources for Adobe Elements. Although some information and tutorials you find online will cover what you already learned in this book, others will magnify what you know and show you new ways of working in Elements. This appendix lists a few of the best resources for expanding your knowledge of Elements.

H•O•T

Photoshop Elements 2

A Few Elements-Related Web Sites

Adobe

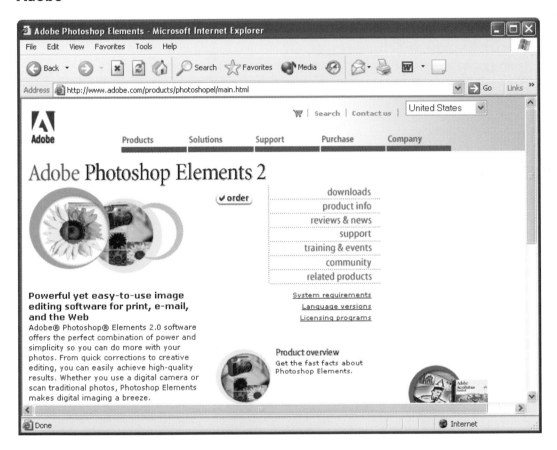

http://www.adobe.com/products/photoshopel/main.html

Jay Arraich's Photoshop Elements Tips

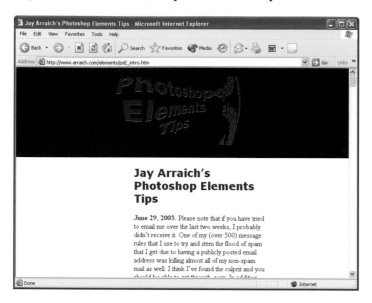

http://www.arraich.com/elements/psE_intro.htm

About.com Photoshop Elements Resources

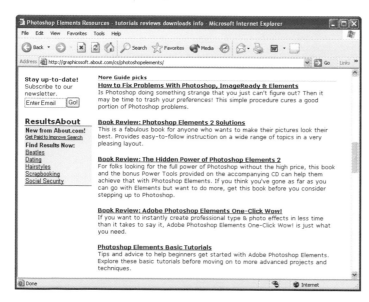

http://graphicssoft.about.com/cs/photoshopelements/

Stock Photo and Clip Art Sites

iStockPhoto.com

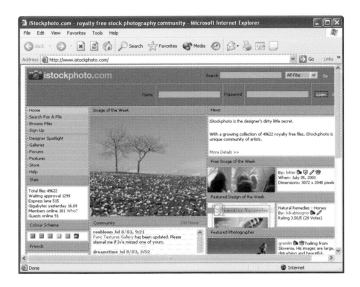

http://www.istockphoto.com

ClipArt.com

http://www.clipart.com

B.

Technical Support

H·O·T

Photoshop Elements 2

If you run into any problems while following the exercises in this book, there are a few places you can turn for help. This document will be maintained and expanded upon at this book's companion Web site:

http://www.lynda.com/products/ books/elm2hot/

Adobe Technical Support

http://www.adobe.com/support/

206-675-6258 (Mac) 206-675-6358 (Windows)

If you are having problems with Elements, please contact Adobe Technical Support at the number listed here. Adobe staff will be able to help you with such typical problems as these: the trial version has expired on your computer; the application crashes when you try and launch it; and so forth. Please note that lynda.com cannot help troubleshoot technical problems with Elements.

Peachpit Press

customer_service@peachpit.com

If your book has a defective CD-ROM, please contact the customer service department at this email address. We do not have extra CDs at lynda.com, so they must be requested directly from the publisher.

lynda.com

http://www.lynda.com/products/books/elm2hot/

elm2faq@lynda.com

We have created a companion Web site for this book, which can be found at **http://www.lynda.com/products/books/elm2hot/**. Any errors in the book will be posted to the Web site, and it's always a good idea to check there for up-to-date information. We encourage and welcome your comments and error reports to **elm2faq@lynda.com**.

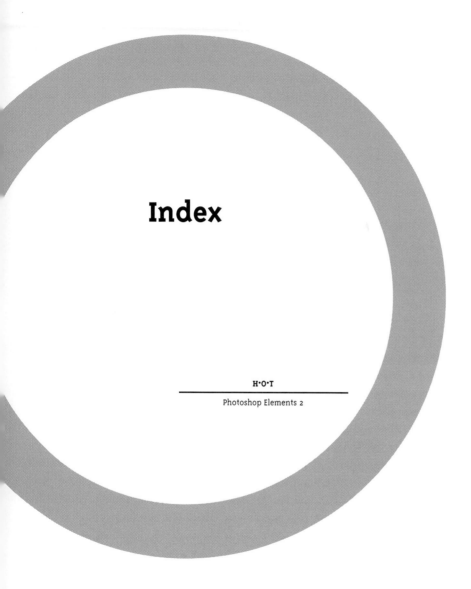

Index

H•O•T

Photoshop Elements 2

A

Acrobat, 304
Acrobat Reader, opening PDF slideshows with, 311
active images, 69
Add to shape area option (Shape tool), 150
adding
    palettes to Palette Well, 22
    to selections, 104
adjustment layers, 72
    deleting, 76
    Hue/Saturation, 240
    levels, 72-74, 241
    viewing/hiding, 74
adjustments. *See also* photo correction
    color adjustments, 201-202
        automatic adjustments, 215
        black-and-white images, 205-206
        Color Cast Correction dialog box, 202-203
        Color Variations dialog box, 210-214
        Hue/Saturation adjustment layer, 204-205, 240
        Levels adjustment layer, 241
        Replace Color dialog box, 207-210
    value adjustments, 184-185
        automatic adjustments, 192-194
        contrast, 185-186
        Dodge and Burn tools, 195-200
        Levels dialog box, 187-189
        overexposure, 191
        shadow details, 190
Adobe Acrobat, 304
Adobe Acrobat Reader, opening PDF slideshows with, 311
Adobe Online, 17
Adobe Photoshop Elements. *See* Photoshop Elements
Adobe Photoshop versus Photoshop Elements, 3-4
Advanced Blending option (Photomerge feature), 263
airbrushing, Enable Airbrush option (Paintbrush tool), 121
aligned option (Clone Stamp tool), 235
aligning text, 168
anchor points (selections), removing, 96
angle gradient fill type, 124
animated GIFs, 303-304
animation options (Save for Web dialog box), 294
Anti-aliased option
    Magic Eraser tool, 133
    Magic Wand tool, 98

Paint Bucket tool, 141
    Type tool, 168
anti-aliasing images, 44
Apple .mac service, 302
associating file types with Photoshop Elements, 32-33
Attach to E-mail button (shortcuts bar), 19
attach to e-mail feature, 10, 19
attaching photographs to email, 285-289
Auto Contrast command versus Auto Levels command, 194
Auto Levels command versus Auto Contrast command, 194
automatic color adjustments (photo correction), 215
automatic startup of Welcome screen, disabling, 14
automatic value adjustments (photo correction), 192-194

B

background color, 136
    setting to default, 116, 136
Background Eraser tool, 131-132
Background layer, changing to normal layer, 128
backlighting, 191
Bitmap dialog box, 56
bitmap graphics, 145-146
    changing vector graphics to, 44
Bitmap image mode, 53
    converting RGB Color to, 54-57
black input level slider (Levels dialog box), 188
black output level slider (Levels dialog box), 188
black-and-white images
    colorizing, 256
    converting color images to, 54-57, 205-206
black-points, 185
blending modes, 85-87, 113
    for tools, 84
    list of, 80, 84
Bloat tool, 277
Blur tool, 253-255
blurring photos, 251-255
blurry photos, sharpening, 243-250
bounding box, showing/hiding, 111
brightness. *See* levels
brightness adjustments. *See* value adjustments
Browse button (shortcuts bar), 18
Browse for File button (Welcome screen), 13

N

Name option (New dialog box), 52
New button (shortcuts bar), 18
New dialog box, 51
new features in Photoshop Elements
  attach to e-mail feature, 10
  dialog tips, 6
  Frame From Video, 8
  help search field, 7
  optimization for Mac OS X and
      Windows XP, 10
  PDF slideshow feature, 9
  Quick Fix, 7
  Selection Brush, 8
  smart error messages, 6
New File button (Welcome screen), 13
non-destructive image editing, 71
Normal blending mode, 80

O

Online Services button (shortcuts bar), 19
Only Web Colors option (Color Picker), 138
opacity. *See also* transparency
  Clone Stamp tool, 235
  Pencil tool, 117
  Preserve Transparency feature, 143
Opacity option (layers), modifying, 62
Open button (shortcuts bar), 18
Open dialog box, 31
opening
  images, 30-33
    with File Browser palette, 34-38
  Layers Palette, 61
  palettes from Palette Well, 22
  PDF slideshows with Acrobat Reader, 311
  Welcome screen, 14
optimization
  JPEG image compression, 296
  for Mac OS X and Windows XP, 10
  Save for Web dialog box, 294
options bar, 23. *See also* preferences
ordering. *See* sorting
orientation of images, 314
overexposure (photo correction), 191
overlapping images on layers, 63
Overlay blending mode, 82
Overlay Color option (Selection Brush
    tool), 101
Overlay Opacity option (Selection Brush tool), 101

P

Page Setup window, 315
Paint Bucket tool, 140-142
Paintbrush tool, 120-122
painting mode (Pencil tool), 117
Palette Well, 21-22
palettes, 20
  adding to Palette Well, 22
  grouping, 20-21
  Hints, 16
  More button, 21
  moving, 20
  opening from Palette Well, 22
  Palette Well, 21-22
  preferences, 21
  removing from Palette Well, 22
  resetting positions of, 21
  resizing, 20
  ungrouping, 21
panoramic photos
  creating, 259-268
  repositioning, 262
Pattern Stamp tool, 235
PDF (Portable Document Format), 9, 304
PDF slideshow feature, 9, 305-311
Pencil tool, 116, 118-119
Perspective option (Photomerge
    feature), 264
photo correction, 182. *See also* photo
    manipulation; photo retouching
  color adjustments, 201-202
    automatic adjustments, 215
    black-and-white images, 205-206
    Color Cast Correction dialog box, 202-203
    Color Variations dialog box, 210-214
    Hue/Saturation adjustment layer, 204-205,
        240
    Levels adjustment layer, 241
    Replace Color dialog box, 207-210
  Sponge tool, 216-220
  value adjustments, 184-185
    automatic adjustments, 192-194
    contrast, 185-186
    Dodge and Burn tools, 195-200
    Levels dialog box, 187-189
    overexposure, 191
    shadow details, 190
photo manipulation, 258. *See also* photo
    correction; photo retouching
  compositing photos, 268
  Liquify filter, 274-281

Snap to Browser-Safe Color option (Color Picker), 138
Snap to Grid feature, disabling, 266
Soft Light blending mode, 82
sorting layers, 70
sponge mode option (Sponge tool), 217
Sponge tool, 216-220
startup, disabling Welcome screen at, 14
Step Backward button (shortcuts bar), 19
Step Forward button (shortcuts bar), 19
Strikethrough option (Type tool), 168
Style picker option (Shape tool), 151
styles. *See* layer styles
Subtract from shape area option (Shape tool), 150
subtracting from selections, 103
supported formats. *See* formats
swapping foreground and background color swatches, 136
Switch Colors option (Toolbox), 136
switching to Hand tool, 230

T

text
adding to images, 165-171
aligning, 168
applying layer styles, 176-177
colors of, 169
editing, 173-176
layers for, 172
accidentally creating, 176
moving, 171
warping, 169, 178-181
Text color option (Type tool), 169
thumbnails
image thumbnails section (File Browser palette), 35-37
of photographs, printing on contact sheets, 318-322
tint adjustments. *See* color adjustments
Tolerance option
Magic Eraser tool, 133
Magic Wand tool, 98
Paint Bucket tool, 141
tonal range option (Dodge tool), 197. *See also* levels
tool tips. *See* Hints palette
Toolbox, 16-17
Adobe Online, 17
background color swatch, 136
Bloat tool, 277
Blur tool, 253-255

brushes
Gradient tool, 123-126
Impressionist Brush tool, 121
Paintbrush tool, 120-122
Pencil tool, 116, 118-119
Burn tool, 195-200
Clone Stamp tool, 234-240
Crop tool, 265-266
Dodge tool, 195-200
Eraser tools, 127-128
Background Eraser, 131-132
Eraser, 129-130
Magic Eraser, 133-135
Eyedropper tool, 142
foreground color swatch, 136
changing, 65
setting to default, 136
swapping with background color swatch, 136
Hand tool, 230
Hints palette, 16
Lasso tool, 231
Move tool, 148, 171
creating composite images, 109
Paint Bucket tool, 140-142
Pattern Stamp tool, 235
Red Eye Brush tool, 224-227
selection tools, 89-91
Elliptical Marquee tool, 92
Lasso tool, 93-94
Magic Wand tool, 98-99
Magnetic Lasso tool, 96-98
Polygonal Lasso tool, 94-96
Rectangular Marquee tool, 92
Selection Brush tool, 8, 100, 102-103
Shape tool, 149-152
Sharpen tool, 247-250
Smudge tool, 269-273
Sponge tool, 216-220
Twirl Clockwise tool, 278-279
Twirl Counter Clockwise tool, 279-280
Type tool, 166-171. *See also* text
tools
blending modes for, 84
hidden tools, 17
options bar, 23
selecting, 17
transforming images, 221
transitions
between selections, 232
for PDF slideshows, 307
transparency in layers, 61. *See also* opacity

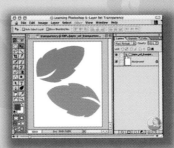